The Gallery of Maps

in the Vatican

ITALIA
ARTIVM
STVDIORVMQVE
PLENA SEMPER
EST HABITA

The Gallery of Maps

in the Vatican

Lucio Gambi

Translated by Paul Tucker

George Braziller • Publisher • New York

First published in the United States in 1997 by George Braziller, Inc.

Originally published in Italy in 1997 by Franco Cosimo Panini Editore under the title *La Galleria delle Carte geografiche in Vaticano.*

English translation and illustrations copyright © 1997 by Franco Cosimo Panini Editore.

For information, please address the publisher:

George Braziller, Inc.
171 Madison Avenue
New York, NY 10016

Library of Congress Cataloging-in-Publication Data:

Gambi, Lucio.
    [Galleria delle carte geografiche in Vaticano. English]
    The gallery of maps in the Vatican / Lucio Gambi; translated by Paul Tucker.
      p.   cm.
    Translation of: La Galleria delle carte geografiche in Vaticano
    Includes bibliographical references.
    ISBN 0-8076-1425-4 (hard-back)
    1. Italy–Maps–Early works to 1800. 2. Cartography–History–Italy.
3. Mural Painting and decoration– 16th century–Vatican City.
4. Decoration and ornament, Architectural–Vatican City.
I. Tucker, Paul. II. Title. III. Title: Gallery of maps. IV. Title: Maps in the Vatican.
G 1983 .G3 1997 <G&M>
911'. 45-DC21   97-28340
                                             CIP
                                        MAPS

Frontispiece Illustration: Detail from *Italia nova* (Modern Italy) showing the cartouche that appears in the upper right-hand corner of the map. See page 25 for an illustration of the complete map.

Designed by Ultreya srl, Milan
The paper is 150 gsm Gardamatt
Typeset in Times ten roman
Printed and bound in Italy

First edition

Contents

Introduction: The Gallery of Maps   *7*

Ancient Italy   *20*

Modern Italy   *24*

Liguria   *28*

Tuscany and Northern Lazio   *32*

The Territories of Perugia and Città di Castello   *38*

Northern Lazio   *42*

The Territory of Spoleto   *48*

Southern Lazio   *54*

Campania   *58*

Southern Campania and Basilicata   *64*

Basilicata and Southern Campania   *68*

Northern Calabria   *72*

Southern Calabria   *76*

Corsica   *80*

Sardinia   *84*

Sicily   *88*

The Jurisdiction of Avignon and the Comtat Venaissin   *94*

Piedmont and Monferrato   *98*

The Duchy of Milan   *102*

The Mainland Possessions of Venice West of the River Piave   *108*

The Lagoon of Venice, Friuli, and Istria   *114*

The Duchy of Parma and Piacenza   *118*

The Duchy of Mantua   *124*

The Duchy of Ferrara   *128*

The Jurisdiction of Bologna   *134*

Romagna   *140*

The Duchy of Urbino   *146*

Marche   *152*

The Territory of Ancona   *156*

Abruzzo   *162*

Northern Puglia   *166*

Southern Puglia   *170*

Civitavecchia   *174*

Genoa   *178*

Venice   *182*

Ancona   *186*

Tremiti Islands   *190*

Corfù   *194*

Malta   *198*

Isle of Elba   *202*

Bibliography   *207*

The Gallery of Maps

As a group, the frescoes in the Vatican Gallery of Maps make up the largest cycle of geographical images in Europe.

The Gallery was created at the wish of Pope Gregory XIII (the Bolognese Ugo Boncompagni, papacy 1572–1585) and was realized at great expense, both in terms of money and manpower, in an extraordinarily short space of time. For if we are to believe the inscriptions in the Gallery, it was begun in 1580 and completed in 1581. However, it seems more reasonable to suppose that it took a little longer than this (though still a comparatively short time if we consider the sheer amount of work), as the building phase probably began as early as 1578.

The architect responsible for the Gallery was the Bolognese Ottaviano Mascarino, who had replaced Martino Longhi the Elder (d. 1591) in 1578 as the pope's personal architect. But the principal figure involved was the cosmographer and mathematician Egnazio Danti, who in 1580 was invited by the pope to leave the University of Bologna and settle in Rome, where he also took part in work on the reform of the calendar. While Danti was responsible for the overall design and himself drew the cartoons for all the maps, he was assisted by a throng of painters and stuccoworkers, notably by two Flemish landscapists, the brothers Matthäus Bril (1550–1583) and Paul Bril (1554–1626), and by Girolamo Muziano (1532–1592) and Cesare Nebbia, who directed and coordinated the painting and stuccowork relating to the noncartographical parts of the design.

The practice of decorating the walls of state buildings with geographical images goes back to ancient Roman times and continued throughout the Middle Ages. But it received new impetus in the second half of the 16th century, as is shown by a variety of instances, among them the maps painted in the Guardaroba Nuova of the Palazzo Vecchio in Florence, also the work of Danti, and those in the Sala del Mapparnondo of the Villa Farnese at Caprarola. However, compared with immediate precedents such as these, the Vatican Gallery is without doubt more original, and not just on account of its unusual size, 131.2 yards long by 6.5 yards across (120 x 6 m). Its great novelty lay in the idea of arranging regional maps of Italy in two parallel lines along the walls of an interminable corridor, so that its rectilinear axis stood for the country's central Apennine ridge, thus producing a sort of three-dimensional analogic model of the peninsula, with the northern regions placed at one (actually the southern) end of the Gallery and the southern regions at the other, and those bordered by the Ligurian and Tyrrhenian Seas on one side and those by the Adriatic on the other. Danti himself explains the sense of this arrangement with great clarity in a letter to the Flemish cartographer Abraham Ortelius (Abraham Oertel, 1527–1598) dated 24 December 1580, when work in the Gallery was already well under way:

> Your eminence, and the profit I have derived from your distinguished labors place me in a position of great debt and warm regard toward you, and as a small token of my esteem I send you these few lines together with a plan taken making diligent use of the instrument [the radio Latino, used to measure angles, invented by Latino Orsini], as I have done for most of the Papal States, at the order of the Pope, who summoned me to Rome to decorate a Gallery His Holiness has had built with a description of Italy. So, having divided the country in two at the Apennines, I placed the half that is washed by the Ligurian and Tyrrhenian Seas on one side and that

bound by the Adriatic and the Alps on the other. I then further divided it into forty separate parts, according to the various States and Prefectures, for the Gallery is divided into forty large panels, each so large that sixty-four sheets of paper royal were needed for the cartoons. I am now preparing scaled-down versions of the maps for a book, in which forty-eight separate regions will be represented together with eighty episodes depicted on the ceiling above the panels, each showing a miracle known to have occurred in that province (BERTOLINI 1908).

From this letter it emerges, then, that Danti intended to reproduce the painted maps on a reduced scale and publish them in an atlas (or "book" as Danti rightly says, as the term *atlas* did not come into use for another fifteen years), and that he turned to Ortelius, author in 1570 of the already famous *Theatrum Orbis Terrarum*, for assistance in its preparation:

I wished to advise you of my intention, so that should it please you to have the book engraved, you might notify me and I might then seek the support of the Pope. Each plate will be accompanied by a note containing detailed new information, together with the inscriptions I devised for the Gallery.

The planned atlas came to nothing: in fact, we do not even know whether Ortelius ever replied to Danti's letter. The work of painting the maps on the walls, on the other hand, was largely completed by 1581–82. According to the plan adopted, the Apennine range, "backbone" of the Italian peninsula, was made to correspond to the Gallery's central axis, while, at the end nearest to the Sistine Chapel, the double series of regional maps was preceded by two general ones, one (on the Adriatic side) representing the country under the Roman Empire (*Italia antiqua*) and the other (on the Tyrrhenian) as it was at that time (*Italia nova*).

Apart from supplying preparatory cartoons for the cycle's 40 panels, Danti may also have had a hand in painting them. But there is no doubt that the work was largely done by skilled painters under his supervision, among them almost certainly Giovanni Antonio Vanosino da Varese, along with the brothers Bril, for the landscape scenes set into the maps, and many other artists for the noncartographical features (the frames of the panels, the elaborate cartouches with their decorative motifs and allegorical figures, the boats depicted in the seas, the grotesques decorating the window jambs, etc.).

The panels are enclosed within white and gold frames with geometrical friezes and figured decorations. Above each frame is the title in Latin (lacking only in the case of some of the smaller panels beside the doors at the two ends of the Gallery). In one of the corners, or in some other part of the frame (sometimes outside of it altogether) are often found the Boncompagni arms of Gregory XIII, a golden dragon on a vermilion ground. More common still are the Barberini arms of Pope Urban VIII (papacy 1623–1644), showing bees with spread wings. This is a sign that the panel in question has been retouched, restored, or repainted. Indeed, the panels underwent a considerable amount of often radical restoration up until the mid-17th century (after which restoration continued, but more discreetly). This is shown by the frequent appearance (not to say occasional swarm) of Barberini bees among the friezes framing the explanatory inscriptions or, as in the case of the *Italia antiqua* (Pl. 2) and *Italia nova* (Pl. 5) panels, in the circular center of the compass roses and above the outer spirals of the very Baroque friezes covering the sea to the west.

The outer frame encloses an inner showing the longitudinal and latitudinal scales graduated in degrees and minutes. In the original panels painted under Danti's supervision, the scale clearly went all the way around, but in the course of restoration it has frequently been deleted or obliterated. Moreover, where repainted, the figures on the scale are often patently wrong.

Another feature common to all the panels, usually found in an isolated zone (i.e., one without chorographic information) whose position varies according to the subject (often in a corner, but also halfway down one of the sides), is a painted label or plaque (or for exceptional reasons a pair of them) with an inscription briefly outlining the physical, economic, or political peculiarities of the region depicted. These plaques are generally rectangular, less frequently circular or oval, and though sometimes plain in design, usually framed by rich Mannerist decorations. Below these plaques, but sometimes in a plaque of its own and in a different area, is the scale of the map in thousands of standard geometrical paces. This measurement, certainly introduced by Danti, is based on the Roman mile, consisting of a thousand paces and equivalent to 1,618.5 yards (1,480 m). A latitudinal minute of Danti's usually corresponds to one of these miles, as may be seen by measuring the graduations along the borders of the panels. In addition to the astronomic graduation and the metric scale, the panels occasionally include the bearings of the principal city in degrees and minutes and more frequently the average longitude and latitude of the region represented.

The larger panels generally feature compass roses, in Roberto Almagià's[1] opinion added after the chorographic elements had been drawn. These show that the regions lying east of the Apennines are oriented with the north upward, those to the west with the south upward, with the exception of the *Italia nova* (Modern Italy), *Etruria* (Tuscany and Northern Lazio), *Patrimonium S. Petri* (Northern Lazio), and *Latium et Sabina* (Southern Lazio) maps.

The panels are painted in bright colors, the most commonly used being an intense blue for the sea (with the effect of the waves reproduced by means of long stretches of foaming crests) and various shades of green for the flat areas. Following standard 16th-century practice, the mountainous regions are represented by more or less tightly clustered cones colored brown or chestnut, and shaded in pale pink, violet, and yellow and occasionally white (which, however, is never used to represent snow or glaciers), so as to enhance the orographic relief. In some cases, the artist who drew the map clearly wanted to reproduce the actual outline or morphological details of a mountain, either because it was well-known or particularly high. These touches of landscape realism are probably also due to Danti, as they are more frequent in the maps of regions he had more thoroughly examined.

Over this basic physical representation stretches the network of human settlements, in some places dense and in others more sparse. The inhabited areas are painted in vermilion and are drawn according to a conventional plan. The lesser centers are represented by a large house or group of houses, those somewhat larger by a minute perspective view apparently intended to draw attention to some important building. But the centers with significant urban functions or that occupy prominent political, military, economic, or religious positions are generally portrayed by a small schematic plan, surmounted, in the case of an episcopal see, by a cross (Latin for a bishopric, papal for an archbishopric). Lastly, at the bottom of the map, usually toward one of the corners, there are often one or two zenithal or perspective plans of the most famous or important cities in the region or else of its main fortalices and ports.

In addition to these graphic elements, which (except, of course, in the case of the *Italia antiqua* panel) aim at describing the country as it was in the last quarter of the 16th century, several maps include imaginary scenes or objects reminiscent of medieval cartography. For example, the land areas show imaginary representations of military or political events (usually taken from classical or medieval history but sometimes more recent) that took place where they are drawn, whose subjects are concisely explained on small scrolls. The seas, on the other hand, are scattered with decorative, or at least highly elegant, depictions of various kinds of boats and ships, or else of monsters and triumphs taken from classical mythology.

A stylistic analysis of the panels as a group and especially of the forms representing the mountain relief, the landscape elements in the plains, the Arcadian backgrounds stretching to their edges to fill in the empty spaces, the

Instrument of the "*primo mobile*," also called "*quadrante*" according to Petrus Apianus (Peter Bennewitz, 1501–1552), who invented it. It was used to calculate sines and cosines.

This one was built in brass in 1568, and it is 11 inches (279 mm) high. It is marked "F.E.D.P.F.," which means "*Frate Egnazio Danti Perusinus Fecit*" ("Friar Egnazio Danti from Perusia made it"). Danti dedicated it to Archduke Cosimo I, as is clear from the Medici coat of arms carved on the instrument.
(Florence, Istituto e Museo di Storia della Scienza)

decorative elements animating the surface of the sea, the plaques bearing the inscriptions, the calligraphy used to inscribe the names of cities, mountains, and rivers, etc., reveals the work of many different hands, not always identifiable and carried out at different times—i.e., not just during the years in which this great sequence of geographical frescoes was originally painted on the walls of the Gallery, but also in the subsequent 50 years of restoration and repainting. But despite the participation of many different artists, each no doubt with his own different degree of experience in the work of transferring chorographic designs from cartoon to fresco, the cycle is a homogeneous and harmoniously articulated whole, thanks to the overall supervision of Danti, especially during the actual painting of the frescoes.

The two long walls of the Gallery are broken up at regular intervals by 34 windows, 17 looking east and giving onto the Belvedere courtyard and 17 west and giving onto the Vatican gardens. Thirty-two of the 40 panels occupy the spaces between one window and the next and are around 10 feet 10 inches (3.3 m) tall and 13 feet 11 inches (4.25 m) wide. The other 8 panels, smaller in size, are placed at the two ends of the corridor, some beside the doors in the two short walls, the others at the extremities of the long.

The cycle begins with the 2 panels entitled *Italia antiqua* and *Italia nova*, which face each other across the Gallery at a short distance from the south entrance, and it continues with the other 30 main panels on the long walls. The last of these, near the north door at the other end of the corridor, represents the territory of Avignon, which had historical links with the Holy See, while the other 29 each represent a region of Italy. However, neither this division nor the way in which the country is represented corresponds to the two main Renaissance sources for Italian history and geography, Flavio Biondo's *Italia illustrata* (1453, first printed edition 1574) and Leandro Alberti's *Descrittione di tutta Italia* (first edition 1550, complete edition 1560). Danti's division was dictated less by geographical than by political considerations, especially where the papal provinces and the many large and small states in the Po Valley area were concerned.

Of the eight smaller panels found at the two ends of the Gallery, the four near the south entrance feature plans of the four main ports (Civitavecchia, Ancona, Genoa, and Venice), while those at the north end show maps of four of the smaller islands (the Tremiti, Elba, Corfù, and Malta) but also depict a number of scenes. The map of the Tremiti Islands, for instance, includes not only a skirmish between Christian and Ottoman ships, but also a view of the remains of the Roman port constructed by the emperor Claudius at the mouth of the Tiber. The map of Elba has a view with a hypothetical reconstruction of the same Roman port. The map of Malta includes a depiction of the Turkish siege of the island, which ended in Christian victory (1565). Finally, that of Corfù represents the famous Battle of Lepanto, which also ended in the victory of the Holy League over the fleet of the Ottoman Empire (1571).

But it is not just in the smaller of the panels that make up the cycle that geography merges with history. Danti (and whoever helped him devise and draw up the iconographic program) decided that in the larger panels, too, battle scenes and other historical events should be depicted in miniature near the places where they occurred. These events were chosen from among the most hazardous of the dangers braved by the country in Roman times, or the various trials faced by Christian Italy as it struggled to overcome internal and external enemies.

This deliberate merging of geography and Christian history reaches its climax, however, in the Gallery's vaulted ceiling, whose 51 sections a whole troop of painters directed by Muziano and his chief assistant, Nebbia, decorated with as many frescoed scenes, featuring apostles, saints, martyrs, and other champions of the faith. It is possible that among those called upon to select these 51 exemplary events or miraculous deeds was the ecclesiastical historian Baronius (Cesare Baronio, 1538–1607), who had already begun writing, though he had not yet published, his *Annales Ecclesiastici* (1588–1607), a monumental Catholic reply to the *Centurie di Magdeburgo* (completed in 1574) compiled by Matthias Flacius Illyricus (Matija Vlačić Ilir, 1520–1575), a Serbo-Croatian Lutheran Reformer, and a team of other Protestant historians.

Carefully disposed on the ceiling so as to align with the maps featuring the city or place where they occurred, these 51 scenes form a sort of picture atlas of Christian history, whose deeds aimed to sanctify every corner of Italy, justifying its claim to be called a new Holy Land, the fountainhead of Catholicism and homeland of the Church.

To return to the maps, it should be pointed out that many of the views or plans of the regional capitals often found along their lower edges were added in the 17th century. Indeed, there are many aspects of the Gallery as it is today that were not present in the Gallery's original state and did not form a part of Danti's design. Perhaps because of the haste with which the work had been done, the frescoes soon required retouching and restoration. Repair work was in fact already necessary during the papacy of Sixtus V (papacy 1585–1590), who succeeded Gregory XIII, and again under Clement VIII (papacy 1592–1605), in the period between 1592 and 1596. We also know that some relatively minor repairs and alterations were carried out from 1647 to 1650, under Innocent X (papacy 1644–1655), and then again in 1720 under Clement XI (papacy 1700–1721), and again in the mid-19th century under Pius IX (papacy 1846–1878). But the most important alterations and most radical restoration work were certainly those carried out in the 1630s under the Barberini pope Urban VIII, who left a memorial to his initiative in this matter by scattering his heraldic bee all over the Gallery (where it joined the myriad Boncompagni dragons), as well as in the inscription on the marble plaque dated 1631, which he had placed over the south door. While this inscription stresses the general range of work done (repairs to the roof and walls damaged by rain and other atmospheric agents; restoration of the paintings, which are described as out of date; the correction and addition of many geographic details, etc.), it does not say who was responsible for the emendations to the maps. On the basis of several firsthand sources, however, it is possible to identify this person as the German humanist Luc Holste (1596–1661), responsible in particular for having revised the two general maps of Italy and several of the regional ones, such as the *Patrimonium S. Petri, Latium et Sabina*, and *Etruria* panels. Other panels repainted at this time were those showing the main ports of Italy (Civitavecchia, Genoa, Venice, and Ancona), and as was previously noted, many of the city plans that are a common feature of the regional maps were now added.

Nevertheless, the general design of the maps remains Danti's. All the regions are represented as though seen from the air, but not always to the same scale (a fact that immediately attracted severe criticism). Indeed the scale can vary quite considerably, ranging from 1:74,000 in the *Sicilia* and *Etruria* panels to 1:23,500 in the *Urbini Ducatus* and 1:13,000 in the *Anconitanus ager*. The colors are basically the same as those used in present-day atlases: blue for rivers and seas, and green for flat land-areas. As a group, these maps give a clear indication of the state of knowledge regarding the chorography of Italy in the last quarter of the 16th century. Of course, as shown in the maps, that knowledge varies in degree from area to area, depending on the sources available to Danti (these included printed or manuscript cartographic material as well as literary or other forms of description of a particular region, such as those already mentioned by Biondo and Alberti).

If we consider the cycle as a whole—that is, the two general maps of Italy (allowing for the fact that they were repainted in the 17th century) as well as the regional ones—we find that the areas represented with the greatest degree of accuracy are the northern plains, Liguria, Tuscany, and the papal provinces between the Adriatic and the Tiber Valley (of which Danti had conducted meticulous cartographic surveys). Much less happy, indeed at times notably unsure or incorrect, is the chorographic representation of the Alpine region, with the exception of the basins of the Ticino and Adige, which were already fairly well documented from a cartographic point of view. The representation of the mountain districts (e.g., the Abruzzi) are adequate only in parts, whereas the areas on the Tyrrhenian coast between the Tiber and the Sele are more accurate. The worst drawn areas are those in the extreme south, especially the islands.

Apart from this unevenness of quality from a strictly geographical point of view, the maps are, with the exception of some southern areas, extremely informative regarding inhabited areas (supplying their location, forms, place-names, and civil or religious importance), and rivers and lakes. They say much less about roads (in many instances they show only the bridges over rivers) and nothing anywhere at all about agriculture or forestry. But one of the most interesting features of this great cycle of geographical images is the close interdependence of the topographical and the pictorial, of a concern for morphology expressed through certain conventional signs, and a tendency toward realism aiming at the sort of effect obtainable today from an aerial photograph, a tendency that refuses to reduce reality to a set of ideograms or symbols (as became normal practice in 19th-century cartography).

The idea of decorating a gallery with a cycle of geographical images was not in itself particularly new. The great novelty and originality of the cycle consist in the decision to represent the whole of the Italian territory on so large a scale—not to mention the physical arrangement of the panels that almost seems to invite the visitor on a metaphorical tour of the entire peninsula, from the Alps down to the islands in the extreme south, along the central Apennine ridge (whose peaks, now bleak and bare, now thickly wooded, and now snow-laden are evoked in the magnificent landscapes forming the background to many of the frescoed scenes on the ceiling).

Maps had always been charged with symbolic meaning. To map a territory was seen as tantamount to possessing it. And not simply in a metaphorical sense, for knowledge of a territory is the indispensable means of gaining access to it, of availing oneself of its resources, and of physically controlling it. Thus, to represent all the regions of Italy in the most advanced and technically precise manner available, in large panels whose fidelity to the physical reality of the territories was guaranteed by their topographical scale, was primarily an assertion of a dominion that the pope exercised directly over the Papal States and as it were by proxy over the rest of Italy.

The Gallery can be seen as an expression of the self-celebration of power. But its creation also meant the perfecting of an instrument necessary for the wielding of that power. For without knowledge it is not possible to act, govern, or plan, as is clearly stated in the inscription on the plaque placed by Gregory XIII above the north door (in praise of the benefits deriving "*ex rerum et locorum cognitione*") and as we are reminded when Danti writes that the pope wished that the ancient port of Ostia be represented in the Gallery "so that he might always have it before his eyes, and consider how best to restore that admirable, indeed marvelous construction to its original state and use."

Of the many projects undertaken by Gregory XIII, the Gallery of Maps is perhaps the one that best shows the ambitions and attitudes, the fears and aspirations underlying a papacy that marked the beginning of a new phase in the Counter-Reformation. In 1572, when a conclave lasting only one day selected Cardinal Boncompagni as successor to the ascetic Pope Pius V (papacy 1566–1572), the pain and conflict the Protestant schism had caused the Catholic Church had largely abated. Its intially defensive reaction and sense of confusion were things of the past. The Church had reformed itself from within, and in the Council of Trent it had reformulated its doctrine. It was now ready to face the Protestant world in a long-drawn-out struggle to recover the ground lost to the enemy. And it meant to use all the weapons that might come to hand: propaganda and political alliance, active hostilities, and the evangelizing tactics deployed by the massed ranks of the new (or reformed) religious orders. Even the "Turkish threat," no less a menace than the Protestant only a short time before, had definitively receded thanks to the liberation of Malta from the Ottoman fleet's siege and the resounding victory won by the Christian forces at the historic Battle of Lepanto shortly afterward (two events still fresh in people's memory and both depicted on the walls of the Gallery).

It is thus a revitalized and combative Church, but one still mindful of past dangers and of enemy aggression that celebrates itself in the blue and green panels of the atlas painted on the Gallery walls, and in the vast, motley crowd of allegorical Virtues and biblical figures, saints and emperors, fictitious and historical characters, birds, and heraldic devices that fill every remaining corner of the

Gallery, from the window jambs to the intrados of the ceiling, with its spectacular profusion of paintings of every kind and size, and white and gilt stuccowork.

It would be wrong to underestimate the predominantly cartographical aims of Pope Gregory XIII in creating the Gallery, whose main purpose was the scientific delineation of space with a view to better controlling and regulating it (an enterprise closely associated with, and whose significance is indeed summed up in the near contemporary construction, by the same team of scientists and artists, of the Tower of the Winds, which closes and crowns the long Gallery, and where Danti's anemoscope indicated wind direction and his sundial measured time). But it would be equally wrong not to emphasize the other ideological connotations of the Gallery's decorative plan as a whole, which, far from contradicting the main cartographical concerns, place them in the context of the broad range of values characterizing the Boncompagni papacy.

We might summarize the pope's deepest intentions in creating the Gallery in a fanciful but not inappropriate metaphor, by saying that he was obeying the wish to gather and review his own certainties, like so many well-ranked troops, along the *passeggiata* of the palace. We see here the same need to regulate and reorder that we find in Gregory XIII's other major projects, such as his reforms of the calendar and martyrology, the philological and doctrinal revision of the Holy Scriptures, and the launching of the vast historiographical undertaking that would result in the 12 monumental volumes of the *Annales Ecclesiastici* produced by Baronius of the Oratory.

So here we have Italy (together with the old Church possessions of the region of Avignon and the Comtat Venaissin), with its provinces, islands, ports, and seas. Politically speaking this was, of course, a very mixed collection, but as a geographical and conceptual entity it was molded into unity by a providential vision of history, which further glorified the role as fatherland to which it was called by the Church. This providential vision of history, confirmed in the eyes of the faithful by the outcome of many, sometimes bloody events and by the divine seal of the many miracles worked by the champions of the faith, is illustrated on the walls of the Gallery by the triumphant representations of victory over the Turks and by the miniature scenes that occasionally enliven the topographical delineation of localities in the maps. But the most spectacular illustration of this vision of history is that which dominates the visitor from above, the 51 miraculous or edifying episodes painted on the ceiling that together make up a true picture atlas of the history of Christian Italy.

Interspersed among the panels of this cycle are those of a smaller one, made up of 24 monochrome scenes painted in a yellowish brown hue so as to resemble gilt bronze reliefs. The subject of this lesser cycle (whose monochrome coloring, in contrast with the polychromatic "atlas of Christian history," indicates the episodes' different origin and greater chronological distance) is the rite of sacrifice in the Old Testament, another theme with marked anti-Protestant connotations, aiming to emphasise the continuity between Old Testament ritual and that of the Catholic Church, founded on Baptism, the Mass, and the Eucharist.

As almost always happens in these Mannerist decorative cycles, the iconographic scheme includes deliberate echoes and symmetries between one scene and another, and one cycle and another. As was said earlier, all the historical episodes connect with the maps placed immediately below them. There are also many complex relations between the multitude of figures that crowd the ceiling. The throng of biblical figures and Christian Virtues—hundreds of small figures painted in the imaginative and eclectic technique known as a *grottesca*— are often placed so as to constitute a sort of marginal commentary on the historical and biblical scenes. They are like so many learned allegorical glosses revealing their hidden meaning and extolling the virtues of the champions of the faith and at the same time those of the reigning pope (whose heraldic dragon looks out from among the sumptuous decoration on all sides). Moreover, deliberate and more or less explicit echoes relate scenes that though from different cycles are spatially contiguous.

But even more surprising—even for those familiar with the sophistication and abstruseness of Mannerist iconology—is the cleverly symmetrical disposition of certain scenes on either side of the center. These recall each other from one end of the Gallery to the other, giving added emphasis to the themes that Pope Gregory XIII and his ideologues felt most strongly about: the primacy of St. Peter and the subordination of temporal to spiritual authority, the battle against the heretics, and the birth of a new Christian era, modeled on the "Golden Age" of Constantine.

There is no doubt that the person who devised this secret pattern was well aware that the vast proportions of the Gallery and the difficulty of reading the images on the ceiling would make it difficult for even the most willing and skilled of scholars to decipher them all. But he did not give up weaving his subtle web of correspondences and iconographical echoes, trusting that, as in the matter of architectural proportion, the erudite harmonies of this "conceptual music" would, nevertheless, capture the minds and ears of the visitor. And perhaps he was right.

---

[1] Roberto Almagià (1884–1962), an Italian geographer, is the author of the first important study on the Gallery of Maps, *Le pitture murali della Galleria delle carte geografiche* (1952). It remains the basis of all later work on the Gallery.

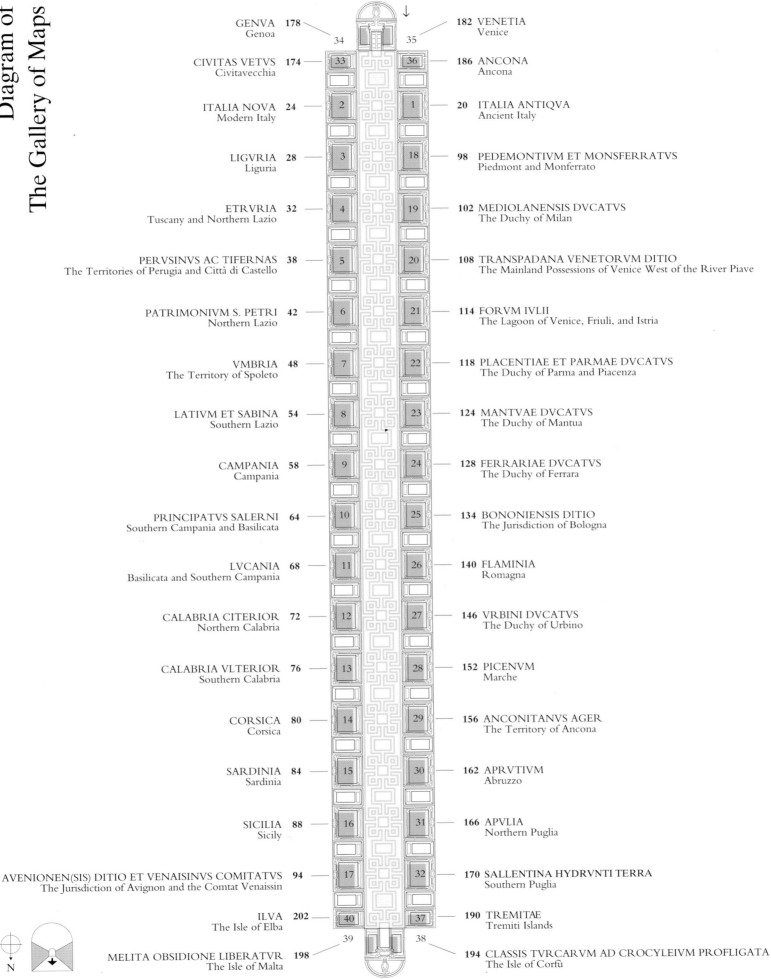

Diagram of
The Gallery of Maps

GENVA **178**
Genoa

CIVITAS VETVS **174**
Civitavecchia

ITALIA NOVA **24**
Modern Italy

LIGVRIA **28**
Liguria

ETRVRIA **32**
Tuscany and Northern Lazio

PERVSINVS AC TIFERNAS **38**
The Territories of Perugia and Città di Castello

PATRIMONIVM S. PETRI **42**
Northern Lazio

VMBRIA **48**
The Territory of Spoleto

LATIVM ET SABINA **54**
Southern Lazio

CAMPANIA **58**
Campania

PRINCIPATVS SALERNI **64**
Southern Campania and Basilicata

LVCANIA **68**
Basilicata and Southern Campania

CALABRIA CITERIOR **72**
Northern Calabria

CALABRIA VLTERIOR **76**
Southern Calabria

CORSICA **80**
Corsica

SARDINIA **84**
Sardinia

SICILIA **88**
Sicily

AVENIONEN(SIS) DITIO ET VENAISINVS COMITATVS **94**
The Jurisdiction of Avignon and the Comtat Venaissin

ILVA **202**
The Isle of Elba

MELITA OBSIDIONE LIBERATVR **198**
The Isle of Malta

182 VENETIA
Venice

186 ANCONA
Ancona

20 ITALIA ANTIQVA
Ancient Italy

98 PEDEMONTIVM ET MONSFERRATVS
Piedmont and Monferrato

102 MEDIOLANENSIS DVCATVS
The Duchy of Milan

108 TRANSPADANA VENETORVM DITIO
The Mainland Possessions of Venice West of the River Piave

114 FORVM IVLII
The Lagoon of Venice, Friuli, and Istria

118 PLACENTIAE ET PARMAE DVCATVS
The Duchy of Parma and Piacenza

124 MANTVAE DVCATVS
The Duchy of Mantua

128 FERRARIAE DVCATVS
The Duchy of Ferrara

134 BONONIENSIS DITIO
The Jurisdiction of Bologna

140 FLAMINIA
Romagna

146 VRBINI DVCATVS
The Duchy of Urbino

152 PICENVM
Marche

156 ANCONITANVS AGER
The Territory of Ancona

162 APRVTIVM
Abruzzo

166 APVLIA
Northern Puglia

170 SALLENTINA HYDRVNTI TERRA
Southern Puglia

190 TREMITAE
Tremiti Islands

194 CLASSIS TVRCARVM AD CROCYLEIVM PROFLIGATA
The Isle of Corfù

N

N

Pl. 1. The south entrance
to the Gallery of Maps
(Scala, Florence).

1

Italia antiqua
Ancient Italy

The *Italia antiqua* panel faces that showing modern Italy (*Italia nova*), which it matches in the area covered, its orientation, and its dimensions of about 10'10" x 14'1" (3.3 x 4.3 m).

The brief inscription on the cartouche in the upper right-hand corner celebrates the wholesomeness of the territory, its mild climate, and its fertile soil. Somewhat more elaborate is the inscription on the large cartouche in the opposite corner, which is placed over a scale in *miliaria romana antiqua* (ancient Roman miles), about 18"(45.5 cm) in length, equal to 10 miles (16.1 km). The graduation along the outer edges of the map is marked at intervals of 5', but the numbering has not survived. The conventions used are the same as in *Italia nova*. However, in their present state, differences between the two maps regarding the treatment of mountainous areas are immediately apparent. In the *Italia antiqua* panel, these are shown by means of a lighter color than in the other, where brown shading is used.

Like *Italia nova*, *Italia antiqua* is the work of Holste, who was commissioned by Pope Urban VIII to restore some of the maps that had been painted in 1580–81 under the supervision of Danti. Holste's design for *Italia antiqua* completely replaced Danti's, so that we unfortunately have no means of forming a judgment of the latter.

The direct juxtaposition of the two Italys, ancient and modern, was already a feature of the Ptolemaic "atlases" of the 16th century, but it had never been attempted on so monumental a scale as here in the Vatican Gallery of Maps. The original cartoons were drawn on 64 large sheets of paper.

The "world eminence of Italy" alluded to in the title to the long inscription echoes one of the themes developed by Greek and Latin literature in praise of Italy (VARRO, *De Ag.* I, 2, 3–8; STRABO, *Geog.* VI, 4,1; DIONYSIUS OF HALICARNASSUS, *Ant. Rom.* I, 36–37; VIRGIL, *Georg.* II, 136–176), taken up again by Pliny the Elder (*Nat. Hist.* III, 39–42) in the introduction to his description of the country. To the "eminence" belonging to classical Italy as the country that first saw the political expansion of Rome was of course added the merit of its including within its shores the center of Christianity, as may be read in the large cartouche in the *Italia nova* panel. The continuity and links with ancient Italy accordingly find expression in the edifying scenes from the lives of Constantine and Pope St. Sylvester that decorate the portion of the ceiling between the two maps.

The northern borders, at the two ends of the Alpine range, are those given by Pliny the Elder (*Nat. Hist.* III, 44), namely the rivers *Varus* (Var) and *Arsia* (Arsa, in Istria). With regard to the territorial composition of the country, the 11 Augustan regions are mostly replaced by earlier ethnic divisions. These are bounded by golden lines that often follow the courses of rivers or the crests of mountain ranges and bear the names of the various peoples inhabiting them (29 are listed in the celebrative cartouche). If the number of place-names (written of course in Latin) is generally speaking so large (around 800, counting those of the islands), this not only is due to the sheer amount of space available in a map of this size, but above all testifies to the knowledge and skill that Holste acquired under the tuition of Philipp Clüver (1580–1622).

Holste was perfectly aware of the fact that a map of ancient Italy needed to give full importance to the network of Roman roads. Since the consular roads are no longer visible in his reworked version of Danti's map in its current state, it is highly probable that they were erased in the course of subsequent restoration. A sketch in Holste's hand in the copy of Clüver's *Italia antica* that he took with him on all his field trips and in which he set down his observations shows a plan of the consular roads north of Rome. Errors concerning the location of ancient sites and in their distance from one another are of course all too frequent. They reflect the current level of antiquarian knowledge and are often due to the habit of uncritically transferring the information gleaned from classical literature directly onto the maps. These same "errors" are found in Holste's most authoritative source, namely the 17 regional maps illustrating Clüver's *Italia antiqua*. An anonymous reviewer of Holste's work drew attention to anachronisms in the hierarchical ordering of the cities, such as the inclusion of centers such as Venice that were founded later. In reality, as stated in the large cartouche, the map covers the period up to the 6th century A.D., for this was the time when Gothic, Lombard, and Byzantine domination brought about a complete change in the political geography of the peninsula.

It is worth noting that Holste in any case endeavored to show the changes in the physical geography of the country, as may be seen by comparing his delineations of the Po Delta in ancient and modern times. The *Italia antiqua* panel, however, has none of the scenes illustrating the famous events of the past, such as the wars with Hannibal, which enhance several of the regional and territorial maps. This is probably not simply due to the fact that the larger scale of the latter facilitated the inclusion of such topographical details. In so far as they are linked with particular places, the famous battles of "ancient" history (extending up to the 6th century A.D.) shown in these scenes, help, no less than the famous battles in "modern" history, to portray the features of a given territory. Thus, the Roman past, which confers a certain unity on the *Italia antiqua* panel, becomes the common background to the various regional and local histories that together make up the mosaic of "modern" Italy.

The fresco on the ceiling corresponding to *Italia antiqua* is *The Emperor Constantine's Vision of the Cross before the Battle of the Milvian Bridge* .

2

Pl. 2. Panel showing *Italia antiqua* (Ancient Italy), and two herms.

3

Pl. 3. *Italia antiqua* (Ancient Italy), detail. Tuscany and the northern Tyrrhenian Sea.

ITALIA REGIONVM ORBIS PRINCEPS
OLIM HESPERIA AVSONIA OENOTRIA ET SATVRNIA DICTA
AB OCCASV AESTIVO IN ORTVM HIBERNV PROTENDITVR
FOLIO QVERNO VEL POTIVS CRVRI HVMANO SIMILIS
SEPTEMTRIONE VERSVS LVNATIS ALPIV IVGIS INTRA VAR ET
ARSIAM FLVMINA A GALLIS GERMANIA ET PANONIA SPARATVR
CAETERA AMBITVR MARI
AB OCCIDENTE LIGVSTICO ET TYRRHENO
A MERIDIE SICVLO ET AVSONIO ABORTV HADRIATICO
MEDIA PERPETVO APENNINI IVGO SE ATTOLLIT
TANDEMQ IN DVAS SECTA PARTES ALTERA SICILIAM
ALTERA EPIRVM VERSVS PROMINET
GENTES PRAECIPVAS HABET AD INFERVM MARE
LIGVRES ETRVSCOS LATINOS SABINOS MARSOS VOLSCOS
CAMPANOS HIRPINOS PICENTINOS LVCANOS ET BRVTTIOS
INDE AD SVPERVM
SALENTINOS CALABROS APVLOS SAMNITES FRENTANOS
PELIGNOS PICENTES VMBROS VENETOS ET ISTROS
INTVS CIRCA PADVM GALLOS
IN ALPIBVS TAVRINOS GRAIOS SALASSOS LIPONTIOS
EVGANEOS RHAETOS ET CARNOS
CAESAR AVGVSTVS IN XI REGIONES EA DIVISIT
QVARVM I CONTINET LATIV ET CAMPANIA II APVLIAM
CALABRIAM ET SALENTINOS III LVCANIAM ET BRVTTIOS
IV SAMNIV V PICENVM VI VMBRIAM VII ETRVRIAM
VIII GALLIAM CISPADANAM VIIII LIGVRIAM
X VENETIAM ET ISTRIA M XI GALLIAM TRANSPADANA
CONSTANTINVS M IN XVI PROVINCIAS DISTINXIT
VNA CVM VICINIS INSVLIS
HARVM PRIMA CAMPANIA II TVSCIA CV VMBRIA
III AEMILIA IV FLAMINIA V PICENVM VI LIGVRIA
VII VENETIA CVM ISTRIS VIII ALPES COTTIAE
VIIII SAMNIV X APVLIA CV CALABRIA XI BRVTTIA CV LVCANIA
XII RHAETIA PRIMA XIII RHAETIA SECVNDA XIV SICILIA
XV SARDINIA XVI CORSICA
ACCESSIT DEINDE XVII VALERIA ET TANDE XVIII APENINAE ALDES
DONEC GOTHI LONGOBARDI ET GRAECI ANTIQVA ITALIA FACIE
IN NOVA REGNA DVCATVS ET EXARCHATVS
TRANSFORMARET

Tiberis   Arnus

STRABO   PTOLEMAEVS

MILLIARIA ROMANA ANTIQVA

4

Pl. 4. *Italia antiqua* (Ancient Italy), detail. The islands of Sardinia and Corsica.

Italia nova
Modern Italy

The map measures 10'10" x 14'2" (3.3 x 4.32 m) and represents the whole of the Italian Peninsula, including the east coast of the Adriatic and the islands, except for Sicily, of which, in accordance with the Ptolemaic tradition, only the northern part is shown.

The adjoining states are *Delfinato* (Dauphiné in southeastern France), *Savoia* (Savoy), and *Svizzeri* (western Switzerland) separated by *Lago di Genevra* (Lake Geneva), *Grisoni* (the Swiss canton of the Grisons, or Graubünden, which at that time held Valtellina), the Austrian regions of *Tirolo* (Tyrol), *Carinthia* (Kärnten), *Stiria*, *Carniola* (Kairen or western Slovenia), *Marcha Vindica*, *Morlachia*, *Dalmatia* (Croatia), and *Albania*. The peninsula is surrounded by the *Mare Adriatico overo Golfo di Venetia* (Adriatic Sea or Gulf of Venice), the *Mare Ionio* (Ionian Sea), the *Mare Tirreno* (Tyrrhenian Sea), and the *Mare Ligustico* (Ligurian Sea).

Two large and elaborately decorated cartouches carry an inscription and a long description of the principal geographical features of the land. In the bottom left-hand corner of the cartouche is a metric scale divided into 20 units, each of which represents 10,000 paces, and measures 23" (58 cm) (approx. 1:510,000).

The map is oriented with the north pointing upward, as can be seen from the compass rose. The fresco is in poor condition: the paint has faded, especially in the lower half; the left-hand cartouche is worn and read with difficulty; and many of the figures are certainly not original.

We have no documentary evidence of restoration or alteration. The panel dates from 1632–33 and is the work of Holste. It replaces Danti's map of *Italia nova*, of which we know nothing, but which was clearly thought unsatisfactory. The map is graduated along its edges at intervals of 5' (152.4 cm), but the numbering has not survived.

Despite its poor condition, the fresco shows that the technique inaugurated by Danti in 1580–81 was still in use when it was painted, as it would continue to be throughout subsequent reworkings and restoration, so as to guarantee at least a semblance of uniformity. The conventional "molehill" form is used to represent mountains, which are lit from the northwest and painted in various shades of green and brown. The plains are green, rivers and lakes blue, and the sea blue, with the waves modeled in blue-green. The courses of rivers and seashores are outlined in pale yellow. Settlements are represented by groups of houses painted in crimson and shown in perspective, though in the case of some cities (Milan, Venice, Pisa, Livorno, Florence, Perugia, Rome, Taranto, Brindisi, and Messina) miniature plans are given. The borders separating one state from another, or one province from another in the Kingdom of Naples, are drawn in gold. The roads, however, are no longer visible. Regional place-names are in gold, local in gold or black. All the place-names, including those identifying areas at sea, are in Italian.

Italy is shown as it was in the last quarter of the 16th century and at the beginning of the 17th. The sources used all date from that period (with the sole exception of Gastaldi's map of 1545, which was used for the portion of Sicily shown). For northern and central Italy, Holste relied on Giovanni Antonio Magini's *Italia nova* of 1608, for southern Italy on the little manuscript atlas of the Kingdom of Naples by Nicola Antonio Stigliola and Mario Cartaro, who began work on it in 1590 or the following year. In the case of Calabria, Holste mostly made use of Magini's *Italia nova* and Prospero Parisio's map of the region of 1589.

As compared with Magini's map, the delineation of the pre-Alpine lakes here is a little out of date, but on the whole the quality of the map is high, being both rich and detailed when it comes to place-names and hydrographically very accurate. It has no historical elements and only portrays the present. It contrasts with *Italia antiqua* in that it shows the changes that had come about in Italy between the time of Augustus and that of Urban VIII. The only slight trace of the past is the occasional archaeological allusion, such as *Luna destrutta* (Ruins of Luna) or *Populonia destrutta* (Ruins of Populonia).

The frescoes on the vault corresponding to the *Italia nova* panel are *Pope St. Sylvester Baptizing the Emperor Constantine*, *The Emperor Constantine Founding the Basilica of St. Peter*, *The Founding of the Basilica of St. Paul*, and *The Emperor Constantine Holding the Reins of Pope St. Sylvester's Horse*.

ITALIA NOVA

Pl. 5. Panel showing *Italia nova* (Modern Italy), and two herms.

6

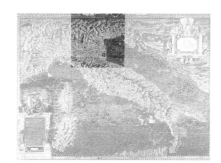

Pl. 6. *Italia nova* (Modern Italy), detail. Northeastern Italy and the northern Adriatic Sea.

7

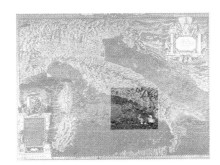

Pl. 7. *Italia nova* (Modern Italy), detail. Southern Lazio and Campania.

Liguria
Liguria

Liguria is represented within a panel of 10′8″ x 14′4″ (3.25 x 4.36 m), of which it scarcely fills a fifth part. The region is a long strip of coast bounded by the Apennines, the sea, and the rivers Varo and Magra. In the bottom right-hand corner, an ornate L-shaped frame, complete with Barberini bee, encloses a scale (now barely legible) corresponding to 14,000 paces and measuring about 11″ (29 cm).

A compass rose in blue and gold placed in the middle of the sea and almost in the center of the panel indicates the southward orientation of the map.

Just within the decorated frame enclosing the panel is a graduated border, but this is now of little use, since, perhaps through careless restoration in the 19th century, the minutes may be read only at intervals and with difficulty and the degrees are no longer legible at all.

This same, unfortunate attempt at restoration has also left its mark on the place-names, where the original can often be seen below the 19th-century repainting. Above all, it is visible in the (unfinished) scale that indicates a ratio of 1:715,000, which is quite out of proportion to a map that is more likely to have one of 1:50,000.

That some restoration work was undertaken for Pope Urban VIII is shown by the presence of Barberini bees in the ornate frames of the scale and cartouche and in the flourish to the place-name *Noli*. However, this is likely to have affected only the decorative features rather than the map itself. The painter Paul Bril, who worked for Pope Gregory XIII Boncompagni, seems to have been responsible for the beautiful mountain landscape that extends across the bottom of the panel, where it decorates the space occupied by portions of the neighboring regions, as indicated by the inscriptions *Pedemontii Pars* and *Mediolanensis D(ucati) Pars*.

Much of the panel is taken up by a large expanse of cobalt-blue representing a slightly ruffled sea, which shows many signs of having been repainted in relatively recent times. This space is filled with numerous decorative and symbolical features, starting with the compass rose and the ornate inscription *Ligusticum Mare*, in letters of gold with elaborate curlicues. In the center is the celebrative cartouche in gold and crimson.

There are numerous ships at sea: a xebec and a galleon off the coast of Nice, another galleon off the Gulf of Genoa, and Andrea Doria's great galley. Directly opposite the latter is an allegory of Christopher Columbus.

Jutting sharply into the sea, the region shows a coastline that if sometimes overjagged, is generally undercurved. More of the Riviera di Ponente is shown than of the Riviera di Levante, which means that Genoa loses something of its central position in the gulf.

The orography is conventional, without any real descriptive character and of use only as a guide to the geomorphological features of the area, which it indicates by means of drawing and color, alternating different shades of green, lightened toward the left, where the light comes from, with touches of ocher.

Nevertheless, a few mountain names are given, though most serve to mark frontier passes. Among these, *Monte della Croce* probably corresponds to Passo di Cento Croci, and *Monte Bravo* to Colle del Braus. The only mountain name not used to mark a frontier pass is Bracco, misspelled *Branco*.

River names are fairly plentiful, though many others may have been lost in the course of modern restoration. For example, the name of the Varo is missing, though this is mentioned in the inscription on the cartouche as one of the two rivers that mark the natural limits of the region. However, the map does show the upper reaches of the Varo with its branches, and these are correctly named, if less correctly drawn: the *Tinea* (Tinée), the *Vesubia* (Vésubie), the *Palion* (Paillon), the *Bibera* (Bévera), and the *Rotta* (Roya), which all meet at Sospello (curiously duplicated, or perhaps added more recently, since in a more accurate position we find *Cespitello*, an older name for Sospello). Finally, there is the *Nerva* (Nervia) and the *Imperiale* (Impero). The Argentina is neither named nor correctly drawn; indeed, it seems to have been swallowed up in *rio S. Lorenzo*, presumably the neighboring river, which has been given too much importance. The complex system of rivers of the Centa, is fairly well rendered, if in places a little crudely. The Lerrone, Arroscia, Neva, and Pennavaire are all quite recognizable, as are, between Oneglia and Albenga, the Armea, the S. Pietro, the Cervo, and the Merula. The river name *Zimora* is no doubt a mistake for *Zinora* or Zinola, and so corresponds to the present-day torrent Quiliano.

Of the two rivers of Genoa, the Bisagno (*Bisagna*) is named, but not the Polcevera, though this is shown on the map. Next come the Lavagna, which corresponds to the Entella, the Varo, and the Magra, on the border with *Etruriae Pars*, while the upper course of the Taro may be seen at the boundary between the Republic of Genoa and the Duchy of Parma.

A golden line marks the regional boundaries, some of which are political—the dominions of the *Serenissima Repubblica*—and some "natural," such as the river Varo.

No roads are visible in the fresco's present condition, but from the grouping of the settlements along the rivers one can deduce the probable routes of the roads entering the valleys. The map is rich in place-names, all in Italian with the exception of *Prugnetum* (Brugnato). The settlements are shown by means of somewhat mannered, though varied, miniature views. Of particular note is that indicating Bobbio, on the border with the Duchy of Milan.

The settlements are fairly consistently indicated throughout the map, though in some places with less frequency, especially as one moves inland, where errors in the drawing of the river courses and hence of the neighboring valleys increase the difficulty of locating them correctly.

The fresco on the vault corresponding to the map of *Liguria* is *The Translation of the Ashes of St. John the Baptist to Genoa*.

8

Pl. 8. Panel showing *Liguria* (Liguria), and two herms.

9

10

Liguria (Liguria), details.
Pl. 9. Allegory commemorating the voyage of Christopher Columbus.
Pl. 10. Mountain landscape.

11

12

13

Liguria (Liguria), details.
Pl. 11. Andrea Doria's brigantine.
Pl. 12. Allegorical figures.
Pl. 13. Two battleships.

Etruria
Tuscany and Northern Lazio

The map, approximately 10'7" x 14'2" (approx. 3.22 x 4.31 m), shows the area bounded by the Magra Valley, the Tyrrhenian Sea (*Mare Tyrrhenum*), the Tiber Valley, and the Tuscan-Emilian Apennines. It also shows the Tuscan Archipelago: Gorgona, Capraia, *Iglio* (Giglio), and *Gianuti* (Giannutri). In modern terms, then, it comprises Tuscany, the part of Lazio lying on the right bank of the Tiber, and parts of Umbria (*Umbriae Pars*), the Marche (*Picenum*), Romagna (*Flaminia*), and Emilia (*Flaminiae Pars*).

The fresco has been restored at least twice. Between 1586 and 1589, during the papacy of Sixtus V, Giovanni Guerra repainted "two thirds, together with the decoration," while in 1596, under Clement VIII, Pietro Oldrado retouched the whole of the bottom half, including all the place-names, a scene, and a scroll ("*una historietta et una cartella*"). Holste, however, does not appear to have made any significant alterations to the map. The Latin names for places in Umbria (*Nar F[luvius]*, or the Nera; *Tiberis F[luvius]*, or the Tiber; *Perusia*, or Perugia; *Narnia*, or Narni; *Interamnia*, or Terni; and *Velinus F[luvius]*, or the Velino) may all have been added at the time of Clement VIII. Under Urban VIII, several place-names, almost all in the lower part of the fresco, were certainly repainted: for example, *Troia I.*, *Capo delle Saline*, *Talamone*, *Iglio*, *Gianuti*, *Civitavecchia*, and *Capo Marino*, which has the Barberini bee on its flourish. Another addition made under Urban VIII is the plan of the port of Civitavecchia, and other names probably rewritten at this time are *Narta F(iume)*, *Lago di Bracciano*, *L(ago) di Bientino*, and *Lago di Fucecchio*. It is quite possible that Holste had a part in these revisions, drawing the roads south of Siena, which were not on the maps Danti used as his sources. He may also have added the ancient place-name alongside the corresponding modern one (*Isola olim Veii* [Isola, once called Veio]; *Civita Castellana olim Falisci* [Civita Castellana, once called Falisci], etc.). The lower part of the fresco, however, does not match the *Patrimonium Sancti Petri* panel, which was certainly drawn by Holste and which shows the same territory. Umbria, on the other hand, has essentially the same form as in the maps of the territories of Perugia and Spoleto, which are certainly by Danti, or as in the printed map of the territory of Orvieto published by Danti in 1583.

Many place-names have been half-erased. And although the coat of arms on the cartouche is that of Pope Pius IX, no names seem to have been rewritten in the 19th century. This may be the reason why there are so few misspelled names (e.g., *Carrese* instead of Caprese in the upper Tiber Valley).

The orography is of the conventional "molehill" type, in various shades of green and brown, lit from the left. The highest mountains are shown in relief in the northern and northeastern areas. Plains and hills are shown in various shades of green. The coastline is picked out in light ocher and pale yellow. The sea is painted deep blue and modeled in green. The settlements are symbolized by small persepective views of groups of houses painted in crimson. Episcopal sees are marked wih a golden cross. Plans are shown of Florence, Lucca, Viareggio, Pisa, Livorno, *Forte* near Orbetello, Porto Ercole, Civitavecchia,

Rome, and *Perusia* (Perugia). Siena is seen in a view showing its towers. The place-names are all written in black and gold and are all in Italian, except for those outside of the Tuscan territory, which are in Latin. The borders are painted over in gold, the roads in white or brown.

No battles or historical scenes are represented on the map. On the whole, despite its being the product of a variety of sources and indeed of different hands, *Etruria* is surprisingly homogeneous, and the picture of the territory that it gives is basically a faithful one, i.e., a region with densely populated hill and mountain areas and marshy valleys and plains, only a small number of fortified ports, several public works still in progress, a well developed road system (in the fresco's present state visible only in the lower part of the map), and a network of waterways often complicated by the presence of marshlands.

The map says little about the human exploitation of the region except with regard to the settlements. It is more informative about those areas where humankind is excluded, such as the frequent stretches of uninhabited woodland, one of which (the hunting preserve of Antimino) is human-made.

The most conspicuous feature in the map is the relief. However, as was customary at the period, the mountains hardly ever have names and their form is merely conventional: they are suggested rather than actually portrayed. The *Panie* (Alpi Alpuane) are not shown at all, and the only hint of their existence is the place-name *Pietra Pana*, as on Gerolamo Bellarmato's map. The Tuscan-Emilian Apennines are effectively painted, but this is a chance result of the point of view chosen. The peaks of the Montefeltro Mountains are much less convincing, indeed wholly conventional. The territories of Urbino and Umbria are not shown; their place is filled by a purely decorative landscape, setting off a delightful view of the Marmore Waterfalls.

Hydrographically speaking, the map is both thorough and accurate. However, the painter—or restorer—represents marshes, lagoons, lakes, and rivers in exactly the same way, and the viewer needs to know the area already in order to interpret its features correctly.

Numerous settlements are shown, some with little plans, others with more or less conventional views. The borders between states are not shown. Regional names are few and far between: *Val di Magra* (Magra Valley), *Garfagnana*, *Stato di Lucca* (State of Lucca), *Flaminiae (Pars)* (Romagna), *Urbini Ducatus* (Duchy of Urbino), and *Umbriae Pars* (Umbria). At its southern extremity, the map ends with a bird's-eye view of Rome, different from the one in the Southern Lazio panel, marking the historical limit of ancient Etruria.

Several ancient sites are shown: *Luni distr(ucta)* (complete with ruins), *Populonia distr(ucta)*, *Cincelle distructa*, etc., but otherwise the map has no archaeological or antiquarian features.

The frescoes on the vault corresponding to the map of *Etruria* are *St. Romuald Founding the Hermitage of Camaldoli* and *St. Francis Receiving the Stigmata*.

14

Pl. 14. Panel showing *Etruria* (Tuscany and Northern Lazio), and two herms.

15

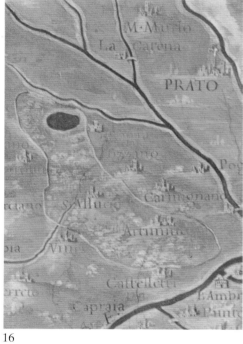

16

17

Etruria (Tuscany and Northern Lazio), details.
Pl. 15. Trompe l'oeil painting with view of Siena.
Pl. 16. Hunting preserve of Artimino.
Pl. 17. Trompe l'oeil painting with view of San Miniato al Tedesco.

18

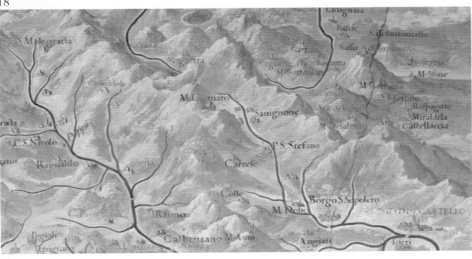

19

20

Etruria (Tuscany and Northern Lazio), details.

Pl. 18. The Maremma coasts with Mount Argentario.

Pl. 19. The upper Tiber Valley.

Pl. 20 The Marmore Waterfalls at Terni.

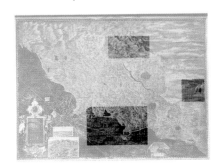

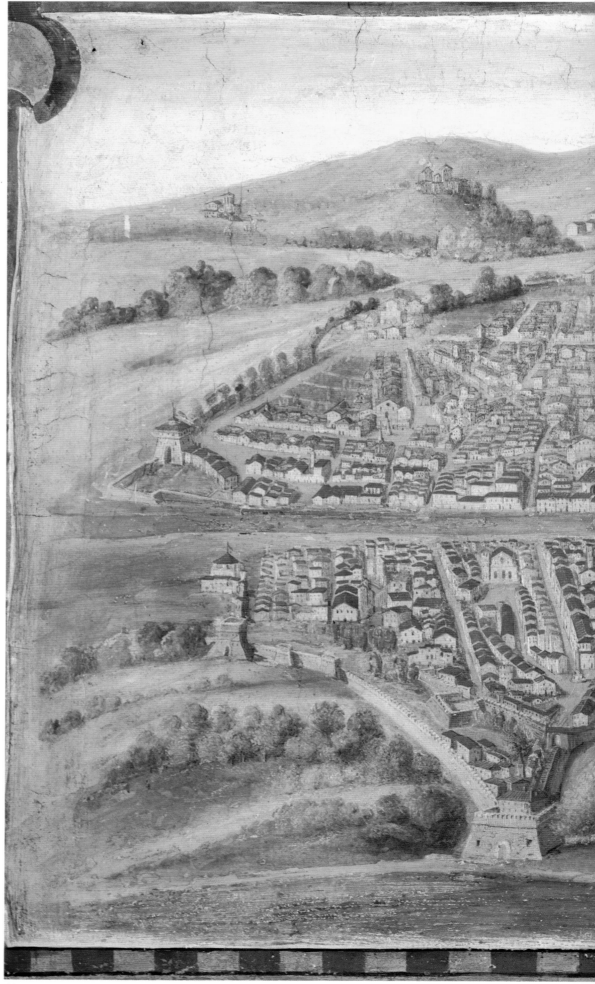

Pl. 21. *Etruria* (Tuscany and Northern Lazio), detail. Trompe l'oeil painting with view of Florence.

21

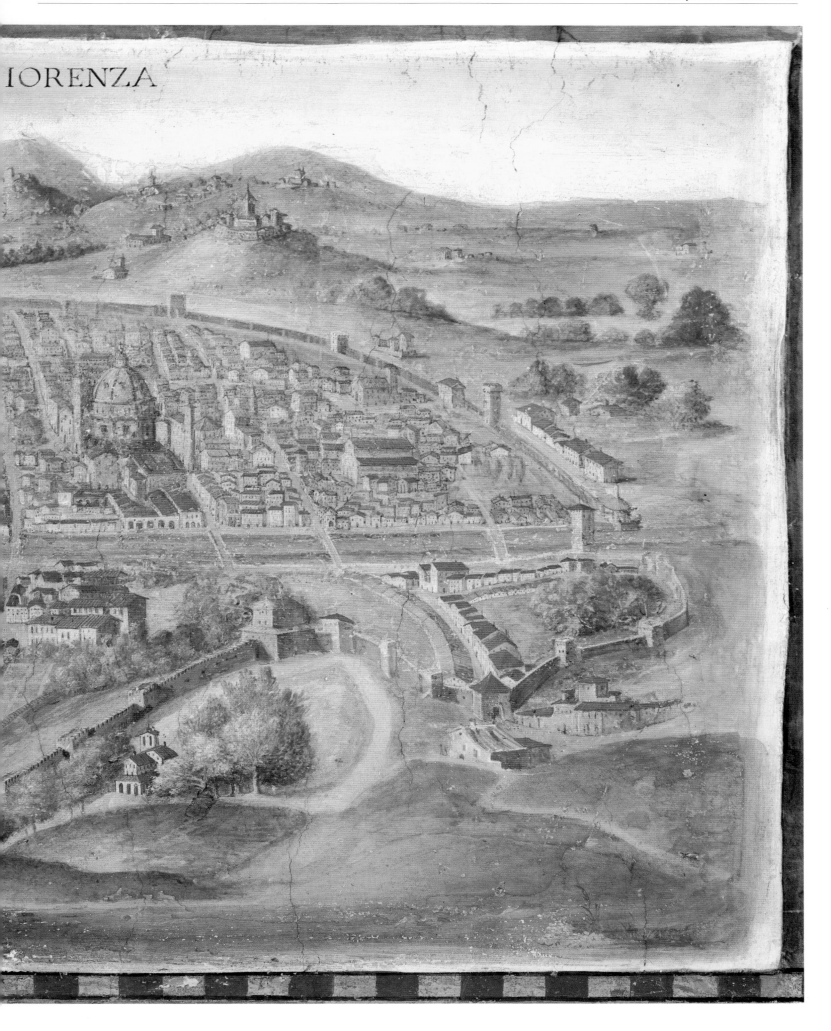

IORENZA

Perusinus ac Tifernas
The Territories of Perugia and Città di Castello

The map, 10'8" x 14'4" (3.25 x 4.37 m), shows the part of the Tiber Valley that forms the territories of Perugia and Città di Castello (*Tifernum*) in Umbria, together with the basin of Lake Trasimene and a part of the Val di Chiana (*Le Chiane Paludi*). The area is bounded by the *Eugubinus Ager* (or country around Gubbio); *Umbriae Pars* (Umbria, that is the territory of Spoleto, since the territories of Perugia and Città di Castello were then considered part of Tuscany); *A Florentinae Ditionis Parte* (territory of Florence); and *Senen(sis) Ditionis Pars* (territory of Siena).

The map is oriented with the south (*O[stro]*) pointing upward, as seen in the compass rose marked with the eight winds traditionally shown on nautical charts in the Mediterranean area: *O(stro)* (south); *A(frico)* (southwest); *P(onente)* (west); *M(aestro)* (northwest); star (north); *G(reco)* (northeast); cross (east), and *S(cirocco)* (southeast).

The map is by Danti. In 1597, it was completely restored by Oldrado, who added the figures, some of them female, and other things to the cartouche, the arms of Pope Clement VIII and a little scene entitled Hannibal the Consul, and other decorative features. Some place-names were rewritten under Urban VIII (e.g., *Lacus Trasimenus*), when Pope Clement VIII's arms were deleted from the cartouche and the Barberini bees added. The inscription, however, remained unchanged at this time. Subsequent retouchings are likely, but are not recorded.

The map was constructed over a grid with a slightly trapezoidal mesh. It is graduated along its border in 5' intervals. The longitudes range from 34°26' to 36°4', while the latitudes have not survived, and the present numbering of the minutes is unreliable. The reference parallel and meridian are not indicated. According to Almagià's calculations, Perugia lies at 43°15' latitude and 35°20' longitude, *Tifernum* at 34°37' latitude and 35°13' longitude.

Danti carried out a survey of the territory of Perugia in 1577 at the behest of the Papal Governor, Monsignor Giovan Pietro Ghislieri and the Priors and Chamberlains of Perugia. The drawings he made at that time were the principal source for this map, together with the fresco measuring around 2 sq. yd. (1.7 m²), which he had painted in the Palazzo dei Priori at Perugia, where it survived until 1798. Danti's drawing for this was also engraved on copper by Cartaro and printed in Rome in 1580, with the title *Descrittione del Territorio di Perugia Augusta ... del P.M. Egnatio Danti da Perugia.* In this map the coordinates of Perugia differ by 20' from those in the Vatican fresco. Other differences include the greater number of smaller places and names of mountains shown, as well as naturalistic details and inscriptions listing, on the one hand, the abbeys and benefices of the knightly religious orders and, on the other, strongholds, castles, large villages, and stone bridges, in addition to the perimeter of the region, 138 miles (222.1 km). Unlike that in the Vatican, the printed map is oriented with the north pointing upward and excludes the territory of Città di Castello (which was certainly absent from the Perugia map too, and for which Danti's source is not known) and the scene of the Battle of Lake Trasimenus (Trasimene) (217 B.C.). Otherwise the printed map resembles that in the Gallery.

The corresponding maps in Ortelius's *Theatrum Orbis Terrarum* (1601 and later editions) and Magini's *Italia* (1608) derive from Danti's.

Mountain relief is shown by means of the convention of cones lit from the left and painted in various shades of green with touches of violet and indigo on the dark sides of the higher peaks. The plains are also shown in green, while the rivers and lakes are a deep blue.

The settlements are symbolized by small plans and perspective views painted in crimson. Also in crimson are the bridges, while the place-names are in black and gold and the borders in gold. The names are almost all in Italian, except for those of the surrounding territories. Episcopal sees are marked by a Latin cross in gold, the benefices of the knightly religious orders by a Greek cross in gold.

The map of the territory of Perugia is one of the most beautiful in the Gallery, even if requirements regarding the uniformity of the cycle as a whole entailed some loss in value. The painter was not able, for instance, to represent the difference between the scattered buildings of the settlements in the plains and the more close-knit fabric of the settlements in the hills and mountains, clearly shown in the original drawing (at least as far as can be judged from the printed map). However, great care is taken over the relation of the settlements to the network of rivers, which constitutes the basic framework of the map, but also to the elevations and the collocation of sites on hilltops or slopes.

The hydrography is detailed and accurate but, unlike the printed map, does not show the difference between running water and marshlands. Here, as in other cases, it is not known whether this is a feature of the original fresco or is due to repainting. Also lacking are the roads, which were shown on the printed map, and the symbols of the abbeys and benefices, although some of these are shown (the Greek cross at Magione, San Giustino, and Monte Alari), giving the impression that the others were omitted in the course of restoration. The symbols marking episcopal sees, on the other hand, have survived (Perugia and Città di Castello). No attempt was made either in the printed map or (probably) in the original fresco to represent cultivated land such as is shown around the plan of Perugia. Woods, on the other hand, are always shown, being the prevalent form of vegetation in the area.

The territory of Città di Castello, which was not surveyed by Danti, is less detailed (the names of many of the tributaries of the Tiber are missing). The little plans of Borgo San Sepolchro and *Tifernum* (Città di Castello), heavily restored in the 19th century, are fairly accurate in outline, but the layout of the streets seems somewhat random, which is not the case in the little and otherwise very schematic plan of Perugia.

The fresco on the vault corresponding to the map of *Perusinus ac Tifernas* is *St. Constantius in Prison Healing the Sick with the Sign of the Cross.*

22

Pl. 22. Panel showing *Perusinus ac Tifernas*
(The Territories of Perugia and Città di Castello), and two herms.

MENVS

I. Magg.ᵉ

Pozzuolo

Petrignano

Borghetto

Pieue di confine

ietra Mala

Hic Hannibal confule interfecto romanos profligauit A.IƆXXXVII

23

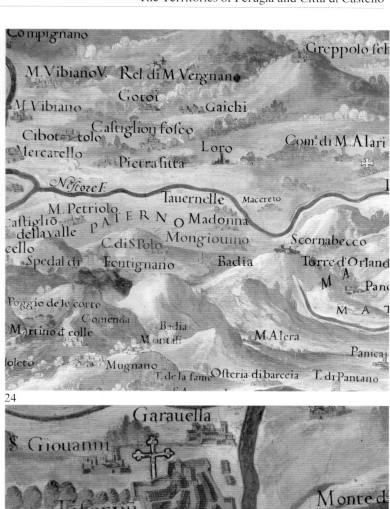

24

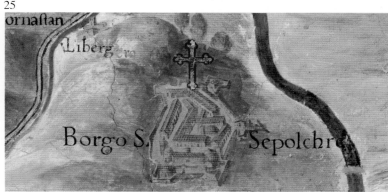

25

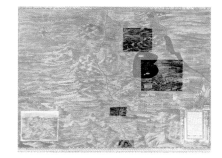

26

Perusinus ac Tifernas (The Territories of Perugia and Città di Castello), details.
Pl. 23. The battle between Hannibal and the Romans at Lake Trasimene (217 B.C.).
Pl. 24. The course of the river Nestore and the border between the territories of Perugia and Siena.
Pl. 25. Plan of Città di Castello (*Tifernum*).
Pl. 26. Plan of Borgo San Sepolcro.

Patrimonium S. Petri
Northern Lazio

The map, about 10′4″ x 13′9″ (approx. 3.14 x 4.2 m), shows the territories lying between the Tyrrhenian Sea (*Mare Tyrrhenum*) and the mouths of the rivers Albegna and Tiber up to Orvieto (*Tiberis Fluvius*) on the coast, and the courses of the Tiber and its tributary the Paglia. This is the area known at that time as *Tuscia Suburbicaria* (the part of Tuscany belonging to the *Urbe*, or City of Rome), or else as the *Patrimonio di San Pietro*. On this map it is shown bounded by the *Maritima Senensium Ditio* (maritime territory of Siena), the *Montana Senensium Ditio* (mountain territory of Siena), the *Urbivetanus Ager* (territory of Orvieto), *Umbriae Pars* (Umbria), *Sabinae Pars* (Sabina), and *Latii Pars* (Lazio).

The scale was originally placed among the folds of the drapes showing the two city plans in the lower left-hand corner but has been painted over in red. There is no compass rose. The map is oriented with the north pointing upward.

The present map was painted between 1636 and 1637, to replace the original one by Danti, which was severely criticized by his contemporaries Filippo Pigafetta and Magini. It ultimately derives from Bellarmato's map *Chorographia Tusciae* (printed from 1536 on), and is not unlike the southern part of Danti's own *Etruria*.

Holste replaced Danti's with his own, very different work. Danti had included a map of the territory belonging to the Republic of Lucca in the same panel, which Holste neither reproduced nor modified, perhaps because of poor relations between Lucca and the Papal States, which would lead to the papal interdict against the former in 1641. The letters L A G in the lower left-hand corner of the cartouche are part of the original painting, but their meaning is not clear (they are too large to refer to Lake Bolsena). There is no record of subsequent restoration, but the arms and portrait of Pope Pius IX over the two city plans suggest that the panel was in part restored during his papacy. Indeed, the whole upper part looks as though it was repainted in the 19th century. The colors are rather faded, despite the repainting of the rivers and lakes. The graduation is missing, having been replaced by a gold band following the edges of the panel.

The conventions are slightly different from those used by Danti, although the colors are the same. The mountains are of the usual "molehill" form, in various shades of green, brown, and violet and lit from the left. However, the painter clearly tried to make the map as scenic as possible—as is clear if we compare it with the corresponding area in Danti's *Etruria*. The plains and hills are colored various shades of green, coasts and watercourses outlined in pale yellow, rivers shown in blue, and the sea in blue modeled with green. The initial portions of the consular roads may be seen spreading out from Rome, while a longer section of

Via Aurelia has survived. The settlements are symbolized by perspective views of groups of houses, painted in crimson: the only city to have a plan is Rome. The painter has tried wherever he can to represent buildings and other human artifacts on a scale as close as possible to that of the map as a whole, making sure that one thing is proportionate to another and not made conspicuous by being painted oversized, as Danti would do. Episcopal sees are marked with a gold cross, and names are written in black and gold, some in Italian and others in Latin.

No battles or other historical events are shown on the map, but there are frequent allusions to the past, through the use of Latin names for some localities and above all the use of both Latin and Italian names for others (e.g., *Civita Castellana olim Falerii*, *Fanum Volumnae Viterbo*, *Civitavecchia olim Centum Cellae*). The principal lakes all have their Latin names beside their modern ones. The ruins of ancient settlements are also marked, such as *Blerae veteris vestigia* near Bieda, *Falari distr(utta)*, *Sabate destr(utta)*, and *Porto*, the ancient Ostia, at the mouth of the Tiber. The map is remarkably homogeneous and offers the best representation of northern Lazio of the period. By today's standards, its orography may be thought disappointing (although the representation of the Cimini range is full of picturesque details), but from a hydrographical point of view it is excellent. Particular care is taken over the volcanic lakes that abound in the area, as well as over the courses of the rivers.

Place-names are plentiful and precise, and the settlements are carefully classified and described: fortified towns such as Bracciano, castles such as Anguillara, towers, villages, and isolated churches. The only real city is Rome, whose vast extent is seen in the bird's-eye view toward the right-hand margin of the map, the starting point for the minutely drawn network of consular roads. The painter's constant effort to represent settlements and roads on the same scale as the rest of the map—more typical of the topographical artist than of the cartographer—gives a faithful picture of a predominantly wooded area in which settlements are not frequent but of extraordinary antiquity. The woods, or *selve*, are common and, unlike the mountains, often given names (e.g., the *Selva di S. Agostino* near Montalto, or the *Selva maccarese*). Along the coast is a series of lagoons, small lakes, spits, land-reclaiming ditches, and lookout towers. The only real port is Civitavecchia.

The frescoes on the vault corresponding to the map of the *Patrimonium S. Petri* are *The Miracle of Bolsena and the Procession Bearing the Corporal Stained with Blood from the Host to Pope Urban IV in Orvieto* and *Countess Matilda of Canossa Donating Her Possessions to the Church*.

Pl. 27. Panel showing *Patrimonium S. Petri* (Northern Lazio), and a herm.

28

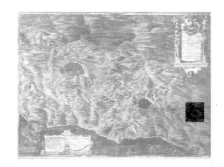

Pl. 28. *Patrimonium S. Petri* (Northern Lazio), detail. Plan of Rome.

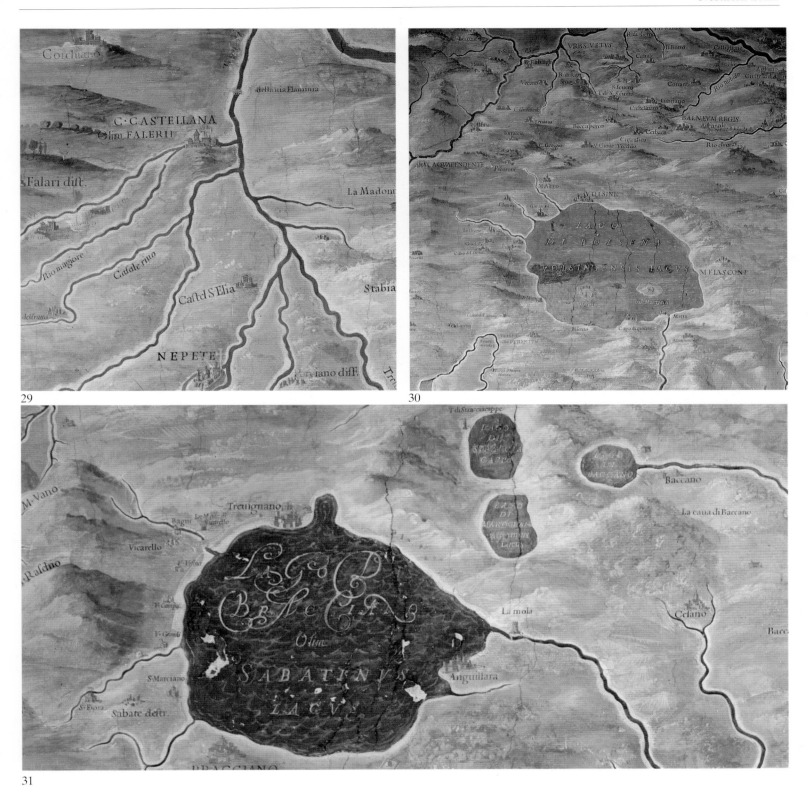

29

30

31

Patrimonium S. Petri (Northern Lazio), details.
Pl. 29. Territory between Civita Castellana and Nepi (*Nepete*).
Pl. 30. Lake Bolsena.
Pl. 31. Lake Bracciano.

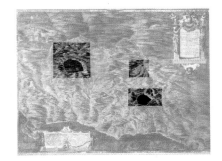

32

T. di Corneto

T. di Bertaldo

URBS VETUS

Pl. 32. *Patrimonium S. Petri* (Northern Lazio), detail.
Cupids with plans of Viterbo (*Viterbium*) and Orvieto (*Urbs Vetus*).

Umbria
The Territory of Spoleto

The map, 10′8″ x 14′4″ (3.24 x 4.36 m), shows the ancient Duchy of Spoleto, with the territory of Camerino, which had been part of it in the late Middle Ages. The territory came under the direct control of the Church in the 13th century. It is bounded by the *Patrimonii Pars* (or Patrimony of St. Peter, the part of Lazio lying on the right bank of the Tiber); *Hetruriae Pars* (*Etruria* or Tuscany, which acccording to Danti also included the territories of Perugia and Città di Castello); *Piceni Pars* (Piceno, now in the Marche); and *Aprutii sive Samnii Pars* (the Abruzzi, territory of the Samnites).

The scale is of 4,000 *passus geometrici communes* (feet used to measure distance), and is 13″ (34 cm) long (approx. 1:26,000).

The map is oriented with the south pointing upward, as can be seen from the compass rose, which shows half- and quarter-point winds: *O(stro)* (south); *A(frico)* (southwest); *P(onente)* (west); *M(aestro)* (northwest); *T(ramontana)* (north); *G(reco)* (northeast); *L(evante)* (east); and *S(cirocco)* (southeast).

There is no record of the panel's having been restored or modified, except for the addition of the view of Spoleto, which probably dates from after 1613. However, Almagià suggests that some minor alterations were carried out by Holste around 1636. The inscriptions on the cartouches are the original ones, although their frames were repainted under Urban VIII, whose heraldic bee they show. In the left-hand cartouche the frame covers the end of two lines in the inscription.

The map is graduated in minutes. The degrees now lack their numbers, but the reference meridian and parallel have survived, which makes it possible to establish the position of the territory mapped at a latitude of between 42°30′ and 43°30′ and at a longitude of between 33°57′ and 35°44′. The map is projected over a rectangular grid.

The conventions adopted are the usual ones: the mountains, painted in various shades of brown and green, have the standard "molehill" form and are lit from the left; the plains and hills are in various shades of green; the hydrography is in blue. The towns are represented by perspective views of groups of buildings painted in crimson (some of which, such as that of Assisi, would seem to have been taken from drawings made on the spot), and in some cases by miniature plans, like that of Orvieto. The episcopal sees are marked with a gold cross. The names are written in black and gold, some in Latin, but mostly in Italian.

At least a part of the territory shown was personally surveyed by Danti in 1580. We do not know what other sources he used, and there are no close analogies with Magini's map of the same area.

Two historical events are depicted in the panel: the siege of Spoleto by Hannibal, and Vinichisius, Duke of Spoleto, freeing Pope Leo III (papacy 795–816) from prison and offering him refuge in the city. The second scene is very probably a later addition.

The cartographer paid particular attention to the relief, as is obvious given the physical character of the region (also evoked in the right-hand cartouche), which includes most of the mountain ranges in Umbria and the Marche. Many of the mountains and valleys are given their names, and some mountain areas, such as that of the Sibillini Mountains are represented in a particularly picturesque manner.

The hydrography is thorough, though the names of many waterways are missing. Numerous lakes are shown. By Lake Piediluco may be seen the coat of arms of Gregory XIII, in memory of his part in the reclaiming of the plain of Terni, by ordering the re-opening of the drainage canal of the Velino, which was still partly blocked despite work done by Antonio da Sangallo (1483–1546) under Paul III (papacy 1534–1549). The Marmore Waterfalls, formed by the Velino as it falls into the underlying valley of the Nera, may be seen a little farther to the right. The Fossa Renosa, an irrigation canal near Bevagna in the plain of Foligno, and the tidy rows of trees and fields emphasize the unusual character of the only real plain to be found in this part of the Umbrian territory.

Elsewhere, as is made abundantly clear, woodland dominates, a fact of which the spectator is also reminded by the trees in the foreground, near the cartouches. The area is densely populated, especially around Camerino, so much so that Almagià thought that this must have been the part surveyed by Danti. Churches, castles, villages, towns, and cities are all well differentiated and easily identifiable. Settlements on slopes, such as Assisi, Cascia, and Nocera, are clearly distinguished from those on hilltops or in the plains. The position of cities like Terni, at the conjunction of two rivers, is well rendered.

Among the other humanmade phenomena shown are the many bridges (including the monumental bridges of Narni and Spoleto, which were drawn on the spot) and the Via Flaminia, backbone of the region.

Only a few ancient sites, such as the ruins of the *theatro* near Spello, are shown. Indeed, this is another essentially modern map, drawn by a cartographer who, as in the case of the country around Perugia, was extremely familiar with the territory.

The fresco on the vault corresponding to the map of *Umbria* is *St. Clare Freeing Assisi from Siege by the Saracens.*

33

Pl. 33. Panel showing *Umbria* (The Territory of Spoleto), and two herms.

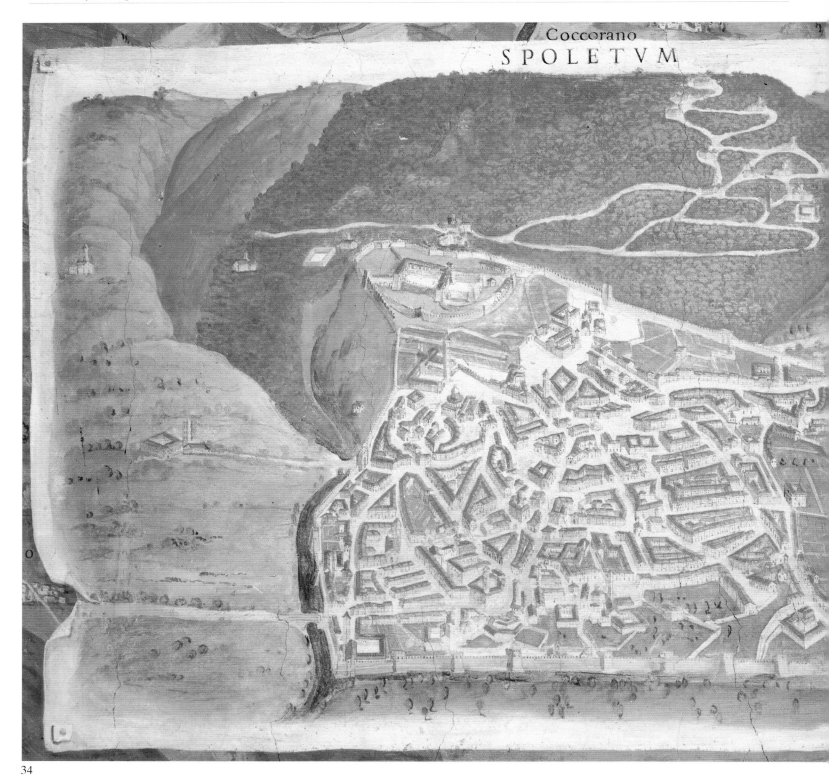

34

35

Frinfana   Pannaiola   Coll
Foliano
Puro

Auenuta

C.S.Maria   Colle d'   A
Ocrichia
Cccacalcia
Saueli
Piederiua   Belueder
S.Martino   Valcaldara   S.Scolaltica

S.Pellegrino   NV

Lago di Nescia

M.Victor

Grotta della
Sibilla

Forcella
Acqua Pagana B.
Sclu

Appennino   V
M.S.Poli

Umbria (The Territory of Spoleto), details.
Pl. 34. Trompe l'oeil painting with plan of Spoleto.
Pl. 35. The Sibillini Mountains with the Sibyl's cave.

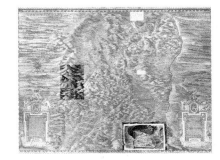

36

37

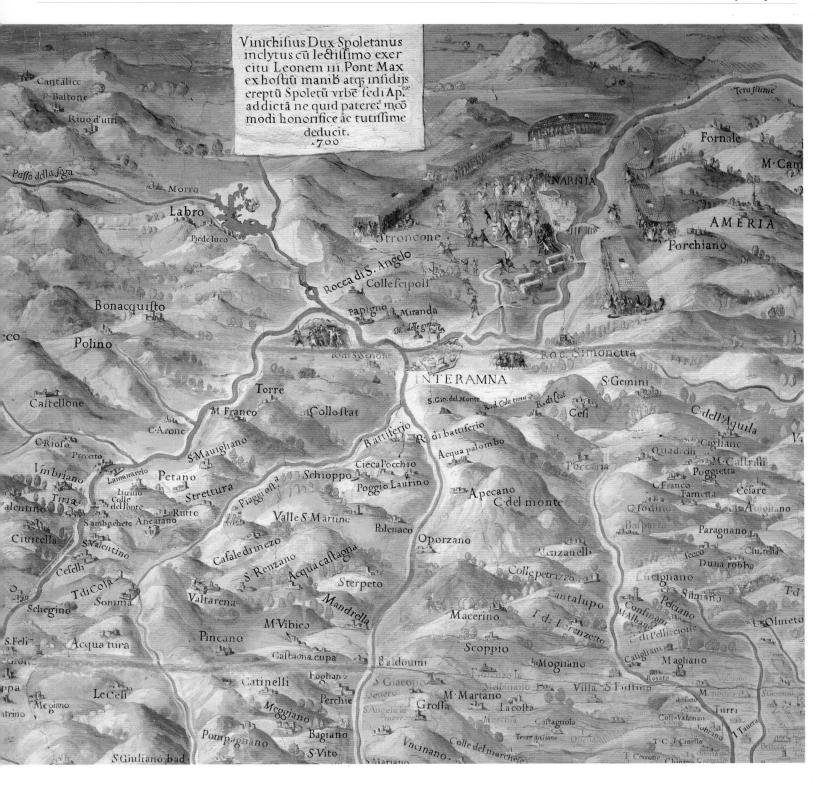

Vinichifius Dux Spoletanus
inclytus cū lectiffimo exer
citu Leonem III Pont Max
ex hoftiū manib atq; infidijs
ereptū Spoletū vrbē fedi Ap.cæ
addictā ne quid pateret incō
modi honorifice ac tutiffime
deducit.
·700

Cantalice
P·Baftone
Riuo d'utri
Paffo della fegu
Morro
Labro
Piedeluco
Bonacquifto
Polino
Caftellone
Torre
C·Riofo
Precetto
Vimbriano
Laimanarelo
Petano
Tiria
Lurino
Colle
delfonte
Strettura
Rutte
Sambochete Ancaiano
Ciuitella
S·Valentino
Cefelli
T·diCola
Somma
Schegino
S·Feli
Acqua tura
Grotte
Le Cefi
Mcogiano
Pincano
Caftaona cupa
Catinelli
Foghan
Perchie
Meogiano
Bagiano
Pompagnano
S·Vito
S·Giuliano bad
S·Mariano

Rocca di S·Angelo
Stroncone
Collefcipoll
Papigno Miranda
R. delle grati
R·di s·Fenore
INTERAMNA
M·Franco
C·Arone
S·Mauigliano
C·dell Monte
Collo ftat
Battiferio R·di battiferio
Ciecal'occhio
Schioppo
Acqua palombo
Poggio Laurino
Piaggi ofta
Valle S·Martine
Cafale di rnezo
Acqua caftagna
S·Renzano
Sterpeto
Valtarena
Mandrella
M·Vibico
Baldouini
Scoppio
S·Giacopo
Mellanano
S·Angelo in
moreorio
Grofa
M·Martano
Lacofta
Caftagnola
Terre di Gian
Fiorenzo la
Villa S·Tuftino
Rofaro
Vncinano
Colle del marchefe
T·C·I·Cinello

NARNIA
Tera fiume
Fornale
M·Cam
AMERIA
Porchiano
S·Gemini
C·dell'Aquila
S·Gio·del Monte R·d·Cola tuna R·di Cefi
Cefi
Cigliano
Quadrdi M·Caftrilli
Porcaria
Poggioretta
C·Franco
Farnetta
Cefare
C·fodino
Augliano
Balparta
Apecano
Paragnano
Oporzano
Cecco
Ciuitella
Menzanelli
Duna robba
Colle petrizzo
Lucignano
Silmano
Cantalupo
Peciano
Macerino
T·di Lorenzetto
Confingni
M·Albauo
T·di Pelliccione
Cagliano
Mogliano
Magliano
Olmeto
T·d
M·necro
Caglianu
Turri
Colle·Valenzo
Sobrano
I·Tauera
T·Cerrone Chiana

R·c·Simonetta

Umbria (The Territory of Spoleto), details.
Pl. 36. The plain between Foligno and Spoleto.
Pl. 37. The lower course of the river Nera with the Reatini Mountains.
Plan of Terni (*Interamna*) in the center.

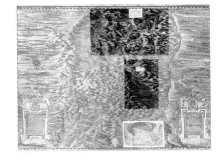

Latium et Sabina
Southern Lazio

The map, about 10'7" x 14' (approx. 3.23 x 4.27 m), shows the territory lying between the Tyrrhenian Sea (*Mare Tyrrhenum seu Inferum*), the courses of the rivers Tiber (*Tiberis Fl[uvius]*), Nera (*Val di Narca*), Velino, Salto, Garigliano (*Garigliano F[iume]*), and Liri. The surrounding territories are *Suburbicariae Pars* (also called *Tuscia Suburbicaria* or the Patrimony of St. Peter, i.e., Northern Lazio), *Umbriae Pars* (Umbria), *Aprutii Ulterioris Pars* (Northern Abruzzo), and *Regni Neapolitani Pa(r)s* (Kingdom of Naples). In modern terms, *Latium et Sabina* is the portion of Lazio south of the Tiber. The scale bar measures around 13" (34 cm) and is equal to 6,000 *passus geometrici communes* (approx. 1:26,500). The orientation, which is not marked, is with the northeast pointing upward.

This panel was painted in 1636 or 1637 from drawings by Holste. It completely replaces the previous fresco by Danti, of which only a sketch made in 1592 by Philip Van Winghe for Ortelius survives. This was oriented with the southwest pointing upward and did not show the territories beyond the promontory of Monte Circeo. The inscription on Danti's cartouche (recorded in Cod. Barb. Lat. 1803), which cited Strabo (*Geog.*, V, 3, 4, 6), only referred to *Latium antiquum* ("*Latium antiquum a Tiberi Circeio servatum est mille passum L. longitudine tam tenues primordio imperio fuere radices …*" ["Ancient Lazio has remained 50 miles in length, stretching from the Tiber to Monte Circeo these the humble origins of the Empire …"]), and not to the modern region, which according to Strabo extended from Ostia to Sinuessa, on the border with Campania. The map also showed Sabina.

Danti's map, severely criticized by Pigafetta (in 1591) and Magini (in 1598), was replaced by one of a very different kind by Holste. There is no record of subsequent restoration, but a large number of toponyms and some hydronyms have been repainted. Repainting may also be the reason for the absence of various geographical names and the disappearance of the compass rose, whose form can just be made out in the top left-hand corner.

The graduation of Danti's original panel has been replaced by a gold band. Holste nevertheless gives the coordinates of Rome in the plaque placed in the lower right-hand corner: 41°56' latitude and 36°30' longitude.

The orography is mostly conventional: "molehill" forms painted in various shades of green, yellow, brown, and violet, and lit from the left. However, the painter has made some effort to produce a more painterly, rather than merely symbolical representation. The plains and hills are shown in various shades of green; coastlines and watercourses are outlined in pale yellow; the rivers and lakes are in blue, deeper where repainted; and the sea is in blue with the waves modeled in blue-green. The settlements are represented by perspective views of groups of buildings painted in crimson. Many, such as *Frascati* and *Praeneste* (Palestrina), were clearly drawn on the spot. Rome and *Tarracina* (Terracina) are represented by bird's-eye perspective views. Episcopal sees are marked with a gold cross

(the one by Rome has three arms). The names are written in black and gold, some in Latin and others in Italian.

The map does not depict battles and other historical events, but the past is evoked, as in the *Patrimonium S. Petri* panel, in the frequent use of classical place-names, e.g., *Praeneste* for Palestrina, *Interamna* for Terni, *S(anta) Petronella olim Annae Perennae Fanum*, and *Nettuno olim Caeno Antium navale*.

Like others by Holste, this map, which was the result of long study and of familiarity with the terrain, is more uniform than virtually any of Danti's, as well as being admirably detailed and precise. Though conventional, the orography is extremely evocative. The names of the mountains are rarely given, as was customary. On the other hand, the omission of the names of many rivers and all the lakes except for *Fucinus Lacus* (Lake Fucino) and *Cutiliae lacus* (Lake Paterno) and the coastal lagoons, is extremely unusual. Indeed the lack of these and other place-names made Almagià think the map was unfinished, but as, was said above, this may also have been due to poor restoration. Great care has been taken over the representation of the settlements, depicted wherever possible on the same scale as the rest of the map, and drawn according to their size and position. Special attention is also paid to the bridges and the Roman roads.

Indeed, just beneath Zagarolo and Palestrina can be made out a faded remnant of the system of consular roads, the surveying of which had been one of Holste's main interests as a historical geographer and, following his lead, most of which were mapped in this period. Almost contemporary with Holste's map of *Latium et Sabina* is Domenico Parasacchi's beautiful survey of the Appian Way. The areas it crosses and the coastal region are considered to be the best parts of the map, both because of the minute detail in which the settlements are shown and also the representation of the irregular disposition of the bodies of standing water, evidence of the land-reclaiming ditches and drainage canals that papal engineers had been working on for more than a century.

This map too gives an overall, effective, and, within certain limits, accurate picture of the territory. Its limitations, it should be noted, are not determined by the use of techniques different from those used today, but rather by its inability to show the population's regular migrations from the mountains to the plains and vice versa, through the lack (still felt today) of a cartography able to represent what is provisional and subject to change. A situation of continual flux thus seems frozen here in an image corresponding only in part to the human reality of 17th-century Lazio: the higher ground densely populated, its plains and coastal areas startlingly empty except for watchtowers, and only one real city, Rome, its importance emphasized in the large plan shown in the trompe l'oeil drawing in the lower left-hand corner.

The frescoes on the vault corresponding to the map of *Latium et Sabina* are *The Appearance of Christ to St. Peter outside Rome* and *Simon Magus Falling to his Death*.

38

Pl. 38. Panel showing *Latium and Sabina* (Southern Lazio), and two herms.

ROMA
PER SACRAM B.PETRI SEDEM CAPVT ORBIS EFFECTA. S.LEO.I.

39

40

Latium and Sabina (Southern Lazio), details.
Pl. 39. Trompe l'oeil painting with plan of Rome.
Pl. 40. Detail of trompe l'oeil painting with plan of Rome showing the Vatican and Castel Sant'Angelo.

Campania
Campania

The map of *Campania* fills a panel measuring 10'10" x 15' (3.31 x 4.29 m). It is oriented with the south pointing upward, as seen in the compass rose painted in gold in the upper center. The territory shown is bounded by the Sorrento Peninsula and the Pontine Marshes, extending inland toward the Frusinate to include the ancient Duchy of Sora, situated between the Volturno and the Liri, and reaching as far as the southeastern spurs of the Monti Ernici.

The scale, at the base of the elaborate cartouche in the lower right-hand corner, is equivalent to a distance of 12,000 paces and measures 15" (37.2 cm), and so has a ratio of about 1:47,700.

Below the scale an inscription—probably added later, since it was not transcribed by Taja—gives the coordinates of Naples.

In the upper right-hand corner is another large cartouche, with winged putti astride an ornate frame, which covers most of the portion of the Tyrrhenian Sea shown. It has no inscription, nor apparently ever had, the space where it should have been being left unpainted and filled with flourishes. Both cartouches are decorated with Barberini bees, testifying to restoration work under Pope Urban VIII, perhaps even to the addition of the unfinished cartouche.

The map is on the whole of rather mediocre quality. The coastline—relieved against a deep blue sea full of cargo vessels—tends to be imprecise, when not blatantly wrong, especially between Gaeta and Capo Miseno. The shape and size of the main islands is also far from accurate, especially Ischia and Procida, of which the map simply supplies the outline. The Gulfs of Salerno and Naples are the only ones named (in Latin).

The orography, represented by heaped cones painted in ocher and umber, with green washes and lit from the left, is entirely conventional in treatment. The Monti Lattari are shown differently here from their depiction in the *Principatus Salerni* panel, but with little improvement. *M. di Soma* (Monte Somma) is the only mountain name given, indeed, *M. Esuvio* (*sic*) appears as the name of a settlement. There is no trace here of the flaming cone symbolizing the volcano in the *Principatus Salerni* panel. The Lepini, Ausoni, and Aurunci ranges are all poorly rendered. This leads to a mediocre description of the Fondi plain, as of the coast between Gaeta and Sperlonga and around Terracina, which the calcareous spurs fail to reach. In the Gulf of Gaeta, in particular, insufficient emphasis is given to the semicircular chain of the Aurunci, while the mountains in the Matese district and the outermost projections of the Ernici are improbably placed at right angles to the coast.

The system of waterways—in two different shades of blue, evidence of repeated restoration—has its center in the river Volturno and in the Liri-Garigliano water system, which is well depicted, though the confluence with the Sacco and Rapido, the ancient *Gari*, is missing. To the east and west of these two major axes few other watercourses are shown, and those few often inaccurately depicted.

The Pontine Marshes are drawn less successfully here than in the *Latium et Sabina* panel. The delineation of the area in the *Campania* panel is based on a vague and only partial knowledge

of the Agro Pontino, even if it is not totally inaccurate. Though they are not named, we can recognize the Amaseno and the Ufente, and the series of torrential rivers, starting with the Ninfa, which all have their sources in the Karst Springs at the foot of Monti Lepini, are well represented. On the other hand, the vegetation, whether of scrubland, woodland, or marshland, is depicted in a merely conventional manner, and no specific symbol or color is used to represent the reddish undulations of the dunes. But most imprecise and incomplete of all are the coastal lakes, here shown as two small rounded lagoons.

An inadequate knowledge of the physical character of the region is also shown in the treatment of the Campi Flegrei. Here too the cartographer was evidently not familiar with the coastal lakes: Lake Miseno has been made little more than an inlet, Lake Fusaro can only be identified thanks to the neighboring *La Gavetta* (Torregaveta), and Lake Patria from the settlement of the same name. Most surprising of all is the total omission of Lake Averno.

There are many gaps and uncertainties in the representation of the human settlements too, which are symbolized by miniature perspective views in crimson. To be more precise, the map is divided into two main areas, the wide band of coastland, where the lack of data is most obvious, and the broad wedge-shaped area extending inland toward the Duchy of Sora, which on the contrary is well delineated and full of detail.

A fairly large part of the coastal strip overlooking the Gulf of Gaeta is occupied by the representation of a historical event and by the simple white cartouche bearing the legend that narrates it. Pope John X (papacy 914–928), succeeded in forming a league together with the lords of southern Italy and Alberic I of Spoleto and arming a force that he himself then led against the Saracens, who were occupying the Valle del Garigliano. The battle took place in August 915 (the legend gives the erroneous date of 914, the year in which John X became pope).

A perspective view of the city of Naples completes the lower right-hand quadrant of the fresco. The city is designed in a calligraphic manner between the waters of the gulf and the hills from Posilipo to Capodimonte, even if the observation point, very high on the horizon, tends to flatten the relief. The result, generally, is a fairly clear topography as far as the form of the *insulae* and the urban plan as a whole is concerned, but no attempt has been made to render graphically any particular building of the city.

The axonometry, simplified as it is, allows us to see the principal results of the urban alterations ordered by the Viceroy Pedro Alvarez de Toledo (1484–1553), even if little importance is given to the walls, which were an integral part of the defensive system of Naples, and the object of considerable attention during the planning stage of Alvarez de Toledo's project itself.

The frescoes on the vault corresponding to the *Campania* panel are *The Miracle of the Blood of St. Jannarius* and *St. Benedict Unmasking the Disguised King Totila.*

41

Pl. 41. Panel showing *Campania* (Campania), and two herms.

Pl. 42. *Campania* (Campania),
detail. Trompe l'oeil painting with
plan of Naples.

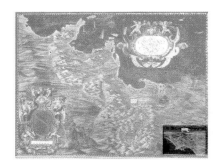

42

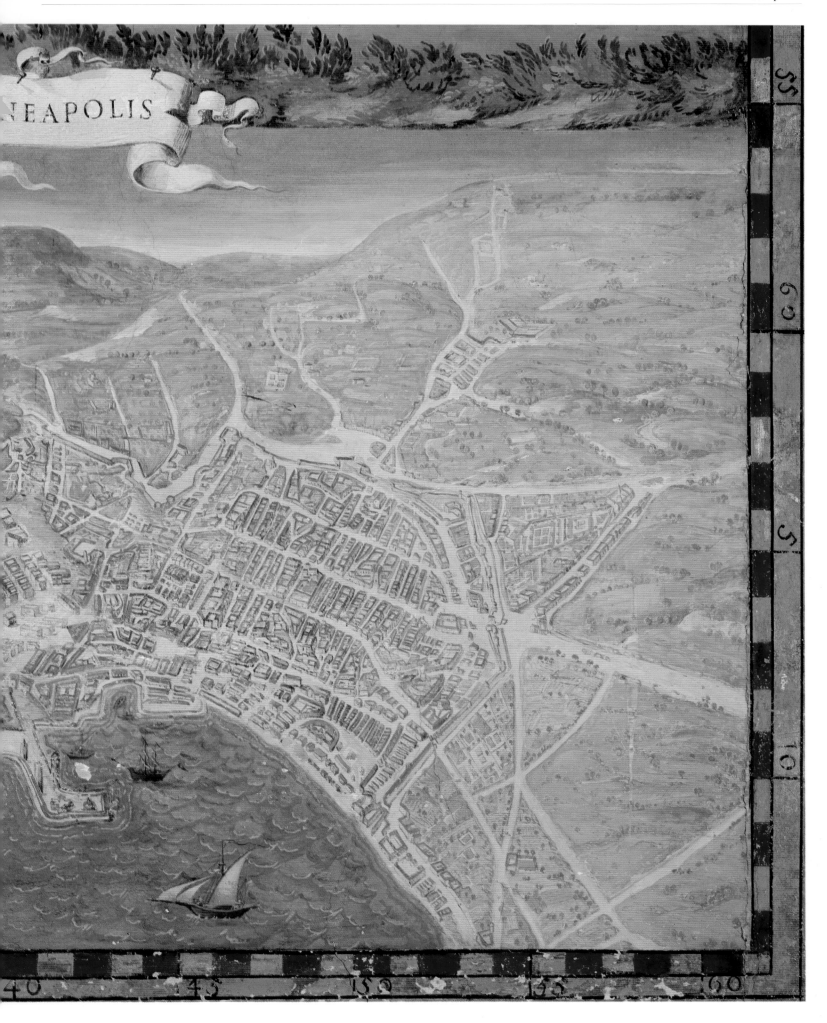

NEAPOLIS

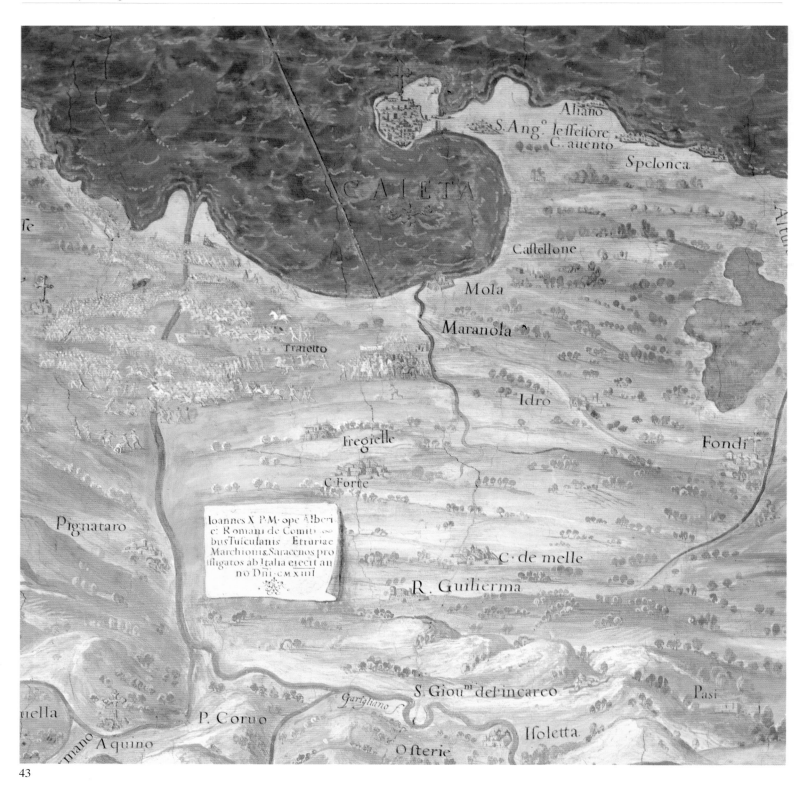

Aliano

S.Ang.º leffettore

C. auento

Spelonca

CAIETA

Caftellone

Mola

Maranola

Traietto

Idro

Fregielle

Fondi

C·Forte

Pignataro

Ioannes X·P·M· ope Alberi
ci Romani de Comiti
busTufculanis Etruriæ
Marchionis Saracenos pro
fligatos ab Italia erecit an
no Dni·cm xiiii

C·de melle

R. Guilierma

S. Gioumᵐ del incarco

Pasi

Gariglianø f.

P. Coruo

Ifoletta

uella

mano Aquino

Ofterie

43

Pl. 43. *Campania* (Campania), detail. The defeat of the Saracens near the river Garigliano (915).

44

Principatus Salerni
Southern Campania and Basilicata

The map of the Principality of Salerno occupies a panel of 10′8″ x 14′2″ (3.25 x 4.31 m) and, aside from some slight changes, uses the same cartographic base as the *Lucania* panel. However, the strip of territory it shows is that bordering on the Tyrrhenian Sea between the Gulf of Policastro and the Gulf of Salerno, extending inland until just beyond the Monti della Maddalena and also including Irpinia. The scale is exactly the same here and is shown, together with the reference meridian and parallel, in a small cartouche at the bottom of the panel; the scale measures 17″ (43 cm) and is equal to a distance of 12,000 paces, so that the ratio is 1:41,300. This map is again like that of *Lucania* in that it is oriented with the south pointing upward, as may be seen from the compass rose in blue and gold in the top right-hand corner. The graduation at the edges, forming a trapezoidal grid, encloses the area lying between 39°52′ and 41°40′ latitude and between 39°27′ and 42° longitude.

The landscape is depicted in a style different from that employed in most of the other panels as regards the rendering of the mountain relief and the use of color. This may be due to restoration carried out between 1647 and 1650 under Innocent X by Giovan Battista Magni. The presence of Barberini bees along with Gregory XIII's heraldic dragon in the lavish frame to the cartouche in the lower left-hand corner suggests there may have been other attempts at restoring the panel before this, although these probably only concerned the ornamental features.

Some stretches of the Tyrrhenian coast are different here with respect to the *Lucania* panel, an improvement that Almagià thought was due to the use of nautical charts. However, there are none of the features normally associated with the latter, such as small islands and rocks; furthermore, as we shall see below, the coastline settlements are not always correct. The coastal area is also poor in place-names. The names of the three principal bays—Policastro, Naples, and Salerno—stand out in gold letters on the blue sea (crossed by a carvel, cargo boats, and fishing vessels). But whereas the Latin name for the last, *Paestanus Sinus*, is also supplied here (as in the *Lucania* panel), we do not find the inscription *Veliates Sinus* marking the Bay of Palinuro. The orography is conventional and shows little ability in rendering the relief.

The geomorphological delineation of the Cilento district is also far from precise. Here the conventionally treated mountain masses trespass on the vast Sele plain, which is much reduced in size, as is the depression of the Vallo di Diano.

The Lucanian watercourses, together with their names, are almost all reproduced from the other panel. In addition to these, the present map includes a large number of rivers on the Tyrrhenian side of the Salernitano, though not all of these are named. On the whole, the cartographer would seem to be reasonably familiar with the rivers, but there are some gaps in his knowledge, especially in the Sorrento Peninsula and in the Cilento district. The Ionian coast of Basilicata here bears the name *Ora Magnae Graeciae*.

No regional names as such are given within the Salernitano, but in accordance with the Ptolemaic tradition (which Danti does not normally follow), the names of two peoples, the *Hirpini* and the *Picentini* (Picentes) are used to designate separate districts.

The settlements are on the whole unevenly distributed. Alongside areas like Irpinia in which the place-names are both numerous and correctly located, there are others where only a vague or even confused idea of the distribution of the settlements is given. The Amalfi coast is especially misrendered, despite the cartouche's celebration of its inhabitants' pioneering use of the magnet for orientation. The settlements in the Cilento district are also incompletely and inaccurately represented. Agropoli, Roccadaspide, Castelcivita, Teggiano, and Vallo della Lucania are also missing, unless the latter is to be identified with a place called *Cornito*, which is represented by a conventional and scarcely noticeable perspective view placed between Tanagro and Calore.

A few archaeological sites are shown, but this is not evidence of a real interest in classical geography, such as is manifested in the *Lucania* panel. With the exception of *Picentia destructa*, the ancient city of the Picentes, which was punished by Galba for opening its gates to Hannibal and later destroyed during the Social War, no classical site (not even Velia) is identified by name, nor are the ancient place-names given. On the other hand, the map does show sites abandoned in more recent times, such as *Capaccio Vecchia* and *Pesti*. The Italianized form of the Roman name *Paestum*, which is that used in the *Lucania* panel, suggests the exclusion of all references to classical times in favor of modern geography. At the same time, the cartographer shows little knowledge of the circumstances in which the town was finally abandoned, which happened in the 9th century as a result of the combined effects of malaria, flooding, and Saracen raids. Among the historical sites, mention should be made of that of the Caudine Forks, whose fame derives from Livy's account of a well known episode in the Samnite War of 321 B.C. It is interesting to note that the Forks are here placed near S. Agata dei Goti (here given as simply *S. Agata*, whereas the name *S. Agata dei Goti* is wrongly given as S. Agata di Puglia). Renaissance historians and geographers took a keen interest in the question of the site's location, and interpreted Livy's not very detailed account as referring to Forchia in the Valle d'Arpaia. It was Clüver who in 1623, in his *Italia Antiqua*, advanced a different interpretation, the one also adopted in the present map. It is not clear, then, whether Danti anticipated Clüver's thesis, or whether the site was not rather added or re-located in the 17th century. In the latter case, however, there might be some doubt as to whether the painter Magni, or Holste, a thorough annotator of Clüver's work on historical geography, was responsible.

The lower right-hand corner of the fresco terminates with a perspective view of the Sanctuary of Montevergine.

The frescoes on the vault corresponding to the map of the *Principatus Salerni* are *The Manna Issuing from the Tomb of St. Andrew at Amalfi* and *The Victory Won by Rainulph, Duke of Puglia, through the Intervention of St. Bernard.*

45

Pl. 45. Panel showing *Principatus Salerni* (Southern Campania and Basilicata), and two herms.

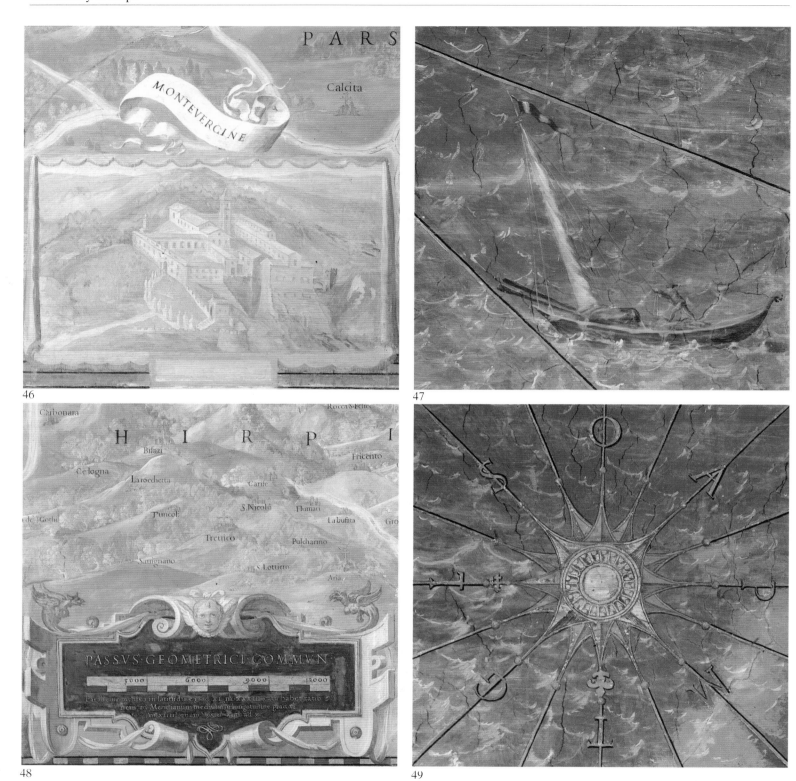

46

47

48

49

Principatus Salerni (Southern Campania and Basilicata), details.
Pl. 46. View of the Sanctuary of Montevergine.
Pl. 47. Fishing boat in the Tyrrhenian Sea.
Pl. 48. Metric scale.
Pl. 49. Compass rose.

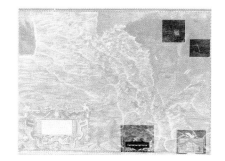

50

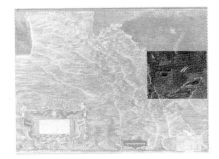

Pl. 50. *Principatus Salerni* (Southern Campania and Basilicata), detail.
The Gulf of Salerno and the Sorrento Peninsula.

Lucania
Basilicata and Southern Campania

Lucania is shown in a panel measuring 10'10" x 14'3" (3.30 x 4.35 m). A gold line separates it from Calabria, the Principality of Salerno, Puglia, and the Terra d'Otranto.

This is the only panel in the Gallery to have its title inscribed on a separate scroll (in the lower right-hand corner); the name used is the ancient one of Lucania rather than the medieval one of Basilicata.

In the lower left-hand corner is a cartouche bearing a celebrative inscription in gold letters on a blue ground enclosed in a splendid frame decorated with putti, caryatids, and allegorical figures and also featuring a gold shell with the Barberini bee. The cartouche also contains the scale, which measures 9" (21.5 cm) and represents 6,000 paces. This would give a ratio of around 1:41,300. In the same cartouche, there is also the indication of mean meridian and parallel, which, however, is not in agreement with the graduation in the margin of 39°46' to 41°4' latitude and 39°40' to 42°15' longitude, which is also hardly readable. In this case, too, a bungled restoration has a misreading of the coordinates.

The red and gold compass rose in the upper right-hand corner shows that the map is oriented with the south pointing upward.

The Barberini bee in the cartouche is evidence that work was done on the panel under Urban VIII, but it is not easy to say exactly what this consisted of. It probably only concerned the ornamental features, including the pleasant pastoral landscape filling in a space along the lower margin of the panel.

The region is shown between the Tyrrhenian and Ionian Seas (the latter bearing the generic name *Hadriaticum Mare*) painted in cobalt blue. Four merchant cargo boats are seen in the Tyrrhenian, the one in the Gulf of Salerno being particularly striking. Most of the coastline shown is outside of Lucania, which includes only a brief stretch of coast in the Gulf of Policastro around Maratea and another slightly longer one in the Gulf of Taranto.

The predominantly mountainous terrain is effectively rendered by covering virtually the entire territory in cone-shaped mountains, lit from the left. Although depicted in a conventional manner, the mountains are on the whole reasonably well represented. The Monti della Maddalena range, which is close to the Vallo di Diano, is positioned with a reasonable degree of accuracy, but the parallel Paratiello-Volturino-Alpi chain can barely be made out, and the line going from Toppo Castelgrande to Monte Caramola, and the northern slopes of the Pollino is broken and unclear. Nor are the highest peaks shown—the Vulture, for example, or Monte Sirino. The only mountain named is the *Mons Alburnus,* which, however, is in the Principality of Salerno and is shown in isolation rather than as part of the short Monti Alburni chain.

The rivers are accurately drawn, though here too there is some uncertainty. All the principal watercourses flowing into the Ionian Sea are drawn and marked with their names. The map shows the karst character of the Tanagro (the river goes underground between *Polla* and *Grotta d'Acque*).

The region's hydrography is completed by a river on the Tyrrhenian side, the *Tardo*, shown as flowing from a large lake that is situated near the town of Lagonegro and so must correspond to Lake Remmo.

The settlements—represented by means of mostly conventional small perspective views painted in crimson—are unevenly distributed. On the whole, the northern part of the region seems the best known, while the towns and villages are inadequately described, especially in the southeast. There are indeed some surprising omissions in the latter area, in which the settlements shown are in any case few and far between. Particularly worthy of note is the absence of Tursi, despite the fact that this had been an episcopal see since the 10th century. Though the panel shows some interest in the sites of abbeys, it does not mark S. Maria d'Anglona, the ancient cathedral of deserted Anglone, which had become an important Benedictine monastery. Nor does it show Montalbano Jonico and Rotondella.

The map not only shows actual archaeological sites but also supplies ancient place-names alongside modern ones. Regarding the latter, it is to be remembered that Forenza is the ancient *Ferentum*, *Cerenza* (Acerenza) the *Acheruntia* mentioned by Horace, whose birthplace at Venosa is also marked (*Venusia Horatii P. Patria*), while the abbey of *S. Maria di Vanza* (Banzi) stands on the site of the ancient *Bantia*.

As to the archaeological sites, distinguished by the presence of the adjective *destructum* alongside their name, the map includes *Metapontum*, *Pastum* (Paestum), already a part of the Principality of Salerno, and a certain *R(occa) distrutta*, which is easily identifiable as the ruins of *Siris-Eraclea*, the two Greek colonies that rose, one on the ruins of the other, on the long ridge of the Policoro hill, here marked as *Pelicoro* and inaccurately positioned on the Agri.

With regard to the modern settlements shown, many are towns that developed from Basilian monasteries, such S. Angelo, Lagonegro, Lauria, Carbone, Noia, which stands for Noepoli, and *Cerciofino*, one of the place-names wrongly retranscribed in the course of restoration in the 19th century and probably corresponding to Cersosimo. Apart from *Maschie*, or Maschito, the Albanian colonies are also missing, even those that had grown into towns with large populations, such as Barile, S. Costantino, and S. Paolo.

In the lower central portion of the panel is a scene depicting an episode—not one of the most famous—of the Second Punic War, the battle fought, with an uncertain outcome, between the Roman consuls Marcus Claudius Marcellus and Titus Quintus Crispinus and the Numidian cavalry, near Venusia (Venosa). In fact, it seems that this illustration does not concern the battle of Venusia, but rather concerns the ambush, shortly after the battle and not far from the battlefield, near Banzi, where the Consul Marcellus was slain while the Consul Crispinus, although wounded, managed to escape.

The fresco on the vault corresponding to the map of *Lucania* is that of *St. Laverius Casting out Devils*.

51

Pl. 51. Panel showing *Lucania* (Basilicata and Southern Campania), and two herms.

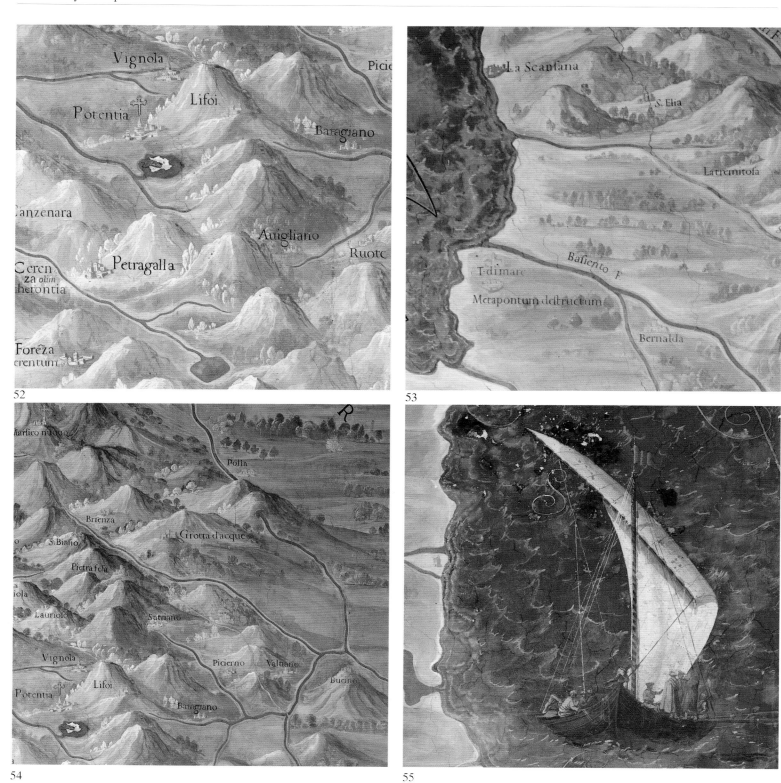

52

53

54

55

Lucania (Basilicata and Southern Campania), details.
Pl. 52. The territory of Potenza.
Pl. 53. The river Basento and the ruins of Metapontum.
Pl. 54. The territory between Potenza and Polla.
Pl. 55. A cargo boat in the Gulf of Salerno.

AGER nunc

PRINCIPA TVS

SALERNO

SALERNVM

CITERIOR

pagano

Compſa

VLIAE

56

Pl. 56. *Lucania* (Basilicata and Southern Campania), detail.
The plain of Salerno and a landscape with pastoral scenes.

Calabria Citerior
Northern Calabria

The map, 10'8" x 13'12" (3.24 x 4.26 m), is oriented with the south pointing upward. In the lower left-hand corner, a cartouche in an elaborately decorated frame, complete with allegorical figures and Barberini bees, bears an inscription repainted in the early 17th century, when several lines were erased. The inscription supplies a list of the region's products, including not only various cereals, but also wine, silk, a sweet syrup produced from the ash tree, and minerals such as rock salt and iron.

In the lower right-hand corner is the scale, measuring 18" (45 cm) and equivalent to 12,000 paces, representing a ratio of 1:40,000. The map is enclosed within a frame graduated in intervals of 5 minutes and covers the area lying between the probable latitudes of 40° 05' and 42° 05' and longitudes of 41° 20' and 44° 05', namely the northern province of Calabria, between Monte Pollino in the north and the isthmus of Catanzaro in the south.

The peninsula is surrounded on both sides by a ruffled sea, on which are seen a variety of vessels, their sails filled by the wind, which comes from all directions. The two seas cut into the coast, forming a series of gulfs: those of Corigliano and Squillace on the Ionian side, and those of S. Eufemia and Policastro on the Tyrrhenian. However, the coastline is very roughly drawn.

From an orographical point of view the map merely hints at the position and size of the Sila plateau and the coastal chain. The only mountains named are Monte Mula, one of the highest peaks of the coastal chain, fairly accurately placed between the sources of the Occido (here *Acido*) and the Grondo, and Monte Pollino, wrongly located to the west of Castrovillari and Morano. Nor is the horizontal barrier of Monte Pollino shown, unless it is meant to be represented by the hillock surmounted by a leafy tree in the foreground. Nevertheless, it should be said that, though the compactness of the range is overlooked, the bulging, slightly pointed forms of the coastal chain as drawn in the map do convey something of their real form. Similarly, the group of whitish peaks emerging from thick woodland between the rivers Crati and Esaro, may be interpreted as representing the erosive phenomena shaping the Tarsia Gorge. On the other hand, the peaks emerging from the valleys of the Sila district, correctly represented as well wooded, are too sharp. And on the opposite side of the peninsula, the map fails to convey any idea whatsoever of the physical character of the Marchesato (quite apart from the poor conditon of this part of the panel).

A large number of rivers are shown, but with the exception of the Crati and a sizeable part of its basin, these are carelessly and sometimes inaccurately drawn. Many of them are marked with their names (often in Latin, in which case they were added later and are written in an ornate hand), which in the Crati basin are usually correct or else easily identifiable (e.g., *Aesies* for Jasso and *Acheron* for Caronte). The Crati is shown as having its own mouth, as distinct from that of the *Sibaris*, or Coscile, which is also joined by the Esaro. Along the west coast the torrent Noce and the river Lao are confused.

The human settlements are only shown in the Crati basin, on the Tyrrhenian coast and north of the Sibari plain on the Ionian coast. Within these districts, they are plentiful, and the views representing them, though in various cases imaginary, are often elegant (e.g., Amantea, Carolei, S. Fili, Celico, S. Agata, Mottafollone, Cassano, Cerchiara, and an unidentified *l'Essequie hostaria*). However, their names and positions are more accurate in the area known as the Casali Cosentini.

The information concerning the settlements along the western coast is less reliable. Here there are several gaps between Amantea and Paola and between Diamante and Maratea. Some places do not have a topographical symbol and are represented by their names only, crowded into the limited space. In other instances, the position is wrong; Bonifati, for example, is shown above Belvedere and in the same valley, while Sangineto is shown north of Buonvicino, which promptly finds itself on a ledge overlooking the sea. Buonvicino is also shown as at a considerable distance from Diamante, which in reality is situated at the foot of its valley.

It should also be pointed out that of the hundred or more watchtowers scatttered up and down the coast and still in use in the 16th century, only two are shown here (as opposed to the number shown on the Salentine coast): the *Torre del Diamante* on the west coast, incorporated into the town of the same name, and the isolated and anonymous tower on the east coast, protecting Rocca Imperiale from the sea.

The place-names are in the vernacular, with the exception, as mentioned above, of Cosenza and Cassano (a diocese since the 9th century) and *Policastro olim Buxentum*, which is shown in an elegant perspective view, with its walls surmounted by the episcopal cross. But the most important allusion to ancient times is the scene of two armies meeting before military encampments, between Montalto and Rende. The scene, which was certainly part of the original map, clearly illustrates the battle between the army of Alexander the Molossian, King of Epirus, and a group of Bruttians and Lucanians, which took place in 330 B.C.

It is interesting to consider the purpose of reevoking this military event of many centuries ago. The area in which the two armies are shown is the same where twenty years previously there had been, with the instigation of the Roman Inquisition, the *manu militari* persecution and massacre of the Waldensians. Therefore, one has the impression that the purpose of this scene is the obliteration of a bloody memory. This impression becomes even stronger when we recall that, not so far from here, in the lower valley of the Crati, a text placed between this river and the Esaro mentions the Albanians, a population that had emigrated to the Cosentino in the 15th century, a little after the Waldensians. The Roman Church was, in this period, working on the religious assimilation of this new population.

The frescoes on the vault corresponding to the map of *Calabria Citerior* are those of *St. Francis of Paola Using His Cloak as a Boat* and *St. Francis of Paola Emerging Unharmed from the Flames of a Furnace*.

57

Pl. 57. Panel showing *Calabria Citerior* (Northern Calabria), and two herms.

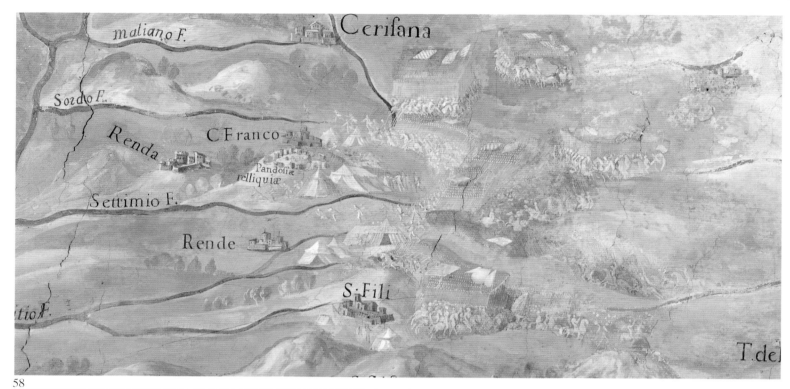

58

59

60

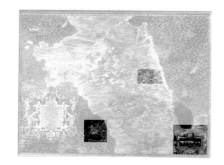

Calabria Citerior (Northern Calabria), details.
Pl. 58. The Battle of Pandosia between Alexander the Molossian
and an army of Bruttians and Lucanians (330 B.C.).
Pl. 59. Metric scale.
Pl. 60. A galleon accompanied by a smaller vessel in the Ionian Sea.

61

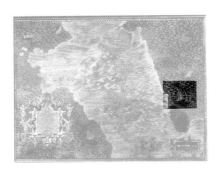

Pl. 61. *Calabria Citerior* (Northern Calabria), detail. Brigantine in the Tyrrhenian Sea.

Calabria Ulterior
Southern Calabria

The panel, 10'4" x 13'9" (3.15 x 4.20 m), shows the southern part of Calabria and is oriented with the south pointing upward. It is in better condition than its companion *Calabria Citerior*.

The cartouche with the inscription is in the lower left-hand corner and like the one on the preceding panel is notable for the richness and refinement of its decoration. The style, the colors (gold for the frame, the underside blue or violet, pink for the ribbons, green for the background to the inscription), and the six figures flying around the frame, in very similar poses to those in the other panel, all suggest that the same artist was responsible for both cartouches.

The fact that there are Barberini bees here too indicates that they are of the same date. The inscription lists the goods produced in the region: cane sugar, rock salt, silk, and wool.

The geometric scale in the lower right-hand corner measures 15" (37 cm) and is equal to 12,000 paces. It therefore represents a ratio of 1:48,000. This means that the two neighboring panels representing Calabria are drawn to different scales, and it would be impossible to join the two maps. Indeed, it should be noted that in the parts the two maps have in common (the Sila plateau and the isthmus of Catanzaro) there are considerable differences in the settlements shown and the place-names given.

The map is almost entirely enclosed in a frame graduated in minutes, which are numbered at intervals of 5—the only break being opposite Cariati (here, as in the map of Northern Calabria, called Cariano). The area shown lies between 38°46' and 40°26' latitude and 40°30' and 43°21' longitude.

The southernmost point of the Italian Peninsula, stretching out almost to touch the northwestern tip of Sicily joins a broader, rounder mass of land at the base of the panel, which itself merges into the wooded dome of the Sila and is surrounded by the sea on both sides: the *Tyrrhenum* to the west and the *Hadriaticum* to the east, their names written in gold letters with curling flourishes. On both sides of the peninsula the sea is stirred by the east wind, which also swells the sails of the many crafts upon it.

Although better preserved, because of repainting (the prevalence of green gives the impression of the area's being more mountainous), the panel is no less deficient in chorographic detail than that of Northern Calabria. In particular, it exaggerates the symmetries of the promontories and bays along the coast. But the relation between the width of those parts of the peninsula to the north of the Strait of Catanzaro—or to be more precise between Capo Cimiti and Capo Suvero—and the isthmus cut out by the Gulfs of Lamezia and Squillace, is correct. From an orographical point of view the map attempts to show the chain that forms the backbone of the peninsula, represented as a long ridge stretching from the southern slopes of the Sila to the Strait of Messina and thus ignoring the large depression at Marcellinara and becoming steeper and steeper the closer it gets to the Sicilian channel, where it suddenly terminates at *Capo dell'Armi*, which also has its Latin name of *Leucopetra pro(munturium)*. Above the mountain ridge are two further names: by Caraffa (misspelled *Corazzo*) near the isthmus of Catanzaro, and almost as though it referred to the mountains that close the isthmus to the south is a *M. Calocrio* (possibly Monte Fallaco); and in the extreme south of the peninsula spreads the name of *Aspromonte*.

Numerous rivers leave this longitudinal ridge for the sea, forming a herringbone pattern. Most of the rivers are identified by name, but they are roughly, sometimes quite incorrectly, drawn. Alongside the river Angitola in the west, for example (and associated with several wrongly located places, such as Valle Longa and Brognaturo), flows the river *Ancinale*, which actually runs through a long valley on the other side of the peninsula. And in the Gioia plain the name of *Metauro* is given to two adjacent rivers, which are to be identified as the Métramo and the Petrace.

The coastline is no less inaccurate: Monte Poro is shown as a conspicuous promontory off which are a series of tiny islands, their names written in gold (*Torricella* lying in front of the mouth of the river Angitola, *Necola* in front of the Briatico, *le Formiche* near Tropea, and *Gadamo* and *Proteria* between Tropea and Capo Vaticano). However, these islands never existed in historical times. On the eastern side, *Capo Stilo*, whose name appears to be associated with the inscription *Cocynthum pro(munturium)*, has the outline of a sharpened hook. And in the Marchesato too much emphasis is given to the promontories terminating the plain of Cutro, which are in any case incorrect and have been confused with one another (*Capo delle Colonne* and *Lacinium pro[munturium]*, for instance, are shown as two separate promontories).

As to the settlements, a fair number are shown, and these are reasonably well distributed (except in the Sila area, where none are shown, partly because it is mainly covered in luxuriant and elegantly painted woodland). The perspective views are carefully, sometimes even expressively, executed. But in some areas many settlements are wrongly located, especially in the Gioia plain and in the Marchesato. The only area in which a fair degree of accuracy is reached is that on the Ionian coast between the isthmus and Aspromonte.

Lastly, of special interest is the inscription *Castra Annibalis* on the Ionian coast between the Castella fortalice and the mouth of the Tacina. Though the location is not exact (the site is now thought to be somewhere near Rocceletta), the reference is perfectly in keeping with the idea that Hannibal struck camp for three successive winters (206–203 B.C.) at Crotone, somewhere above the Ionian isthmus.

The fresco on the vault corresponding to the map of *Calabria Ulterior* is that of *The Emperor Henry II Taking Communion and Having his Soldiers Take Communion before the Battle*.

62

Pl. 62. Panel showing *Calabria Ulterior* (Southern Calabria), and two herms.

63

64

65

Calabria Ulterior (Southern Calabria), details.
Pl. 63. The Sila Mountains and metric scale.
Pl. 64. The strait of Messina.
Pl. 65. A vessel in the Ionian Sea.

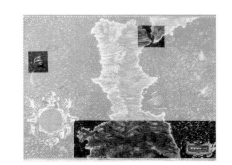

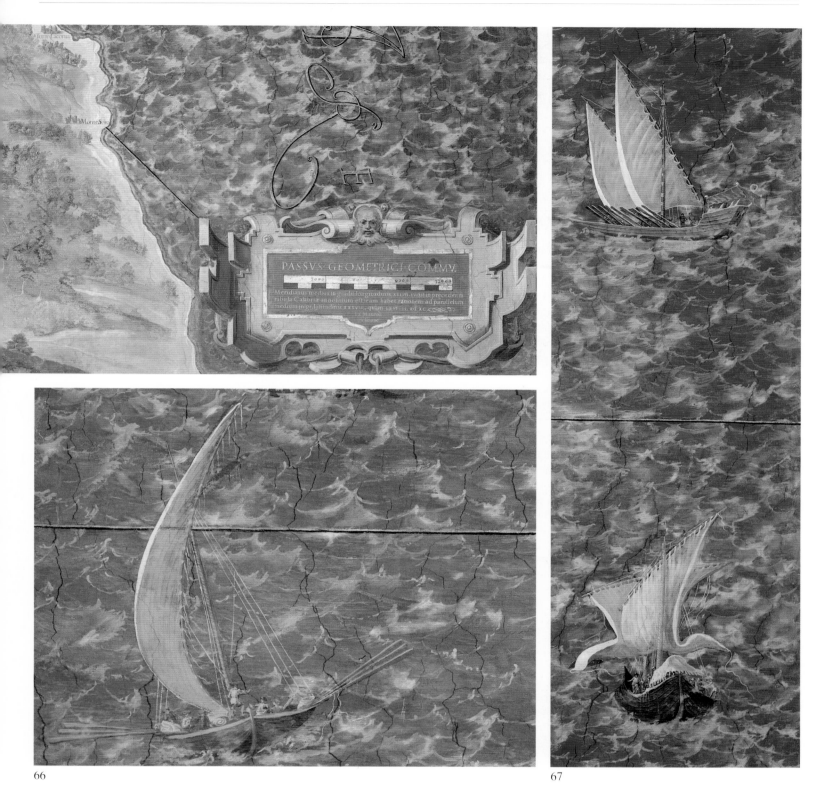

66
67

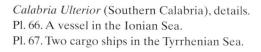

Calabria Ulterior (Southern Calabria), details.
Pl. 66. A vessel in the Ionian Sea.
Pl. 67. Two cargo ships in the Tyrrhenian Sea.

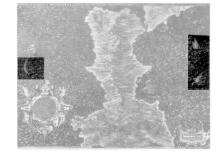

Corsica
Corsica

The island of Corsica is contained in a panel measuring 10'1" x 13'8" (3.08 x 4.16 m). The graduations along its edges range from 40°36' to 42°10' latitude and from 29°50' to 32°57' longitude. In the lower right-hand corner a small cartouche with an ornate frame in pink and gold decorated with winged putti and a trompe l'oeil bas-relief, encloses the metric scale, shown on a blue ground. The scale measures 18" (45 cm) and is equal to a distance of 15,000 paces; the ratio is thus 1: 49,300.

The 16-point gold compass rose—placed, somewhat unusually, on the island itself, in the exact horizontal center of the panel and about a third of the way down—shows that the map is oriented with the south pointing upward. Its rays spread in every direction, crossing the cobalt-blue sea to intersect the gold letters and ornate flourishes of the inscriptions *Tyrrhenicum Mare* and *Ligusticum Mare*. A number of vessels are shown at sea: five cargo boats, an armed caravel, and a galleon flying standards with the Barberini bee.

The latter detail makes it likely that the panel was restored under Urban VIII. But if it was so, the work done was probably not extensive, given that the form of the island here is different from that in the *Italia antiqua* and *Italia nova* panels, for which Holste supplied new cartoons. Recent restoration has certainly affected the colors and the inscriptions, especially the numbering of the degrees and minutes (one of the degrees along its lower edge is marked 70 instead of 32).

In the upper center of the map, a small piece of the Sardinian coast may be seen, which has exactly the same form, and shows exactly the same place-names, as in the panel specifically devoted to Sardinia.

The western coastline is mostly accurate, but the eastern coast projects too sharply at Aleria, and the northern follows too straight a line between Punta di Revellata and Punta Mortella. On the whole, however, the map succeeds in conveying the difference between the eastern littoral, low, unvaried, and dotted with bodies of standing water, and the *rias* (fjords) typical of the western, which is jagged and penetrated by some deep gulfs. Indeed, the slightly overemphasized jaggedness of this coastline, together with the wealth of place-names relating to the coast (over a hundred are given, including those of islands, promontories, rocks, and watchtowers), lead one to suspect that the map may derive from a nautical chart.

Geomorphologically, the map is fairly accurate. It gives a faithful picture of a largely mountainous terrain with a main ridge running from northwest to southeast. The mountains are mannered and represented by means of the usual agglomeration of cones, the lightening of whose summits and sides make them stand out against the green background. No mountains are named, and no idea, be it ever so formal, is conveyed of the highest peaks, such as Monte Corona, Monte Rotondo, and the three peaks of Monte Renoso.

The map shows a large number of waterways, of the same blue as the sea, but not many are named (those that are being rivers whose mouths are on the east coast). The most conspicuous feature of the hydrography represented on the map is a substantial lake situated between Corte and Niolo, out of which flow three rivers. One of these is patently the Golo, and its mouth is indeed inscribed *Fiumara di Golo*. The lake is probably Lake Nino, therefore one of the other two rivers must be the Tavignano, which is an effluent of the former. The third of the rivers flowing out of Lake Nino flows toward the west coast, where it enters the sea in the Gulf of Sagona. This might therefore be the Liamone, even if its real course is not at all as shown.

The settlements are represented by means of small perspective views in crimson for the minor ones, and more elegant ones for the urban centers (the most notable among the latter include those representing *Agiazo* [Ajaccio], *Bonifatio* [Bonifacio], *Porto Vecchio*, *S. Fiorenzo*, and Calvi).

Very few settlements are shown in the Piana d'Aleria, which is dotted with coastal pools, and none at all in the Balagna Deserta or in the strip of badly painted coastland between Punta Mortella and the mouth of the *Ostriconi* (Strigone), which bears the appropriate name (not recorded by Danti) of *Deserto degli Agriati*. But along the western coast, the map successfully conveys a picture of settlements mainly concentrated on the foothills a short distance inland.

The buildings are more realistically grouped, particularly in the case of some scattered houses near Porto-vecchio, marked *Ventimiglia la Nuova*, a reference to the recolonization of Porto-vecchio in 1577 by 200 Ligurian families.

The usual gold pastoral cross is used to indicate the six episcopal sees: Ajaccio, Aleria, Bastia, Mariana, Nebbio (*S. Pietro di Nebro*), and Sagona. The latter had in fact been destroyed in the 12th century, and Gregory XIII had himself reestablished the bishopric, authorizing the bishop to reside in nearby Vico, which was farther inland and therefore safer, instead of in the by now deserted Sagona. In 1625 Urban VIII transferred the see to Calvi. The presence of Sagona as a bishopric here is internal evidence that the panel has survived in its original state, as drawn by Danti, and not as revised by Holste.

Nebbio had also been destroyed and was an episcopal see in name only, and Aleria too was in a state of abandon; it is clear that the map avoids showing these major settlements in a state of decline. Only *Accia* is correctly marked *destructa* and shown as a group of ruins scattered over a wide area.

The map takes special care to mark thermal springs. Three are shown, including the sulphurous springs of *Bagni di Vico* and *Bagni di Pietrapaula*. The third place is simply marked *Bagni medicinali* and probably refers to the Carozzica Springs in the Valle dell'Asco.

The fresco on the vault corresponding to the map of Corsica is that showing *The People of Corsica Paying Homage to the Papal Legate in Recognition of the Sovereignty of Pope Gregory VII* .

Pl. 68. Panel showing *Corsica* (Corsica), and two herms.

Pls. 69–72. *Corsica* (Corsica), details. Cargo ships off the island.

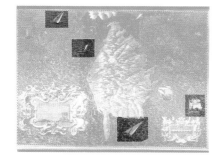

Tiuoli

Perifiobo

C. d'Orminio

Salogno

Monti Rofi

Monte di Sagro

73

Pl. 73. *Corsica* (Corsica), detail. Galleon in the Gulf of Porto.

Sardinia
Sardinia

The map of Sardinia is enclosed in a panel measuring 9′12″ x 13′8″ (3.04 x 4.16 m) and graduated along its edges at intervals of 2′: from 36°20′ to 40°43′ latitude along its right-hand edge and from 36°22′ to 40°40′ latitude along its left-hand edge; from 27°58′ to 36°4′ longitude along its bottom edge and from 28°6′ to 35°54′ longitude along its upper edge.

The island is shown with a large stretch of sea to the east and west, this last side being occupied by a compass rose and metric scale. The latter is shown in the bottom right-hand corner, on a topgallant sail, which together with its yard is sinking into a whirlpool formed by a marine dragon thrashing its tail in the water. The scale measures around 18″ (46 cm) and is equal to a distance of 4,000 standard geometric paces. The sail also gives the reference parallel and meridian.

The compass rose is in the top right-hand corner and shows that the map is oriented with the south pointing upward.

Halfway up the eastern side of the panel is a fine cartouche, its ornate frame decorated with allegorical figures and enclosing an inscription in gold letters on a dark green ground. The inscription would indeed seem to be the original one and does not appear to have been modified. The same is true for the rest of the panel, except perhaps for the rewriting of some place-names and general restoration where the poor condition of the fresco required it. It was presumably in the course of restoration—probably in the 19th century under Augusto Bianchini—that the bar scale was repainted. In its present state, representing 4,000 paces and measuring 18″ (46 cm), it gives a ratio of 1:12,800, which is clearly impossible. The restorer was probably unable to make out the inscription and may have thought it read 4,000 rather than 40,000. The latter figure would give a ratio of 1:128,000, which is much more likely.

The sea is in cobalt blue, its surface ruffled by winds blowing from various directions and ploughed by a number of vessels, especially in the area under the cartouche along the northwest coast of the island: a carrack with a cannon on its forecastle, two small merchant galleys, and a caravel. A xebec sails to the northwest of the island of S. Pietro.

The form of the island is far from accurate; the unlikely coastline is extremely jagged on the east side, where the city of Cagliari overlooks its gulf, and where five other bays penetrate the coast to form lagoons. The north coast is broken by four large headlands (possibly left over from the earliest foot-shaped representations), making the Gulf of Asinara unrecognizable, squeezed as it is into the northwestern coast.

This means that the gulfs of Alghero and Oristano are shifted southward, while the southern part of the island is twisted to the east, so that the islands of S. Antioco and S. Pietro lie too far to the southeast. Moreover, the map displays little knowledge of the small islands off the coast, some of which are not named, while others are not shown at all. Of the two islands of Caprera and La Maddalena, only one is shown, and judging by the form (it is not identified by name), it is Caprera.

From the orographical point of view, the map is pictorially effective though mannered, the entire mainland being filled with a succession of cone-shaped mountain ranges, without any regard for position, size, or shape. Alternating browns and greens both render the chiaroscuro and at the same time evoke a mountainous though not infertile terrain covered in woods and scrubland. Few mountains are named, the most notable being *Li Sette Fratelli*, a vernacular name that in its Italianized form has survived to the present day and that is far more evocative of the seven peaks dominating the Sarrabus plateau than their depiction on the map.

The riverbeds are also drawn in a fairly haphazard way. Although the valleys are full of watercourses, represented by means of thick blue lines, most are unnamed. Indeed, the names of only three rivers are given: the *Themus, Tirus* (i.e., the *Tirsus*), and *Sepus* (i.e., the *Seprus* also known as Flumendosa). While the mouth of the latter is in more or less the right place, the Tirso is mistaken for the Temo and so its mouth forms the channel of the port of Bosa, whereas the Temo is clearly mistaken for the Coghinas and is incorrectly shown as flowing into the sea in the north. Thus, though emphatically and not too inaccurately drawn, the river flowing into the Gulf of Oristano also remains nameless.

A large number of coastal pools are shown, for the most part correctly positioned, although once more their names are not provided. The human settlements are represented by a series of finely painted views in crimson, which show the island to be neither too densely nor too sparsely inhabited. The names of the larger settlements—such as *Carallis* (Cagliari), *Villa di Glesia* (Iglesias), *Oristanum* (Oristano), *Bosa, Lalger* (Alghero), and *Plubtum* (Sassari)—are more elaborately written. These are also the episcopal sees of the island and as such are marked by a golden cross. Numerous watchtowers are shown on the coasts.

Danti's map is by no means free from errors, sometimes owing to the form of the island and so to the drawing of its coastal perimeter. The placing of Cagliari on the east coast, for instance, leads to a series of further mistakes, such as the transferral of Iglesias to the south coast and a general shifting southward of settlements on or just inland from the west and north coasts. But the real problems regarding the identification and placing of settlements are encountered inland, where most of the settlements in the midwest of the island—Orgosolo, *Bitamano* (to be identified with Bitti), Oliena, Meana, *Nori* (Nuoro), Mamoiada, Monte Santo, and others—are incorrectly located. On the whole, the place-names are evenly distributed, except in the Sulcis area and in the extreme tip of Gallura, which are shown as quite uninhabited.

The fresco on the vault corresponding to the map of *Sardinia* is that showing *Pope St. Symmachus Sending Clothing and Other Aid to the Exiled Bishops in Sardinia.*

74

Pl. 74. Panel showing *Sardinia* (Sardinia), and two herms.

75

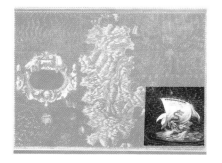

Pl. 75. *Sardinia* (Sardinia), detail. Sea monster and metric scale.

76

Pl. 76. *Sardinia* (Sardinia), detail. The southern part of the island.

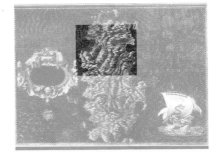

Sicilia
Sicily

The map, about 10' x 13'7" (approx. 3.05 x 4.15 m) shows Sicily with the archipelagos of the Egadi and Lipari Islands, Ustica, and a brief stretch of the Calabrian coast beyond the Strait of Messina. It is surrounded by the following seas: *Aphricum* (Strait of Sicily), *Tyrrhenum* (Tyrrhenian), and *Adriaticum* (Adriatic).

The scale is equal to 15,000 *passus geometrici com(munes)* and measures around 12" (30 cm) (approx. 1:74,000). The map is oriented with the south pointing upward. It includes a compass rose with direction lines. There is no record of the map's being restored or modified, though the numbers on the cartouche seem to have been repainted.

The map is graduated along the edges in minutes from latitudes 36º3' to 38º30' and from longitudes 37º32' to 41º50'. Below the scale is an inscription stating that according to Maurolico the parallel of Syracuse is placed at 38°0' latitude while the meridian is placed at 41°26' longitude "as 70.55 is to 90." The meaning of the latter phrase is unclear. However, there is no record of Maurolico's having suplied the coordinates of Sicilian localities in his geographical writings. On the map, Syracuse lies at 36º36' latitude and 41º8' longitude.

The mountains, represented in the conventional "molehill" manner, are lit from the left and are painted in varying shades of green and brown, as are the plains. The volcanoes spout flames. The coastlines are outlined in pale yellow. The hydrography is in turquoise, like the sea, which has foaming waves modeled in green and is crossed by cargo boats. The settlements are represented by means of groups of buildings of varying sizes, or else by conventional bird's-eye views (except for Messina [*Messana*] and Palermo [*Panormus*], which are shown in plan and evidently taken from drawings made on the spot). No settlements are shown on the smaller islands. The watchtowers along the coast are marked, but no roads or bridges, except the two crossing the *Leontini F(iume)* (Lentini) to the north of Syracuse. No boundaries are shown. The place-names are written in black and gold.

The map is derived from Giacomo Gastaldi's *Descrittione della Sicilia con le sue isole …*, published in Venice in 1545 and reprinted in Rome by Vincenzo Lucchini in 1558. It is therefore very similar to the *Sicilia* in Ortelius's *Theatrum Orbis Terrarum* (1570). All the place-names featured in Gastaldi's map have been retained, though some have been garbled in the process of transcription.

No historical events are depicted. The inscription *Raptur* (i.e., *raptus*) *Proserpinae* marks the place where the daughter of Demeter was abducted by Pluto according to Greek myth. The inscription was already included in Gastaldi's map.

The depiction of the Sicilian territory is purely conventional, the only impression created being that of extreme roughness of terrain. No mountains (not even the volcanoes) are named, nor are the regional divisions of the island, except for *Mazzara* (Mazzara del Vallo) and some of the small islands off it. But the map may originally have given the names of the *Valle di Demona* and the *Valle di Noto*. According to Alberti, the author Danti referred to for information on Sicily, these three valleys mark the modern divisions of the island (see Alberti's *Descrittione di tutta Italia et isole appartenenti all'Italia*).

Settlements are numerous, and the hydrography is detailed, as is usually the case in Gastaldi's maps. The most up-to-date and "informative" part of the map is found in the three additional views (Messina, Syracuse, and Palermo), painted at the same time as the map itself and therefore an integral part of it. These are very recent images of the cities and show the changes currently underway, such as the construction of Spanish city walls and port machinery. Except in the case of Messina, they also give an evocative glimpse of the surrounding countryside.

The frescoes on the vault corresponding to the map of *Sicilia* are those entitled *Pope St. John and Symmachus, Father-in-law of Boethius, Hurl the Soul of King Theoderic into Hell* and *The Veil of St. Agatha Stopping the Lava on Etna*.

77

Pl. 77. Panel showing *Sicilia* (Sicily), and two herms.

MESSANA

78

79

R A C V S A

Strampachi

Carrano

Ylouis

Cast° di Dionilie

Ar enale

Periera 'A G R A T I N A

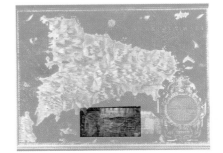

Sicilia (Sicily), details.
Pl. 78. Trompe l'oeil painting with plan of Messina.
Pl. 79. Trompe l'oeil painting with plan of Syracuse.

80

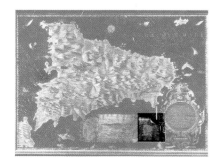

Pl. 80. *Sicilia* (Sicily), detail. Trompe l'oeil painting with plan of Palermo.

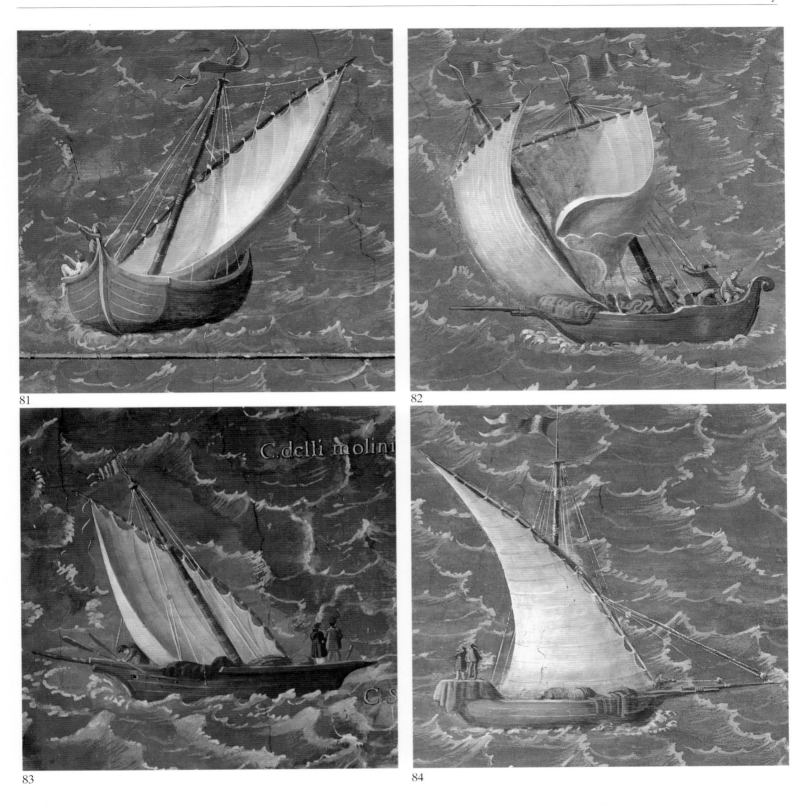

81

82

83

84

C. delli molini

C. S

Pls. 81–84. *Sicilia* (Sicily), details. Cargo vessels and fishing boats off the island.

Avenionen(sis) Ditio et Venaisinus Comitatus
The Jurisdiction of Avignon and the Comtat Venaissin

The map of Avignon and the Comtat Venaissin appears in a panel measuring 10′3″ x 13′9″ (3.13 x 4.19 m), graduated in minutes along its edges, from latitudes 43º45′ to 44º 22′ and longitudes 22º36′ to 23º45′. In actual fact, the territory shown—clearly delimited by the Rhône, the Durance, the Vaucluse plain, and the Baronnies mountains—occupies only the central part of the panel.

The scale is set in the base of the cartouche and is equal to 5,000 standard geometrical paces, or 3,000 Gallic leagues, and measures about 16″ (40.5 cm). The ratio is therefore about 1:18,300. A 16-point compass rose in gold in the upper right-hand corner shows that the map is oriented with the north pointing upward. In the bottom left-hand corner is a lavishly decorated cartouche with a celebration of the region inscribed in gold on a blue ground.

The mountains are represented as cones, which stand out from the green of the plains through the use of a paler hue and touches of ocher where the light is supposed to catch them on the left. There is an attempt to go beyond a merely conventional representation of the mountains through the realistic displacement of their masses, but the result is not always convincing. The eminences to the east of Avignon are overemphasized, as are those on whose edge is located Châteauneuf-du-Pape. Similarly, the plain between Orange, Carpentras, Cavaillon, and Avignon is wider than in reality.

No mountains are named, not even Mont Ventoux, conspicuous here on account of its size and shape. There is an attempt to represent its majesty and isolation from surrounding mountains, but the map once again fails to convey the east-west direction of its crest. It is shown as a rocky mass, bare of vegetation and without the woods that actually furnished lumber to the shipyards of Toulon. On its peak is the chapel of Sainte-Croix, founded at the end of the 15th century by Pietro Valetario, bishop of Carpentras.

The hydrography—painted in blue—is accurate. It centers in the confluence of the Rhône (*Rhosne*) and the Durance (*Durence*), with the tributaries on the Rhône's left bank spreading between them. The anastomosis of the Rhône both above and below Avignon is well rendered, and among the river islands resulting from this phenomenon is the Ile de la Barthelasse, which is fairly well drawn even though unnamed. Two other small islands, each with a building, possibly a small castle, are shown farther up-river, in the stretch near *Rochemaures* (Roquemaure). They may be meant to represent the Ile de l'Oiselet.

The hydrography is more accurate in the north, whereas there are some discrepancies closer to the confluence, where the course of the Rhône has indeed considerably shifted over time. Almost all the tributaries bear their names and most are well drawn.

The country plains are represented by means of the usual wash of green, which though slightly varying in hue makes no attempt to differentiate between various types of vegetation or crops. The low trees on the farther side of the mountains are also conventionally drawn. But some forests are shown using distinct, rounded masses of trees. Especially noticeable here are the forests of Orange, Modène, and Sérignan.

Settlements are shown by means of miniature perspective views in crimson, sometimes, but not always, mannered in style. Among the more realistic are *Riches chances* (Richerences), in the middle of its now almost vanished forest, *Valcluse* (Fontaine-de-Vaucluse), *Vaison*, and *Bedorides* (Bédarrides), with its arched bridge. On the other hand, *Pernes* (Pernes-les-Fontaines), capital of the Comtat Venaissin until 1320, is given little prominence.

Great care is taken in the representation of the bridges on the Rhône and also of the river's tributaries, particularly near Avignon. Especially notable are the bridge of St. Bénézet, which joined Avignon to Villeneuve-lès-Avignon (here called *Montaus latone*), and the *Pont-Sainct-Esperit* (Pont-St-Esprit) farther north. The representation of the settlements on this stretch of the Rhône is particularly interesting, as it conveys an idea of their original position with respect to the river, whose course has considerably changed and parts of which have recently been straightened. Equally noteworthy is the view of *S. Roman* (Saint-Roman-en-Viennois), with the arches of its Roman aqueduct. And the representation of Isle-sur-la-Sorgue (*Lisle*), surrounded by the Sorgue's numerous branches, is also realistic.

Some place-names are followed by the terms *Daulfine*, *Provence,* or *Languedoc*, to show that they belong to seigniories different from the Comtat Venaissin. The term *principault* refers to the fiefs of the Principality of Orange, which formed a kind of enclave within the Papal State. So as not to break up the territory, the Principality of Orange is also included in the map, even if only the capital, Orange, and a handful of urban centers on the border between the two states are marked.

The few religious sites shown are of little importance. The travelers shown walking or riding across the peak of Caumont, between the rivers Durance and Coulon, are certainly an allusion to the role of the nearby Carthusian Monastery of Bonpas in aiding travelers who crossed the river there. Travelers had no choice but to take this route, a favorite haunt of bandits, so much so that before the friars settled there in 1320, transforming the original 12th-century chapel into a charterhouse, it was known as *Mauvais pas*. On the map, however, the site is only marked by a meager chapel, and the name *Bonpas*, which it had acquired on the founding there of the monastery, is not followed by the term *chartreuse*.

On the lower course of the Rhône, down-river from Avignon, a rich procession of ships is seen leaving the city and following the current downstream in a variety of vessels, while two groups of knights escort it on both sides of the river. This illustration refers to a specific historical event, as is recorded in the simple white scroll above the scene: the return of the Holy See from Avignon to Rome in 1377, during the papacy of Gregory XI (papacy 1370–1378).

The fresco on the vault corresponding to the map of *Avenionen(sis) Ditio et Venaisinus Comitatus* is that showing *The Emperor Valentinian Compelled by Divine Force to Revere St. Martin, Bishop of Tours.*

85

Pl. 85. Panel showing *Avenionen(sis) Ditio et Venaisinus Comitatus*
(The Jurisdiction of Avignon and the Comtat Venaissin), and two herms.

R hofne F

S Andre

Montaus latone

S Veran

AVENIO

Lator

Gregorius xi sedem Pontificiam di_
uino numine permotus Avenio
ne Romam post annos LXX redu
cit Pont sui anno VII SMCCCLXXVII

S Rulz

Port

Barbentaue

Graueffon

86

Pl. 86. *Avenionen(sis) Ditio et Venaisinus Comitatus*
(The Jurisdiction of Avignon and the Comtat Venaissin), detail.
The return of the Papal Court from Avignon to Rome (1377).

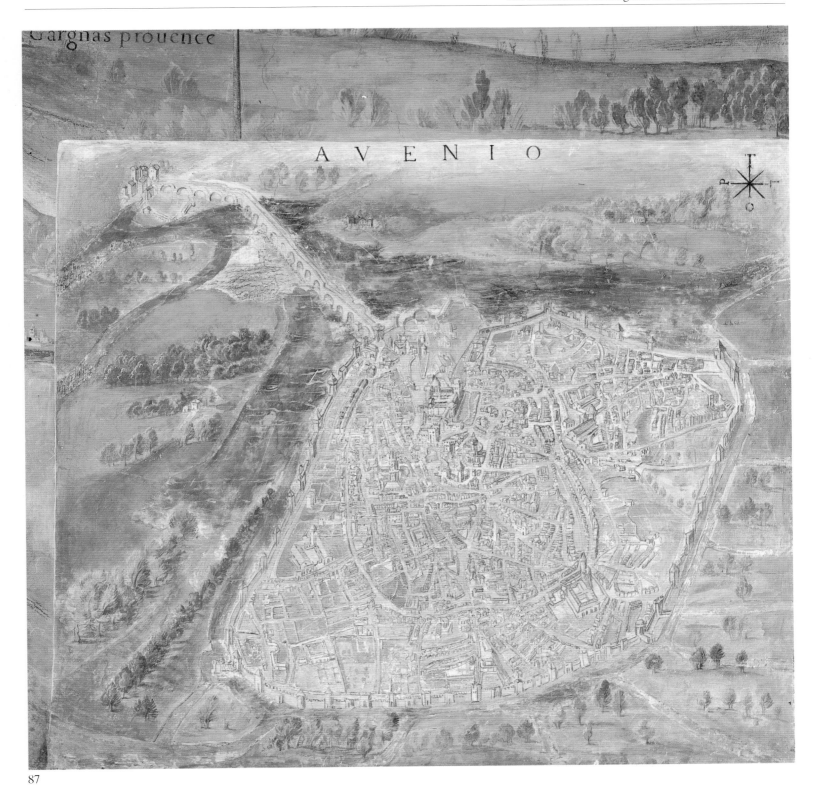

Gargnas prouence

AVENIO

87

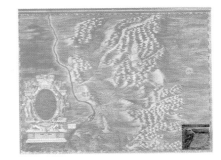

Pl. 87. *Avenionen(sis) Ditio et Venaisinus Comitatus*
(The Jurisdiction of Avignon and the Comtat Venaissin), detail.
Trompe l'oeil painting with plan of Avignon.

Pedemontium et Monsferratus
Piedmont and Monferrato

The map is enclosed in a panel measuring 10'10" x 14'6" (3.3 x 4.42 m) and shows the foothills up to the rivers Agogna and Tanaro and is bounded by the western Alps and part of the Ligurian Apennines. This territory, called *Pedemontium* or Piedmont from the 15th century onward, in reality comprises two political regions: Piedmont proper, the cisalpine portion of the Duchy of Savoy, and Monferrato, which was subject to the Duke of Mantua. A small cartouche in bottom left-hand corner of the panel shows the scale: 1,000 paces to 19" (48.3 cm), giving a ratio of about 1:30,600.

A small 8-point compass rose in the middle of the fresco shows that the map is oriented with the north pointing upward.

The map is graduated in minutes along its edges, using alternate bars of purple and gold, but the numbering of the parallels has not survived, having possibly been erased together with the graduations along the upper edge during restoration. Coordinates are between 28°58' and 31°5' longitude and 44°9' and 45°13' latitude.

The cartouches are decorated with the Barberini bee, meaning they were probably repainted, together with the inscriptions, under Pope Urban VIII.

On the whole, the map gives a fairly convincing picture of the region, with the Alps bounding the plain and the rows of trees painted over the green washes that represent the plain. However, there is no attempt to render the hilly area of the tertiary Piedmontese basin.

The orography is represented by means of an agglomeration of cones painted in green and ocher and lit from the left. The northern chains are painted in a slightly different manner, being represented as bleaker and more broken in places. There is a generous selection of the mountain names usually found in contemporary maps, not so much the highest peaks as the passes then most in use: the *Colle delle Corna*, or Colle di Tenda, the Colle delle Finestre (*Colle della Nostra Donna della Fenestra*), the Colle dell'Agnello, the Colle della Croce (*Col del la gros*), Mont Cenis (the only mountain with its name in Latin, *Mons Cenisius*), the Little and Great St. Bernard, Monte Galese (*Passo Galisio*), and Mont Jovet, wrongly transcribed as *M. Gionet*.

The waterways are painted in cobalt-blue and are shown with a large number of names. The system's main axis is the Po, from *Monte Visulo* (M. Viso) to its junction with the Sesia, whose course marks the state border. Of the rivers branching out from the left bank of the Po, those either marked or else identifiable are the Agogna, the Sesia, the Dora Baltea (*Doria*), which is joined by the Chiusella (not named here) at Vische and flows into the Po at Crescentino, the *Valperga* (Orco), the Stura di Lanzo, and the Dora Riparia (which meets the Po at Turin).

The tributaries on the right bank of the Po are a little less accurate, though they are generally fairly faithful. The river of which only a short stretch is shown as it enters the Po, but whose upper reaches are not shown at all, is probably the Varaita. After this come the Maira and the *Malea* (Mellea-Grana). Next comes the Stura di Demonte, joined by the *Grez* (Gesso). The names of the next tributaries and subtributaries are now hardly legible.

Of the many lakes in the area, the panel shows only Lake Mont Cenis and two others, neither of which is named—Lake Adret del Laus, also called Lungo, in the upper Val Pellice, and Lake Viverone, south of which flows the Naviglio d'Ivrea.

The settlements are represented by means of miniature perspective views in crimson, which though conventional, are considerably varied and sometimes deceptively convincing.

The settlements seem numerous and evenly distributed, but in reality the place-names are often mistaken, when not changed, and this cannot always be the fault of clumsy 19th-century restoration.

The cartographer is clearly not familiar with the geography of the Alpine valleys, especially those around Pinerolo, where the reformed Waldensian religion was widespread. There is no trace of the settlement in Val Germanasca. In Val Perosa, on the other hand, all the settlements, including S. Germano, are on the right bank of the Chisone, except for Perosa, which has been mistakenly transferred to the left. Moreover, the position of some settlements is quite random. Val Pellice is apparently uninhabited to the north of *Luserna* (Lucerne) and Torre, since Villar is not shown and Bobbio (its name repeated, appearing once as *Bobi C.* and another time as *Bobi V.*) is associated with Val d'Angrogna, which, as we have already seen, is wrongly placed and badly drawn, and at whose foot is Salutia, a Latinized form (given that it is an episcopal see) of Saluzzo.

The Susa Valley is no better described. Apart from similar mistakes in the location of settlements, of which there are too few and which are sometimes inaccurately named, there is a curious duplication of the upper valley, with lexical variants. Thus, after Susa, the valley continues for a short stretch, finishing at *Anciglies* (Exilles), *Orso* (Oulx) (on the wrong side of the Dora), and a little farther on, *Serana* (Cesana) together with the mysterious *Pravello*. A little farther to the west, however, we find Exilles again, this time shown as *Esiglies*, and then another Oulx, this time written *Urseo*, Cesana, which becomes *Cresana,* and instead of Pravello but in the same position, Salbertrand (*Salabertono*).

There are similar mistakes in the positioning and naming of the plains. Throughout southwestern Piedmont, especially in Val Tanaro, the place-names have been erased and corrected. The view of Mondovì, bearing the Latin name *Mons Regalis*, is noteworthy, whereas Cuneo is given little importance.

At the center of the fresco, a scene depicts an episode that took place at a rather unfortunate moment in the history of the Duchy of Savoy; during the seigniory of Charles III, it became the fighting ground for France and Spain, whose armies clashed in 1544 at Ceresola, on the Turin plain, in a desperate battle that resulted in the division of the Piedmontese regional state between the two powers, after Monferrato had already been assigned to the Gonzaga family.

The fresco on the vault corresponding to the map of *Pedemontium et Monsferratus* is that of *The Exposition of the Holy Shroud in Turin.*

Pl. 88. Panel showing *Pedemontium et Monsferratus* (Piedmont and Monferrato), and two herms.

Tidi

Borgo de Fornari

TAVRINVM

PARS

89

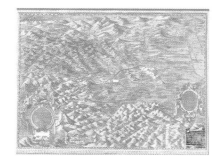

Pl. 89. *Pedemontium et Monsferratus* (Piedmont and Monferrato), detail.
Trompe l'oeil painting with plan of Turin.

91

92

93

94

Pedemontium et Monsferratus (Piedmont and Monferrato), details.

Pl. 90. Part of the plain and the Langhe Hills.

Pl. 91. Plan of Vercelli.

Pl. 92. Plan of Casale Monferrato.

Pl. 93. Plan of Ivrea.

Pl. 94. The Little and the Great St.Bernard Mountains.

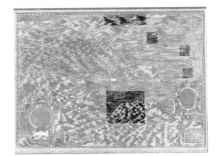

Mediolanensis Ducatus
The Duchy of Milan

The map, about 10′6″ x 13′11″ (approx. 3.2 x 4.25 m), shows the Po Valley as delimited by the river's junctions with the Sesia and the Tanaro to the west and with the Oglio to the east, and by the two natural barriers of the Alps and the Apennines. The Milanese territory is surrounded by Monferrato (*Montisferrati Pars*), the Duchy of Mantua (*Mantuani Duc[ati] Pars*), and the territory of the Republic of Venice to the north of the Po Valley (*Transpadanae Venetorum Ditionis Pars*).

The scale is in the lower right-hand corner, surmounted by cherubs with land-surveying instruments (rod, square, and compass). The numbering of the miles has disappeared, but on the basis of Almagià's calculations, the average scale works out at about 1:50,000, while various sections of the map are in different scales, varying between 1:55,000 and 1:66,000. The mile is taken as having a length of 1/60 of a degree, i.e., 1,480 m.

The lower part of the panel was repainted under Pope Clement VIII, but on the basis of the original. The frames of the cartouches were repainted under Urban VIII, but the inscriptions are the original ones. The place-names show signs of 19th-century repainting, which is the probable cause of the many garbled geographical names. The plan of Milan was badly repainted at the same time. The panel's general condition is good.

The mountains have the usual "molehill" form, painted like the plains in varying shades of green and lit from the left. The hydrography is in blue, while the coastlines and riverbeds are picked out in pale yellow. The settlements are represented by buildings painted in crimson, sometimes isolated and sometimes in groups of varying numbers. Many cities are shown in views, most of them stylized and from a bird's eye perspective. The episcopal sees are marked with a cross.

The map is oriented with the north pointing upward. There is a 16-point compass rose in the top right-hand corner that marks the following winds according to Mediterranean practice: *G(reco)* (northeast), *L(evante)* (east), *S(cirocco)* (southeast), *O(stro)* (south), *A(frico)* (southwest), *P(onente)* (west), and *M(aestro)* (northwest). As was customary, the north is indicated by means of a fleur-de-lys.

The map is graduated at the edges in minutes, which are numbered at intervals of five. The coordinates range from latitudes 44°12′ to 46°6′ and from longitudes 29°32′ to 32°56′. Milan is located at 45°7′ latitude north. The parallel and mean meridian are missing and were certainly erased in the process of restoration.

Four scenes, each with its own scroll or inscription, record four battles that took place in Lombard territory. They show some of the principal events in the history of the region, which was repeatedly snatched back from the barbarians or forced to defend itself against their attacks. The history of the Milanese is also outlined in the main cartouche, which recalls the founding of Milan by the Insubrians, the succession of its dukes, and the contemporary Spanish domination.

All in all, neither the wealth and abundance of the Duchy of Milan—almost a commonplace at the time and duly emphasized in the cartouche—nor its densely inhabited character, are brought out in Danti's map, which is clearly not derived from personal knowledge of the region. The abundantly fertile duchy shows odd patches of semidesert land (the Pavese and the Lodigliano), areas that already had flourishing economies based on irrigation and the connection between agriculture and husbandry and where there were numerous villages. Moreover, though well drawn, the network of canals is not differentiated from that of the rivers.

The regularly disposed fields and trees that appear here and there, apparently meant to evoke the Po plain, are merely a means of enlivening the lower part of the map, one adopted in all the panels in varying contexts. The orography is also purely evocative and conventional. The river courses and the directions of the valleys are arbitrary and the mountains are hardly ever named. Place-names are supplied for the regions (e.g., *Montisferrati Pars*, Monferrato), for some valleys (but Val Chiavenna is mistaken for Valtellina), rivers, and settlements. Mountain passes are rarely marked, even though these were fairly common in maps of northern Italy, e.g., Gastaldi's. Another unusual feature, but this time its inclusion is innovative, is the boundary line.

The pre-Alpine lakes are here represented with a quantity of details that varies from zone to zone. The drawing of the Lario abounds in place-names, almost all of them badly transcribed, and the same is true of Lake Lugano, whereas there are very few place-names around Lake Maggiore. Only three lakes have their names, given in Latin: *Verbanus Lacus Maior* (Verbano Lake Maggiore), *Larius Lacus Comensis* (Lario Lake Como), and *Orta Lacus* (Lake Orta).

Near *Viglebanum* (Vigevano), on the river Ticino, the army of Hannibal with its elephants faces that of Publius Cornelius Scipio (218 B.C.). The view of Vigevano is conventional. The Milanese territory east of the Ticino (*Ticinus fl[uvius]*) is reproduced in great detail, but the *navigli* (waterways) are not identified as such, the largest of them, the Naviglio Grande, itself being represented as a tributary of the Ticino.

The French troops of Count Saint-Paul surround *Papia* (Pavia), which, according to the inscription, they took and sacked in 1523 (in reality in 1528), during the war between France and Spain.

Further south, near Pinerolo (*Pinarolo*), the victory of the consul Marcus Claudius Marcellus over the Insubrian Gauls at Clastidium (222 B.C.) is commemorated, together with the Roman conquest of the region.

Between Castel San Giovanni and Piacenza is a scene depicting the defeat of Desiderius, king of the Lombards, by Charlemagne, and the restitution of the lands usurped by Desiderius to Pope Adrian I (774).

The fresco on the vault corresponding to the map of *Mediolanensis Ducatus* is *St. Ambrose Refusing the Emperor Theodosius Admittance to a Church* and *St. Ambrose Driving the Heretics from Milan.*

95

Pl. 95. Panel showing *Mediolanensis Ducatus* (The Duchy of Milan), and two herms.

Melia

Clanzano

Valle de Mola

Grondera

Belanzano

Gemuelona

S donne

Nauale

Cifera

Domafio

Dio

Nubiale

Dorio

S.Maria

Ascona

Lacarno

Berzago

Miragnia

Lacarno

Mufcie

Prezonico

Corêno

Doro

Perfio

Bellano

Canolio

Valtraua

S.Maria

Acqualeria

Nobialo

Menafco

Valena

Tierna

Olico

Ma

Canaro

Ogliabi

Rocca

Agu

Trezza

Morco

Mili

Forena

Lugano

Porto leriziá

Cinio

S.Maria

Caftagnola

Fredda

Griano

Tremozo

Gandrin

Capo

Oftia

Azegno

Ostia

Limonta

Pefcallo

Pellano

Onno

Sezeno

Malgr

Veftaliano

Piganzo

Lermignaca

Porto

Capian

Orieno

Lagnora

Quarátano

Ranci

Conardo

Cuio

Brino

Bedre

Porto

Biffon

Merogia

Nelbio

Vrro

Moftrafeo

Codilago

Cauato

Lalio

Pognano

Torno

Berlafca

Canzo

Breuen

Porto

Torzo

Coco

Ifpolla

Prebia

Befozzo

Vela

Baras

S.Maria

S.Alquino

Garouo

C.S.pietro

Cernobia

Balerna

Marobio

Chiaffo

Zuccotta

Pizzo

Plenio

Mirabello

Sezegno

Oietta

Erba

Stila

Poeno

Auoia

Biuiro

Eduin

Malindo

Vico

Mufeo

SGio

Ligurno

Canzone

S.Ant

Morlano

Cantú

Sneri

Crucion

Cazoaga

Gaia

Bodio

Caforigo

Calcana

Bruno

Cagiada

Vedano

Lapides molacei

hic in monte et

folis per totá fca

Italiá ducitum

A toffo

Montolire

Giu

Vo

Meno

Gogna

Aroda

Anghiera

Aza

Caluazina

Vergia

Somma

Orago

Arfago Albigi

Caftiglione

Abia

Leca

Tomazzo

Gorla

Carbona

S.Martino

Germeni

Lenta

Cefa

Carima

Bofco

Ma

Barlafina

Contafco

B.Maine

Cafel

Befna

Crona

Moza

Siflago

Cafteller

Mafcas

quaro

Foifaneto

Borro

Sefto

Galara

Golafecca

Lona

Caftrona

Gio

Caft lanza

Gnora

Geranzano

D

Ci

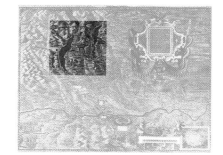

Pl. 96. *Mediolanensis Ducatus* (The Duchy of Milan), detail. The pre-Alpine lakes.

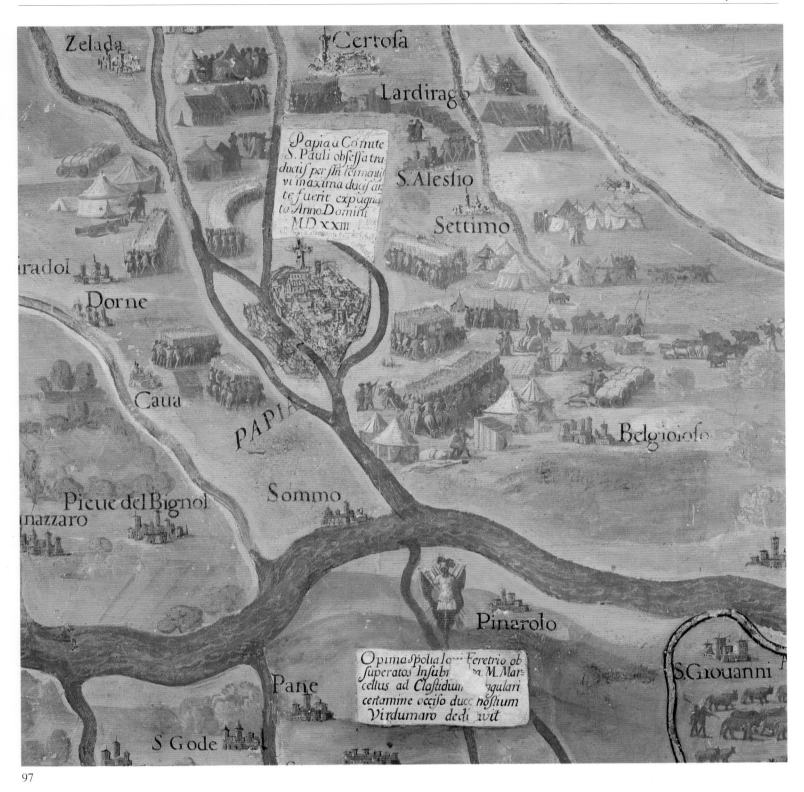

Zelada

Certofa

Lardirago

Papia u Co̅mute
S. Pauli obfeffa tra
ducti ſ per ſ̅n ̅ ̅ to̅rmentiſ
vi maxima ducis an
te fuerit expugnat
ta Anno Domini
MDXXIII

S. Aleſtio

Settimo

iradol

Dorne

Caua

PAPIA

Belgioiofo

Picue del Bignol

inazzaro

Sommo

Pinarolo

Pane

Opima Spolia Io̅ ̅ Feretrio ob
ſuperatos Inſubr̅ ̅ ̅a M. Mar
cellus ad Claſtidu̅ ̅ ̅ngulari
certamine occiſo duce no̅ſtium
Virdumaro ded̅ ̅ ̅ ̅ avit

S. Giouanni

S. Gode

97

Pl. 97. *Mediolanensis Ducatus* (The Duchy of Milan), detail.
The French army besieges Pavia (1528). In the lower center, a scroll and trophy commemorate
the Battle of *Clastidium* (Casteggio) between the Romans and the Insubrian Gauls (222 B.C.).

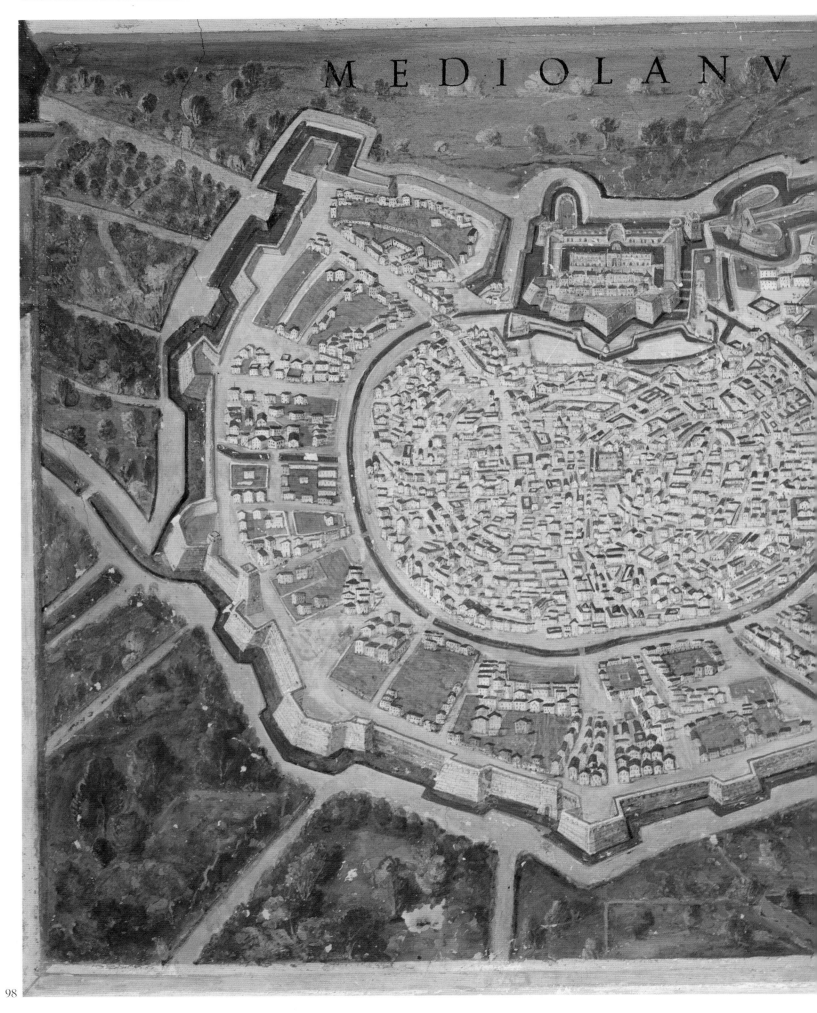

MEDIOLANV

CREMA

Pandino

LODI

Mairana   Olmetto

Coltarito

Riuolta

99

$Hanc Mediolani latitudinem a peritiſſimo uiro
obſeruatam, cum aliis quoq; probari uiderim
hic ponendam duxi, licet ab uniuerſali deſcrip
tione aliquantulum diſcrepare uideatur

100

Mediolanensis Ducatus
(The Duchy of Milan), details.
Pl. 98. Trompe l'oeil painting
with plan of Milan.
Pl. 99. Lodi and Crema,
with the border between
the Duchy of Milan
and the Venetian Republic.
Pl. 100. Inscription
with the latitude of Milan.

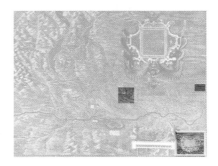

Transpadana Venetorum Ditio
The Mainland Possessions of Venice West of the River Piave

This map, 10'6" x 14' (3.21 x 4.27 m), which portrays most of the dominions of the Venetian Republic—except for the Dogado and Friuli—is one of the richest and best preserved in the Gallery. It is surrounded by a border graduated in minutes between the latitudes of 43°57' and 46°03' and the longitudes of 30°35' and 34°24' along the lower edge and 30°28' and 34°31' along the upper (it has a slightly trapezoidal projection).

In the lower left-hand corner is a cartouche surmounted by the Lion of St. Mark framing a long inscription on an ocher ground, whose sober style suggests it was part of the original design. The text, which reminds the reader of the Mediterranean fruits of the Garda basin, is certainly original. On the other hand, the cartouche in the lower right-hand corner, decorated with the figure of a girl in country dress holding up a Platonic regular polyhedron, and that originally contained the scale, has lost its inscription. However, a comparison with the real distances between various localities gives a ratio of between 1:50,000 and 1:60,000 for the most part (in Val Camonica it is around 1:30,000). The map is oriented with the north pointing upward, as shown by the compass rose in the top left-hand corner.

The predominant color is green, extending even into the mountainous areas through the long valleys. But this green is embroidered all over (except in the spaces not pertaining to the republic) with dense constellations of vermilion marks that correspond to the inhabited areas. These are uniformly distributed on the plains and on the morainic elevations. In the mountains (except for some parts around the basins of the lakes and, outside of the Venetian dominions, on the sunny left slopes of Anaunia and Val di Sole, where they spread to areas of exceptional altitudes), they are aligned in long rows almost exclusively on the valley floors or nearby. The major towns are shown in greatly exaggerated proportion; see in particular Padua, Verona, Brescia, and Crema (and outside the Venetian dominions Mantua and Trento). In general, an effort has been made to give these towns, as well as numerous minor ones, their actual form, albeit in a schematic manner. In many cases the results are satisfactory (for the minor ones see Adria, Este, and Peschiera).

The mountains are strikingly painted and give a reasonable idea of the basic orographical structure of the region. The densely packed "molehills" at the top of the map clearly illustrate the poor accessibility of the Alpine barrier. Very few mountains are named: Monte Presolana (*Corna Presolana*), Monte Baldo (written in italics, so perhaps a more recent addition), and the *Pertica* peak at the head of Val d'Illasi in the Lessini Mountains. To these might be added the indication on the Orobie Mountains of more than a dozen passes, some of which are identifiable (the S. Marco, Tartano, Dordona, etc.). Ice domes, rarely found in this period even in the backgrounds of paintings, are ignored. But the map is better than others at depicting parts of the Alps, in that the mountain area is in several places covered in woods that thicken correctly, especially between Lake Idro and the Adamello, on the Asiago plateau and from here to the head of the Valle del Cismon and then on the left side of the Valle del Piave.

The hydrography is intricate and detailed in the plains, and particular care is taken over the description of swampy or poorly drained areas (e.g., the Valli Veronesi, the long marshy strips around the Gorzone hollow between the Adige and the Euganean Hills, the valleys between Anguillara and Adria) as well as those between the rivers Chiese and Adda with a branched system of irrigation. The names of the rivers are very rare and refer to lesser watercourses (the Serio, the Garza, the Menago, and the Noce). Bridges span the minor rivers on the plain. In the mountain areas—particularly in Val Camonica—they are built over larger rivers too. The scalloped western shore of the Lagoon of Venice is clear, and on this side of it the Brenta is shown as newly chaneled in 1504. In the mountain areas, although detailed, the hydrography is not so well represented. In certain areas it is recognizably and minutely drawn and shows numerous branches with springs. In other areas—especially those to the east of Val d'Adige—the hydrography is less accurate, with incorrect courses and imaginary junctions.

Admirable care has been taken over the description of the lakes. One of the largest included is Lake Garda, which is the largest in area. It has clearly been slightly reduced in comparison with the others. Their forms are, however, outlined with sufficient accuracy, as is also true of the minor lakes (even the mutable Lake Andalo is shown in Anaunia).

As seen elsewhere in the cycle in other political areas, none of the borders of the Venetian State are shown. The only such reference is the inscription near the village of Pozzolengo on the morainic Garda hill chain, which briefly indicates the positions of the border with the Territory of Mantua to the south, the Territory of Brescia to the west, and the Territory of Verona to the east (although here *contadi*—rural districts—and not states are considered).

Two isolated border stones between states are shown only at the head of Camonica Valley (*Preda de'confini*) and on the slopes of Mount Resegone between the heads of the valleys Taleggio and Imagna (*Termine del grase*).

At the bottom of the map, to the south of the course of the river Po—which has villages on its banks only after Ostiglia (here shown as *Osteria*)—and placed on a plain in the Po delta dotted with more woods than settlements are plans of Padua and Vicenza, drawn in trompe l'oeil as though on sheets nailed to the wall. The plan of the former is similar to the schematic plan of the city found in the relevant regional panel; the plan of the latter is different.

The fresco on the vault corresponding to the *Transpadana Venetorum Ditio* is that showing *The Miraculous Appearance of St. Francis during a Sermon by St. Anthony.*

101

Pl. 101. Panel showing *Transpadana Venetorum Ditio* (The Mainland Possessions of Venice West of the River Piave), and two herms.

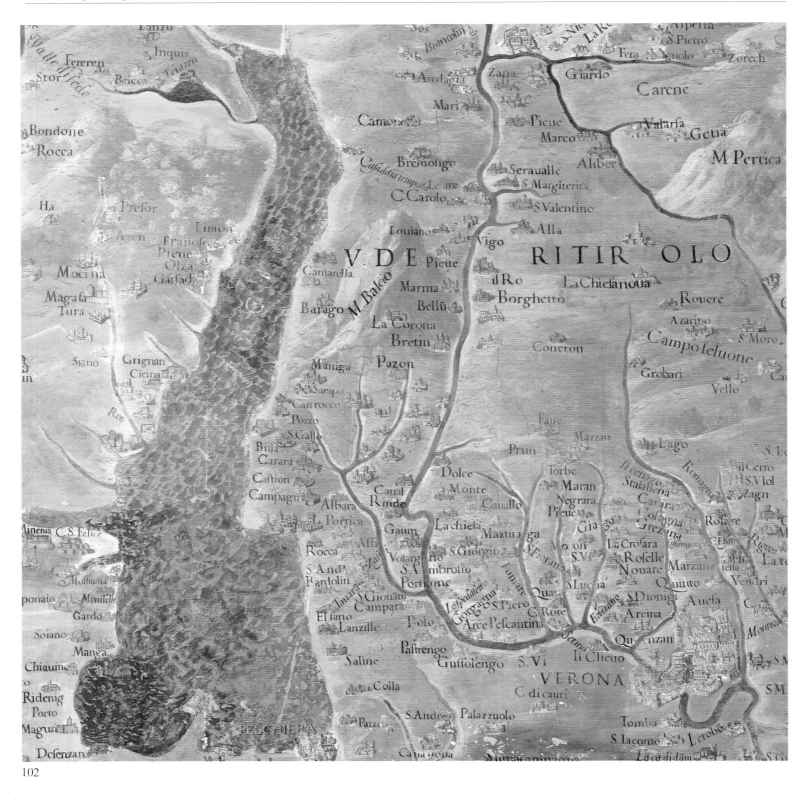

102

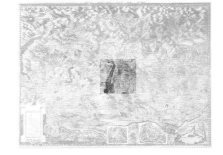

Pl. 102. *Transpadana Venetorum Ditio* (The Mainland Possessions of Venice West of the River Piave), detail. Lake Garda, the river Adige, and view of Verona.

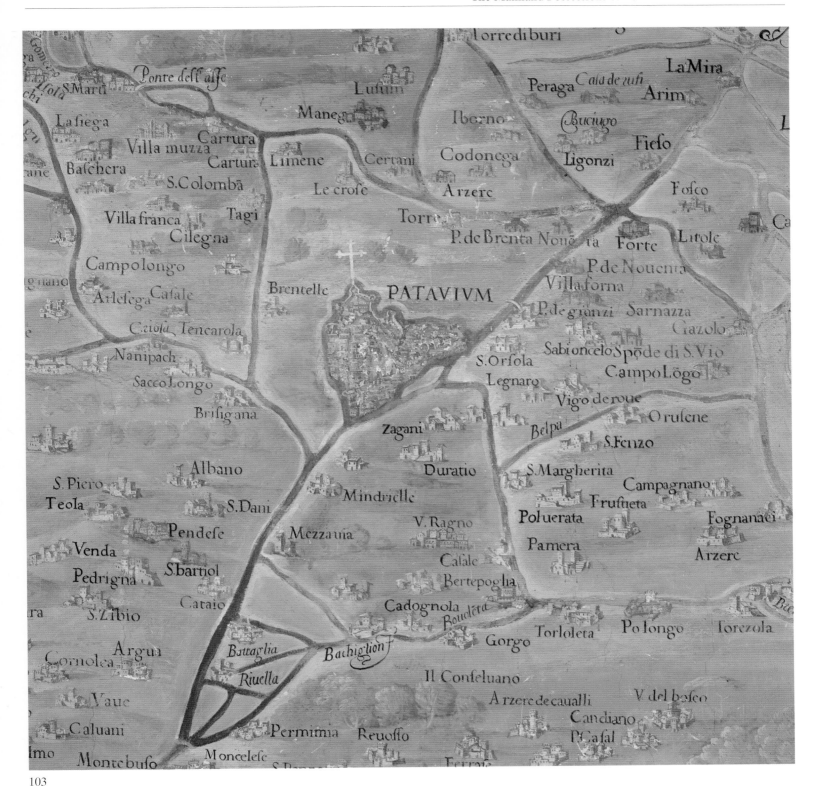

Torre di buri

LaMira

Peraga Cala de rufi Arim

Ponte dell'alfe

S.Marti

Lufum

Manega

Iberno Buciugo

Fiefo

Lafiega

Villa muzza Carrura

Cartura Limene

Certani

Codonega Ligonzi

Bafchera

S.Colombā

Le crofe

Arzere

Fofco

Villa franca Tagi

Cilegna

Torre

P.de Brenta Noue ta Forte Litole

Campolongo

Brentelle

PATAVIVM

P.de Nouenta

Villaforna

Arlefega Cafale

P.de granzi Sarnazza

Grazolo

Cacola Tencarola

Sabioncelo S.pode di S.Vio

Nanipach

S.Orfola Campo Lōgo

Sacco Longo

Legnaro

Brifigana

Vigo de roue

Zagani

Belpa Orufene

S.Fenzo

Albano

Duratio

S.Margherita

S.Piero

Mindriclle

Campagnano

Teola S.Dani

V.Ragno

Poluerata Trufueta

Pendefe

Mezzania

Cafale Pamera Fognanaci

Venda

S.bartiol

Bertepoglia Arzere

Pedrigna

Cataio

Cadognola

S.Libio

Bouclera Polongo Torezola

Argua

Battaglia

Bachiglion Gorgo Torloleta

Cornolea

Riuella

Il Confeluano

Vaue

Arzere de caualli V.del bofco

Caluani

Permimia Reuoffo

Canciano

P.Cafal

imo Montebufo

Moncelefe

103

Pl. 103. *Transpadana Venetorum Ditio* (The Mainland Possessions of Venice West of the River Piave), detail. Padua and surrounding country.

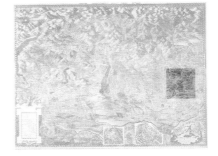

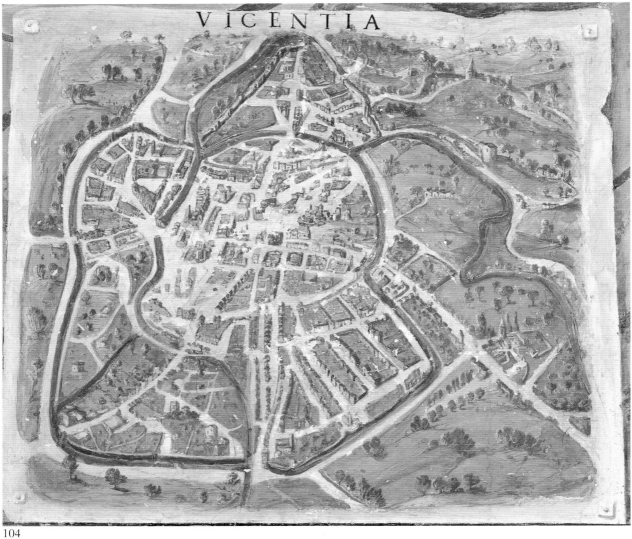

104

105

106

Transpadana Venetorum Ditio (The Mainland Possessions of Venice
West of the River Piave), details.
Pl. 104. Trompe l'oeil painting with plan of Vicenza.
Pl. 105. The lower Po Valley from Mantua to Badia Polesine.

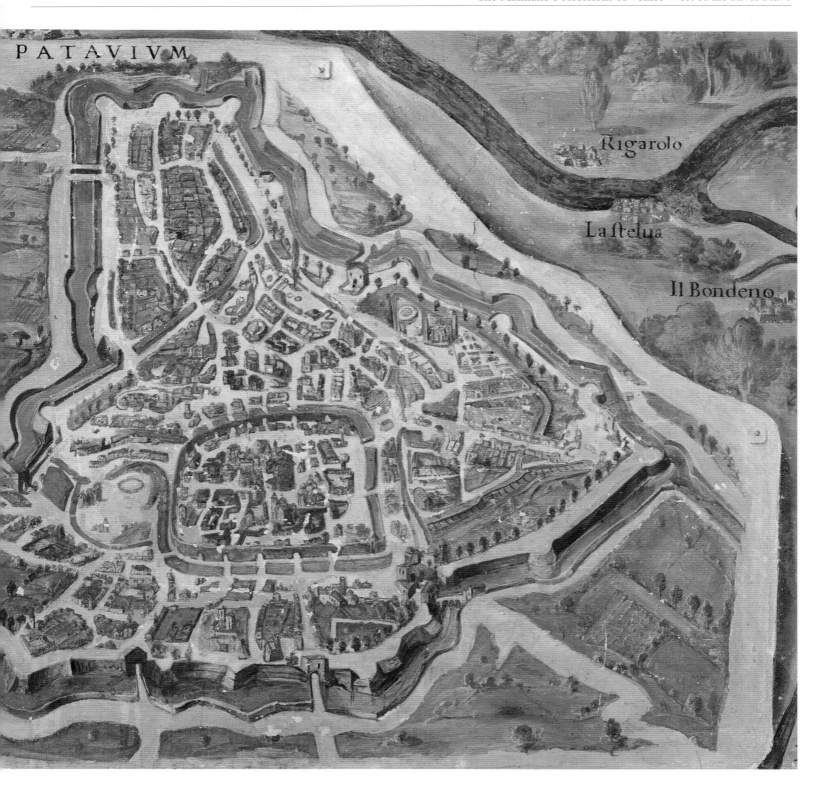

PATAVIVM

Rigarolo

La stelua

Il Bondeno

Pl. 106. *Transpadana Venetorum Ditio* (The Mainland Possessions of Venice West of the River Piave), detail. Trompe l'oeil painting with plan of Padua.

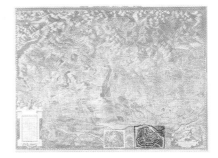

Forum Iulii
The Lagoon of Venice, Friuli, and Istria

This panel, framed by a border marked in degrees, 10'10" x 14'3" (3.31 x 4.35 m), comprises the Patria del Friuli, almost the whole of the Venetian lagoon, the plain of Treviso, and the whole of the Istrian Peninsula.

The center of the Gulf of Venice (*Hadriacticus sinus*) is dominated by a large and extremely ornate cartouche, its frame embellished with Barberini bees and enclosing an inscription in gold letters on a scarlet ground. The cartouche in its present form thus dates from the time of Urban VIII. The original inscription, which particularly stresses the mines of white stone used for important large-scale buildings, seems not to have been altered.

The depiction of the sea ruffled by a strong southwesterly wind is of considerable artistic effect. Winds blowing from different directions (in two cases northern and in another two southern) swell the sails of the vessels—two cargo ships, a fast small galley, and a fishing boat—sailing in various parts of the sea. Near the Istrian coast a raft, towed by three Tritons and carrying cupids holding topographical instruments, carries a standard bearing the bar scale and accompanying inscription in which 10,000 paces correspond to 10" (25 cm). Directly below the cartouche to the south—namely toward the Venetian dominions—is a representation of the winged Lion of St. Mark flying over the sea carrying the evangelist and a Counter-Reformational personification of Faith on its back.

The scale of the map is 1:70,000. The graduations in minutes on its border, ranging from between 44°05′ and 46°10′ latitude and between 34°12′ and 38°08′ longitude along its lower edge and between 34°06′ and 38°10′ longitude along its upper, show that it is projected over a slightly trapezoidal grid. It is oriented with the north pointing upward.

The landmass is predominantly green, the color used to represent the plains. Yellowish and whitish brown (the latter possibly a reference to the calcareous rocks) are reserved for the mountains, which are mainly arranged in long rows. The orography effectively conveys the impression of a harsh, barren relief, but is not very faithful when it comes to position and form. The hydrography is reasonably correct where the general character of the area is concerned, and shows a considerable number of watercourses on the plain between the rivers Piave and the Isonzo, while very few are given within the Istrian Peninsula. Here, however, the map shows some lakes that do not actually exist or are a mistaken interpretation of the seasonal marshes that form on the bottoms of the *uvalas* (sinks).

One is immediately struck by a certain disparity between Istria and Friuli. Thanks partly to its compact and pronounced relief, the former dominates the right half of the map. However, its peninsular nature is far from clear, emerging only at its extreme southern tip where the coastline projects over the graduated border. The coastline is dotted with many settlements, most in the correct position—although Trieste is marked twice, with the Roman *Tergestum vetus* separated by a few miles from the maritime settlement. Capo d'Istria (*Iustinopoli*), Pirano, Umago, Parenzo, Orsera, Rovigno (*S. Evagrio*), and Pola stand out on account of their size and the representation of their walls

(but their names are at times slightly garbled). Inland, the few places named are wrongly positioned (among those recognizable are Crnikal, Buje, Groznjan, Montona, Pinguente, Dragué, Pisino, and Prem) and not even one mountain name is supplied. In the northern part, wide flat hollows, closed by mountains—certainly *uvala* bottoms—can be seen, meticulously marked with regular grids symbolizing arable crops.

Friuli occupies a much smaller surface area than Istria and gives the impression of being far less mountainous. The reliefs closing it to the north (painted in some places with touches of violet that distinguish them from those of Istria) are more scattered and less steep. Indeed, the mountains of Friuli are almost non-existent, or reduced to a pre-Alpine band, from which numerous rivers flow down into the plain. This network of rivers (apart from the bizarre character of some of their names) is reasonably faithful but is often inaccurate. The names of the villages scattered over the flat area and the morainic reliefs are mostly hard to identify and places are marked with symbols that do not correspond to their real importance: Udine (*Vtinu*), Cividale (*Ciuidal*), and Portogruaro (*Porto*) cannot be distinguished from the nearby country villages. Grado is not shown, and the only sign of a walled, episcopal settlement is at Aquileia but carries the name of Ruda. The complicated, broken boundary line between the Venetian state and the Hapsburg Empire on the plain to the west of the Tagliamento River and as far as the Isonzo delta has been ignored. Indeed, the only boundary between the two states shown on the map is to the east of Trieste, a *confine dell'Arciduca,* which passes along a little valley identifiable as the Rosandra (or S. Servolo) from where it turns inland, but extending too far, toward the Karst. This is the boundary that divided the Austrian dominions in the north of the Istrian Peninsula from the Venetian ones in the south.

All in all, the only area of the map to give a satisfactory picture of the chorographical situation is that showing the lagoon between the Po and Isonzo deltas. The sandy shores, the ports, islands, canal systems, and fringes of the lagoon basins, as well as the Doge's settlements, among which Venice stands out for its accurate detail, are clear and faithful.

This map must already have been in poor condition only a few years after its completion, for under Sixtus V half was restored and repainted by Giovanni Guerra of Modena. The large cartouche shows that it was again retouched during the Barberini papacy. It is certain that Holste had no part in this, because a manuscript map of his, dating from between 1644 and 1648 and partly dealing with the same regions as this map, represents these in an entirely different manner, one showing a more accurate knowledge of the area. It is also significant that when the panel was repainted during the Barberini papacy—with conspicuous results as regards the ornamental parts—there should have been no attempt to include the newly founded Palmanova (1593).

The fresco on the vault corresponding to the map of *Forum Iulii* is that showing *The Emperor Frederick Barbarossa Pledging Obedience to Pope Alexander III in Venice.*

107

Pl. 107. Panel showing *Forum Iulii* (The Lagoon of Venice, Friuli, and Istria), and two herms.

108

109

110

Forum Iulii (The Lagoon of Venice, Friuli, and Istria), details.
Pl. 108. The lagoons between the river Tagliamento and the river Isonzo.
Pl. 109. The lagoon of Venice and the lagoons west of the river Piave.
Pl. 110. The Lion of St. Mark the Evangelist and an allegory of Faith.

111

Pl. 111. *Forum Iulii* (The Lagoon of Venice, Friuli, and Istria), detail. Cargo ship on the Adriatic Sea.

Placentiae et Parmae Ducatus
The Duchy of Parma and Piacenza

The panel, 10′8″ x 14′4″ (3.25 x 4.37 m), showing the duchy, which had been in the possession of the Farnese family for about thirty years, features, in its bottom right-hand corner, a cartouche executed in high Mannerist style with an inscription in gold, apparently original, on a sky-blue background. After a reference to the continuity of the urban settlements founded by the Romans, the inscription describes irrigation as typical of agriculture in this area with the production of cheese as the result.

The map is oriented with the north pointing upward, and as may be seen from the geometric scale, where 9,000 paces correspond to 17″ (42 cm), it is drawn to a scale of 1:32,000. It is surrounded by a border graduated in minutes, numbered at intervals of five, ranging from 43°40′ to 44°50′ latitude and from 30°33′ to 32°41′ longitude along its lower edge and from 30°31′ to 32°44′ longitude along its upper.

The upper part part of the panel is prevalently green in color (occasionally shading into yellow, in some instances in reference to the faces of the Insubric Pleistocene terraces, more visible at that time than today). In the lower part, the green mostly gives way to a reddish brown color used to highlight the western sides of the "molehill"-shaped mountains representing the Apennine range. The map suffers from a paucity of information as well as from considerable inaccuracies and lacunae. One of the most striking, in this recently constituted state, is the lack of any indication of its political boundaries.

The oro-hydrographical delineation of the Apennines is even more inadequate. Thus, in the Valle del Trebbia (identified by name, while the adjacent Valle del Tidone is called the *Valle di Tibo*), the map fails to show the forking of its mountain basin in Val d'Aveto and also omits the minor valley joining it from the Perino, which, marked as *Val Prina*, is here made to join the Valle del Nure. The areas with the sources of the rivers Taro and Parma are rather confused, owing to their topographical links with the adjacent basins being mistaken. Only the central basin of the Taro and that part of its course where it crosses the plain are shown with reasonable accuracy. Also fairly accurate, although graphically indistinguishable from the rivers, are the mill canal from Fornovo to Parma and the shipping canal from Parma in the direction of the Po River (where it incorrectly joins the Enza).

Equally unsatisfactory is the representation of the settlements, of which fewer are shown, and with a higher degree of inaccuracy, in the Piacentino, while they are more plentiful around Parma. A fair number are shown in the foothills. In this same area, between the rivers Enza and Tidone, is shown a continuous stretch of Via Emilia (its name, written in italics to the east of Parma, was perhaps added at a later date), crossing the main rivers and many lesser ones on bridges (near which are written the names *Ponte di Lenza*, *Ponte Taro*, *Ponte Tidone*).

Special care has been taken over the views of the towns situated on the road (see San Giovanni, Ponte Nure, Fiorenzuola, Borgo San Donnino, Castel Guelfo), which appear to grow along it. A good number of those lying along the Po River, much used by ships at the time, are also named—although sometimes the name is garbled—and some are well described (see Guastalla, Brescello

[here *Berzei*], Sissa [here *Siffa*], Roccabianca). The villages in the mountain area are rather more scarce—especially around Piacenza—where they are rarely illustrated and almost exclusively in the Parmigiano, with far from negligible examples of realism: see in Val di Taro Pietramogolana, Belforte, Tiedoli (*Taiedolo*), the bridge at Piana de Molino, Borgo di Taro, and, lastly, Compiano, which, however, is mistakenly shown at the mouth of the Ceno. Other examples are Vianino, Varsi, and Bardi in Val di Ceno, and, at the two ends of Val Baganza, Sala and Berceto. In the Piacentino, among the few views of note are the Rocca d'Olgisio (here *Rocca d'Arcese*), which, however, faces Val Trebbia instead of Val Tidone. Lastly, we should not forget the frequent mentions of abbeys and monasteries, especially in the Parmigiano: e.g., Chiaravalle, Castellina, and Fontevivo in the plain; Torchiara and Cavana in Val di Parma; and Carpadasco in Val di Ceno.

While the map may be chorographically mediocre, pictorially it has some value. The method used to draw and shade the mountain reliefs using color and here and there some fine hatching makes the modeling of the valleys very striking. The two large battle scenes included in the panel, both original, refer in one case to antiquity, and in the other to less than a hundred years previously.

The first one is the Battle by the Trebbia River (218 B.C.) won by the Carthaginians against the Romans. It took place on the Piedmont plain to the west of the river, about 4 miles (10 km) past its outlet on the plain. The scene showing it here has two mistakes: the battlefield is to the east of the Trebbia River, between this river and the Nure, completely reversing the deployment of the two armies in battle and the location of their quarters.

The second one is the Battle of Fornovo (July 1495), where the Val di Taro joins the plain. It was a battle without winners—only a large number of victims—with one side and the other singing victory, as the historian Ludovico Antonio Muratori (1672–1750) was to say later. Charles VIII's French army, returning from the Kingdom of Naples and marching along the medieval *via francigena* toward the Po Valley, managed with a disciplined attack to break the circle laid by the League of Italian States and to continue their march toward Piacenza and Asti.

The names on the plain between Via Emilia and the Po River have in many instances been repainted at a later date, the original writing being visible below the present. The same is true of the river names written in italics in this same area, which certainly date from more recent times. The views of a group of settlements on the lower Po Valley along the river are clearly marked with minute consecutive numbers (16 for Soarza, 17 for Vidalenzo, 18 for the Po delta, etc., up to 26 for Roccabianca, 31 for Caorso, 34 for Mezzano, 41 for Fontanelle). These very probably refer to a numbered chorographic list used for the preparation of the map.

The fresco on the vault corresponding to the map of *Placentiae et Parmae Ducatus* is that showing *Pope Innocent IV Intervening to Free Parma from a Siege by Emperor Frederick II.*

112

Pl. 112. Panel showing *Placentiae et Parmae Ducatus*
(The Duchy of Parma and Piacenza), and two herms.

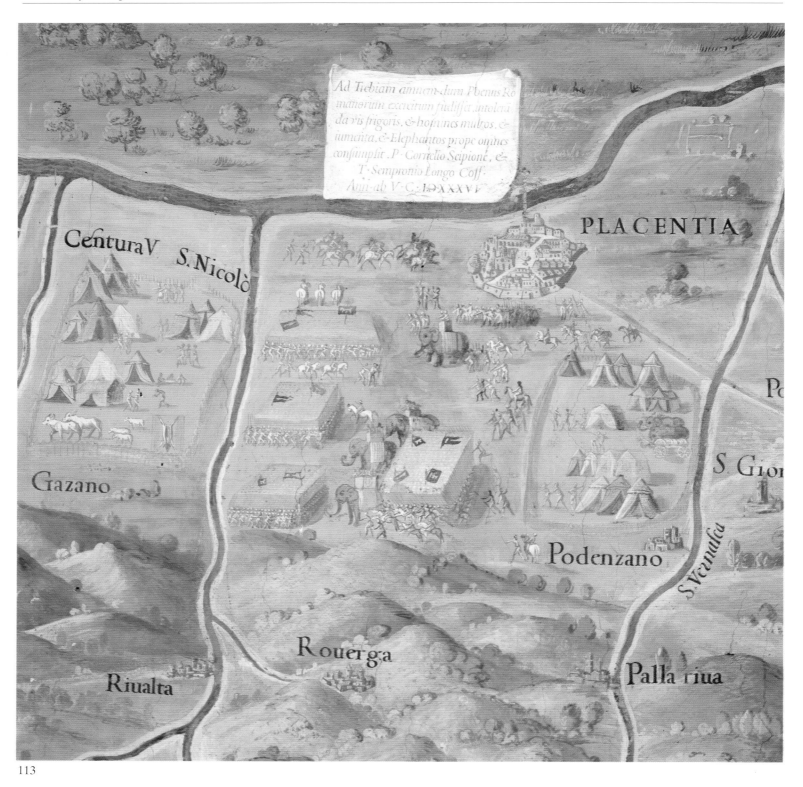

Ad Trebiam amnem dum Pœnus Romanorum exercitum fudiffet intolerandavis frigoris, & homines multos, & iumenta, & Elephantos prope omnes confumpfit .P. Cornelio Scipione, & T. Sempronio Longo Coff. Ann. ab V. C. ID XXXVI

113

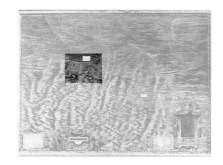

Pl. 113. *Placentiae et Parmae Ducatus* (The Duchy of Parma and Piacenza), detail. Hannibal defeats the Romans by the river Trebbia (218 B.C.).

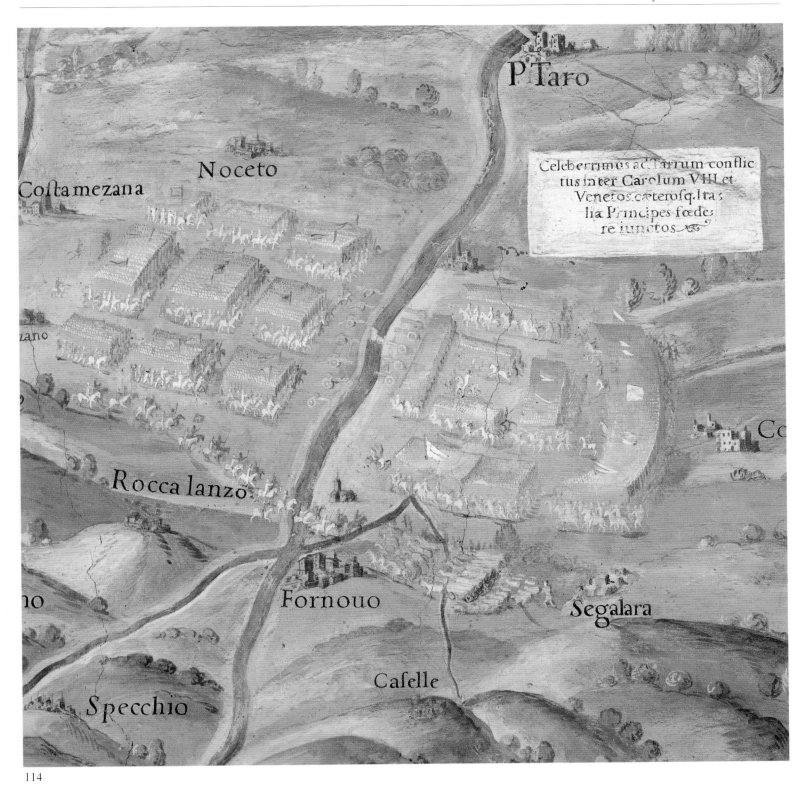

Costa mezana

Noceto

P. Taro

Celeberrimus ad Tarrum conflic
tus inter Carolum VIII et
Venetos cæterofq. Ita:
lia Principes fœde:
re iunctos

zano

Rocca lanzo

Co

Fornouo

Segalara

Cafelle

Specchio

114

Pl. 114. *Placentiae et Parmae Ducatus* (The Duchy of Parma and Piacenza), detail.
The Battle of Fornovo between Charles VIII of France and the Italian Princes (1495).

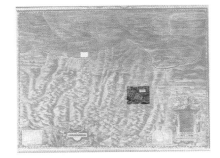

115

116

117

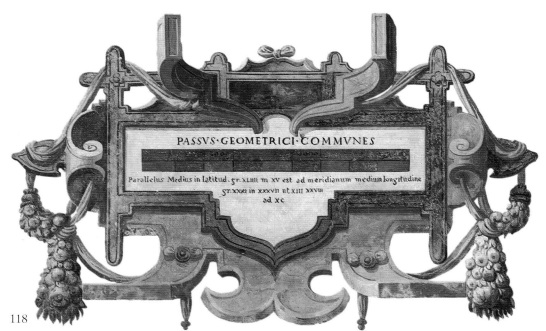

118

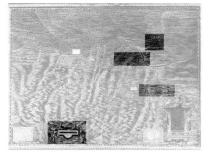

Placentiae et Parmae Ducatus (The Duchy of Parma and Piacenza), details.
Pl. 115. The lower plain of Parma near the river Po.
Pl. 116. Compass rose with Aldobrandini arms of Pope Clement VIII.
Pl. 117. Parma and a part of Via Emilia towards Reggio Emilia.
Pl. 118. Metric scale.

PLACENTIA

119

Pl. 119. *Placentiae et Parmae Ducatus* (The Duchy of Parma and Piacenza), detail.
Trompe l'oeil painting with plan of Piacenza.

Mantuae Ducatus
The Duchy of Mantua

The panel, 11′1″ x 14′2″ (3.33 x 4.31 m), shows no sign of more recent additions, and so would appear to represent the original design, which was certainly included the inscription in a geometrical gold cartouche with an ornate frame decorated with classical masks and cherubs. The inscription celebrates the region's antiquity, the security of its position, excellently defended on all sides by lakes, the cultural splendors of its court—which in those years were indeed at their most magnificent—and the fertility of the surrounding countryside.

The map is oriented with the north pointing upward. The scale, in the bottom left-hand corner, in a fine vermilion cartouche, measures 18″ (45 cm) and is equal to 6,000 paces, giving a ratio of around 1:20,000. The graduation in minutes along the edges, numbered every five, goes from 44°08′ to 44°50′ latitude and from 32° to 36°16′ longitude.

This is the earliest known topographical map of the Mantovano. However, it is uneven in quality. A large part of the panel conveys the impression of a slightly rolling area, even where it should be decidedly flat such as between Mantua, Gazoldo, and Asolo.

The hydrography is also poor in the area to the west of Mantua between the rivers Mincio and Oglio. Nevertheless, the Po River is drawn with tolerable accuracy from Casalmaggiore to Sermide, despite a certain latitudinal emphasis and longitudinal contraction. The course of the Mincio—crossed by bridges at Valeggio and Goito—is also correct so far as its orientation and meanders are concerned (except that the map unwarrantedly makes a fluvial island out of the section between Salionze and Valeggio, which cuts through the morainic reliefs where the river is flanked by various mill canals profiting from the tilt of the riverbed). There are good descriptions of the Mantuan lakes, of Te Island between the city and Lake Paiolo (dried up in the middle of the 18th century), and—before the Mincio River flows into the Po—the medieval Governolo lock controlling the river's downflow.

The area to the north of Mantua has few settlements, their number increasing only very slightly in the area around Mantua. Here, between Cittadella and Marmirolo, is a curious tree-lined avenue that might be taken as an allusion to the road leading to a wood, the Bosco della Fontana, except that there is no trace of the latter. Indeed, the half of the map north of Mantua, with its long series of undulating hills fringed by curtains of trees, which only exceptionally form tiny woods, showing bare arable land or meadows, gives a good and elegant idea of what, very probably, was the typical landscape of this area.

The part of the map to the south and the east of Mantua is of greater value as a chorographical document. To the east of the town the hydrography of the lower plain, partly filled with marshes and sloping down toward the Grandi Valli of Verona, is shown effectively and in detail. Both the river Tartaro (the only

watercourse named) and the tangled network of its streams and the areas invaded by water are marked. Care is also taken over the settlements (some of which had pioneering roles: see *Bastion delle Zinzale* and *P[onte] Molino*). Around twenty are marked on either side of the Po River, after its confluence with the Mincio.

To the south of Mantua is an area almost wholly lacking in settlements—at the extremity of the lakes is a solitary *Pietoli patria di Virgilio.* But the straight line in pink on a yellowish ground that leaves the site of Curtatone (not named) for the high lake at Borgoforte on the Po, which is surrounded by a square walled enclosure, represents the 4.7-mile-long defence line (12 km) that was called the seraglio and was formed of canals and embankments, a fortification system created in the 13th century.

A little further on, an equally straight diagonal line represents a road joining Santa Maria delle Grazie on the high lake with Marcaria on the river Oglio, where there is a bridge and where, between this river and the Po, begins another area whose hydrography (the Ceriana and the Navarolo) and densely packed settlements are also well described.

Trim perspective views enclosed by polygonal walls represent Casalmaggiore and Viadana by the Po, Bozzolo by the Oglio, Asola by the Chiese, and then Sabbioneta, already with its definitive hexagonal form, dating from between 1555 and 1568.

In pronounced contrast to the well described areas south and east of Mantua are the possessions of the Gonzaga family beyond the Po River, where the best-known places (Suzzara, Reggiolo, Gonzaga) are not marked at all, and those shown are very few (among them, some outside the area, are Rolo and Concordia). Only San Benedetto is given with some prominence, with its huge abbey of Polirone. On the other side of the Po River, isolated but drawn in such a way as to stand out, is Guastalla.

Lastly, on the eastern side of the panel, between the Po and the drained marshes of the Tartaro, is a scene evoking the halting of Attila's army (an army supplemented by farming wagons and herds of sheep) after the encounter in 452 with Pope Leo I, which apparently took place in this area.

At the bottom of the map is a plan of Mantua.

Danti's panel underwent large-scale restoration by Oldrado, who, by his own account, restored the colors and repainted the reliefs and rivers as well as the towns, villages, and boundaries. The boundaries are no longer visible, although they can be made out by following the line of defence formed by castles that, in the morainic area, beyond the Chiese to the west and beyond the Mincio to the east, mark the limit beyond which no further information is given.

The fresco on the vault corresponding to the map of *Mantuae Ducatus* is that with *Pope St. Leo the Great Stopping Attila, King of the Huns.*

120

Pl. 120. Panel showing *Mantuae Ducatus* (The Duchy of Mantua), and two herms.

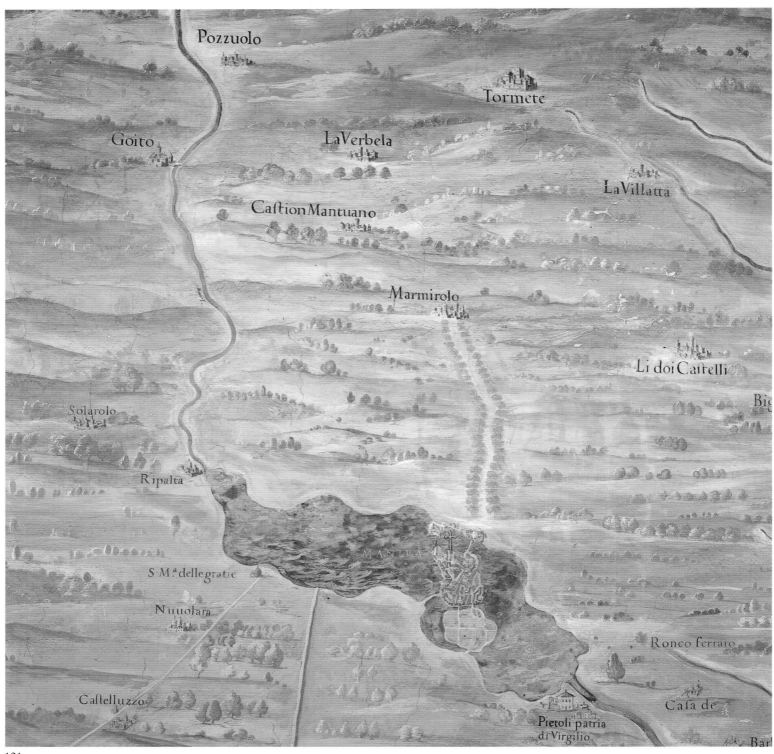

Pozzuolo

Tormete

Goito

LaVerbela

LaVillatta

CaſtionMantuano

Marmirolo

Li doi Caſtelli

Solarolo

Big

Ripalta

S·Mªdellegratie

MANTVA

Nuuolara

Ronco ferraro

Caſtelluzzo

Caſa de

Pietoli patria
di Virgilio

Barl

121

Mantuae Ducatus (The Duchy of Mantua), details.
Pl. 121. The lake of Mantua.
Pl. 122. Trompe l'oeil painting with plan of Mantua.

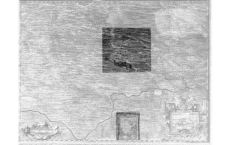

MANTVA

Ferrariae Ducatus
The Duchy of Ferrara

This panel, 11′ x 15′ (3.36 x 4.31 m), follows by just a few years the first topographical portrayal of the Este Duchy, which was shown in or around 1580. The inscription in the impressive cartouche placed on the lower edge in the middle recalls the transferral of the duchy to the Papal States in 1598. The inscription is therefore not the original one, of which nothing is known. The cartouche certainly dates from the time of Urban VIII, as shown by the three bees adorning it above and below the inscription.

The area included on the map is vast, spreading from the *contadi* (rural district) of Cremona and Padua in the north, to those of Ravenna and Lucca in the south. Except for some small areas beyond its borders, the Este Duchy is the only area to be represented chorographically.

The most attractive part of the map is certainly the plain, with its detailed and accurate description of the hydrography and the exceptionally dense network of roadways. The hydrography, only slightly distorted in the center, is almost perfect at the map's western and eastern extremities (the Reggiano and the Ferrarese with its river islands, respectively). Particularly well represented are the Comacchio lagoons, with their "embankments" (coastal strips or delta channels of Etruscan-Roman times) dividing them into ten or so "fields," the names of which survived to the beginning of the twentieth century. The roadways are shown as minute white threads forming a kind of web that is complete to its outermost terminations. Thus all the town and country villages in the plain are reached by roads. It should also be remembered that at this time much traffic went by water. And, in addition to the vigorous course of the Po, terminating in its branches the Levante and Goro, and other rivers that saw a fair amount of navigation (the Secchia, Panaro, Volano, and Primaro), the map also marks shipping canals: that of Modena, which at *Buonporto* flows into the Panaro, and that of Bologna, which toward Malalbergo, at *Torre della Fossa*, joins the Primaro.

Roads and canals frequently intersect in reclaimed areas: great emphasis is given to the *Bonificazione* of the Polesine di San Giovanni, undertaken by Alfonso II (1533–1597) in 1564 and in 1580 almost completed. See also, at the other side of the duchy, between the rivers Enza and Crostolo, the *Bonificazione del Bentivogli* (i.e., Cornelio Bentivoglio), commenced in 1561 and completed in 1576. Lastly, see the area in the Oltrepo, which had begun to be reclaimed by Cornelio Bentivoglio a few years earlier (around 1570) among the marshes of the Zelo (here *Gelo*).

The lower delta plain meets the Adriatic (sailed by two coasters only) in a series of crescent-shaped bays. Apart from the old towns of Ravenna and Comacchio and the abbey of Pomposa, founded in the 8th century, few settlements are shown on this strip of coast. This further brings out the roads winding along the long, deserted sandbars that link the villages along the channels of the delta beds, and make still more prominent the large mass of the castle of Mesola—built according to a design by Marco Antonio Pasi almost at the same time as the map was being painted (between 1579 and 1583).

Decidedly different are the number and distribution of the settlements shown on the map to the west of the delta areas. The positioning and names of these places are given with remarkable accuracy. Attractive plans are provided of the principal towns (Ferrara, Mirandola, Modena, Reggio nell'Emilia, Carpi, and Brescello) and of places of particular importance for the Este court. Examples of the latter are the Belriguardo complex, the first *Este delizia*, founded by Nicolò III (1384–1441) in 1435 alongside the canal of the same name that followed the course of the old Po di Sandalo, or another *delizia*, the Villa di Copparo, commenced by Ercole II (1508–1554) in 1548, or else the rural town of Diamantina with its large farm, the result of land-reclamation carried out in the first quarter of the 16th century.

The mountainous area of the duchy is a little compressed and represented by means of massed cones. Along the Apennine range—with altitudes here always exceeding 4,921 feet (1,500 m)—these become massy and bleak and also stand out thanks to their purple coloring and accentuated shading. The hydrography is on the whole fairly correct.

There are many settlements, but they are often rather inaccurately described. Exceptions include the better known ones among the foothills, such as Vignola, Spilamberto, Sassuolo, and Scandiano. The impression one gets from the map is that on the Emilian side settlements are predominantly on high ground. On the Garfagnana side, on the other hand, the map highlights the greater breadth of the valley. The orography and hydrography of the Garfagnana holdings are more faithful than that of the Frignano—and here there are also references to mountain passes. Above Careggine on the inner slopes of the Apuan Alps, a *Valico di sopra* is marked, which to judge from its position is meant for Vagli di Sopra. Again, above the Apennine range two much-used passes are indicated by means of the double occurrence of the name *Hospidaletto*, standing for two medieval guesthouses, one at Ospitaletto near the source of the Leo, on the way to the Croce Arcana pass, and the other at Ospedaletto near the source of the Serchio springs, on the way to the Pradarena pass. Halfway between these two guesthouses, the name *S. Pelegrino in Alpe*, almost at the end of the range on the Garfagnana side, and those of other places at high altitudes opposite the Frignano indicate the path followed by the mountain road know as *Bibulca*, which up until the 13th century was dominated by the abbey of Frassinoro.

The political boundaries are not shown. However, a clear vermilion line marks the border between the Ferrarese and the Bolognese from the village of Dosso on the river Reno to the Marmorta valleys opposite Argenta.

Between the Secchia and the Panaro there is a large scene depicting the end of the long siege of Mirandola and the entry into the town of Pope Julius II (papacy 1503–1513) in January 1511.

Lastly, toward the bottom of the panel, plans of Ferrara and of its citadel, and to their right, plans of Comacchio, are drawn as though on sheets nailed to the wall.

The fresco on the vault corresponding to the map of *Ferrariae Ducatus* is that showing *St. Geminianus Delivering Modena from Attila*.

123

Pl. 123. Panel showing *Ferrariae Ducatus* (The Duchy of Ferrara), and two herms.

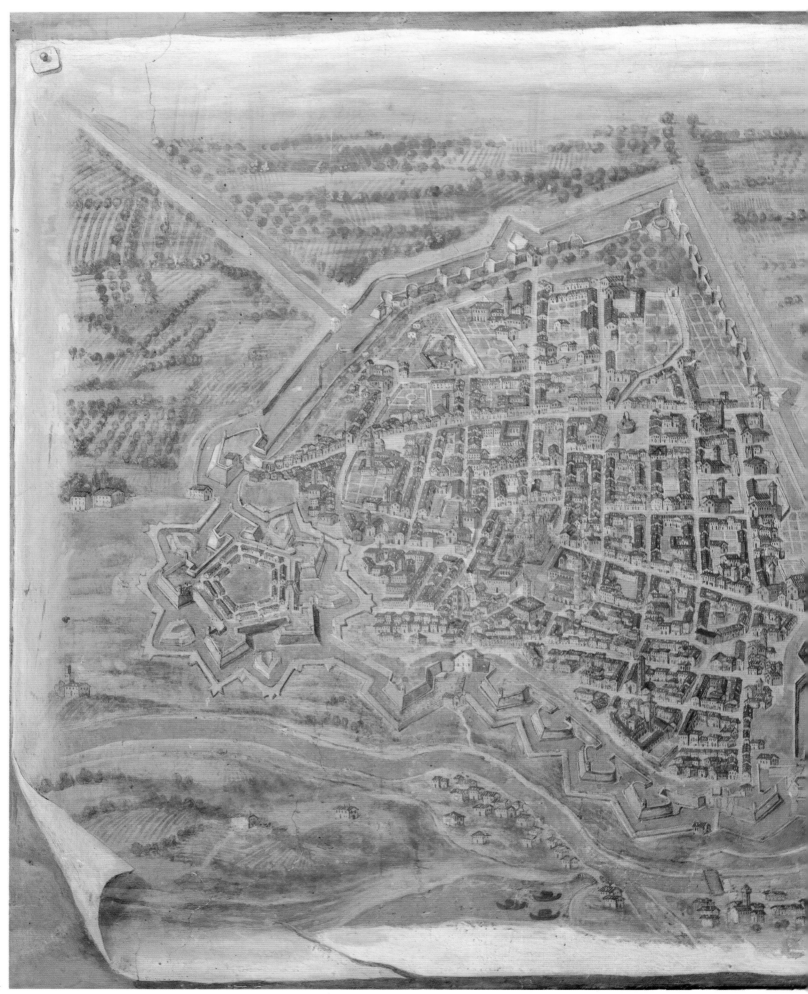

125

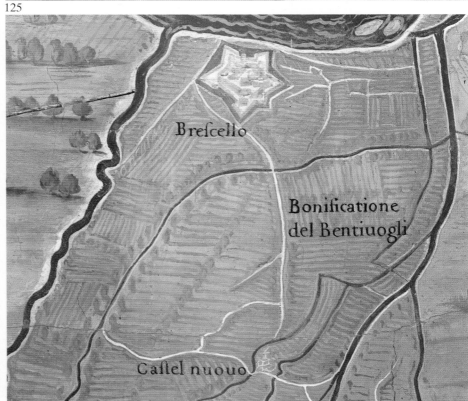

Brefcello

Bonificatione del Bentiuogli

Caftel nuouo

126

Ferrariae Ducatus (The Duchy of Ferrara), details.
Pl. 124. Trompe l'oeil painting with plan of Ferrara.
Pl. 125. Trompe l'oeil painting with fortress of Ferrara.
Pl. 126. Plan of Brescello with the land reclaimed by Cornelio Bentivoglio, Lord of Gualtieri (1561–1576).

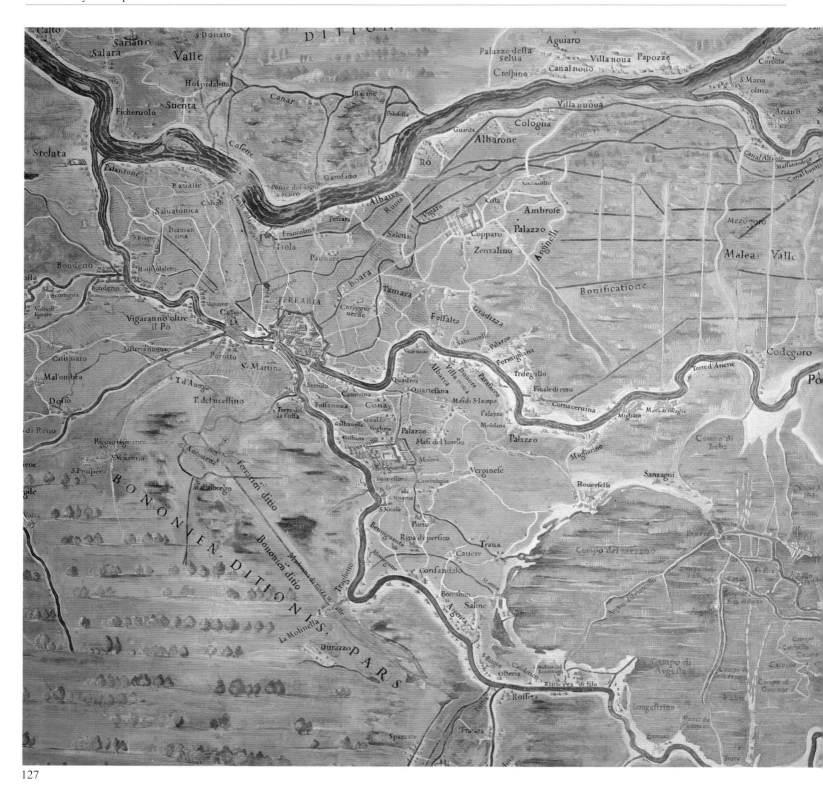

127

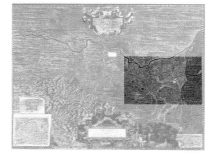

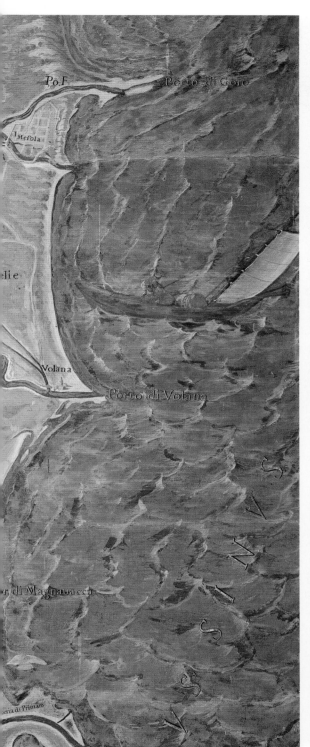

128

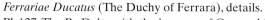

Ferrariae Ducatus (The Duchy of Ferrara), details.
Pl. 127. The Po Delta with the lagoons of Comacchio and the large area of land reclaimed by Alfonso II of Este between 1564 and 1580.
Pl. 128. The Este province of Garfagnana and the mountain course of the river Serchio.

Bononiensis Ditio
The Jurisdiction of Bologna

The panel, 10′9″ x 13′9″ (3.27 x 4.18 m), is the earliest chorographical representation of the Bolognese to survive intact to the present day. It is also one of the best maps in the Gallery in terms of pictorial effect and topographical accuracy.

In the top left-hand corner is an elegant cartouche with an inscription in gold letters on a sky-blue ground. This mentions the Roman colonization of Bologna and, after a reference to the fertility of the land and to the fame of the *Studio* or university, celebrates the events that at the height of the Middle Ages had marked the end of the city's subjection to Imperial rule, and in 1361, the end of Bernabò Visconti's (1323–1385) lordship. The cartouche, enriched with a gold frame and surmounted by two winged dragons—a clear allusion to the Boncompagni arms of Pope Gregory XIII—and surrounded by figures of Muses (perhaps Clio and Erato) and by children suspending bundles of fruit on ribbons, is certainly the original.

On the other side of the panel, a cartouche of the same size and of very similar design carries an inscription on a sky-blue ground regarding the definition of the border with the Duchy of Ferrara.

As can be seen from the compass rose, the Bologna panel is oriented with the north pointing upward, but shifted to the left by 28°. The grid formed by the degree lines is not rectangular but cuts the panel crosswise. The graduation for the latitudes goes from 43°57′ to 45°14′ along the left edge and from 44°02′ to 45°18′ along the right edge, and for the longitudes from 32° to 34°18′ along the bottom edge and from 32°52′ to 35°10′ along the top. The scale, shown in the bottom right-hand corner in an elaborately worked and colored plate, decorated with cherubs carrying surveying instruments, measures 15″ (37.8 cm) and is equal to 8,000 standard geometrical paces, giving a ratio of 1:31,300. In the same cartouche, below the scale, are the coordinates of Bologna—44°16′ latitude and 33°30′ longitude—which agree with those obtained from the graduations along the edges of the panel.

The most original part of the panel is that of the lower plain, with the extensive strip of marshy areas and well defined bodies of standing water (called *Valli* on the map) that follow the Po di Primaro southward, extending toward the central plain, which is strewn with villages and hamlets. This is also the area crossed by the vermilion line marking the boundary agreed upon some years earlier by the Senate of Bologna and the Este court.

The topography of the plain is drawn with great care and is of great interest on account of the distinctions made in the descriptions of the walled and open towns, the old watchtowers placed at intervals along the edges of the marshy areas, and—especially in the foothills—the areas with scattered settlements.

The map also gives a fairly broad picture of the network of roads in the plain. Firstly, it shows the whole length of Via Emilia from Romagna to the *contado* (rural district) of Modena. Then it marks the roads radiating out from Bologna in all directions. Bridges are frequently shown where the roads in the plain cross a river, and in the case of Via Emilia, this occurs repeatedly.

Of equally high quality is the representation of the mountain region, where between the basins of the Panaro and the Santerno the hydrography is knowledgeably described. The conventional device of massed cones is used with taste and skill—drawn in perspective, emphatically shaded, and painted in realistic contours—to highlight the ridges separating the valleys.

The orographic and hydrographic names are fairly numerous. Also shown are morphological curiosities that had impressed travelers for more than a century, such as the Sasso crags overhanging the Reno and narrowing the valley at the end of its mountain course, or the *Pozzi d'olio di sasso* (the name is still in use today) marked near the village of Monte Bonello—a site where two of six wells in a circle eject flames (a white petroleum used for medicinal purposes was extracted here during this period).

The settlements are also accurately and not conventionally described, special attention being paid to the layout of places on high ground and the fortifications dominating them; see, for instance, Serravalle, Savigno, and Montetortore in Val Samoggia. Pains have also been taken over the forms of the villages lying at the bottom of the valleys, which at times have a geometrical layout.

Equally recognizable are the areas where the settlements are more scattered and unwalled, such as that around Vergato in the central valley of the Reno and the hills in general.

No other panel in the Gallery is so rich with scenes depicting historic events and with details. Between the rivers Lavino and Samoggia to the northwest of Bologna, a scroll is placed beside Via Emilia to mark the place where Octavian, Mark Anthony, and Lepidus met to set up their Triumvirate in 43 B.C. About 18.6 miles (30 km) from here, to the south of Bologna and between the rivers Reno and Savena, a second scroll recalls the battle lost here in 1361 by the Visconti, a defeat that restored Bologna to papal rule. The scene reproduces the decisive phase of the battle.

In the bottom left-hand corner of the map is a fine plan of Bologna, an unusual combination of zenithal projection, tilted perspective, topographical drawing, and landscape painting. On the opposite side of the panel, is a horizontal panorama of Bologna, seen from the lower slopes of Monte San Luca. Lastly, in this same corner of the panel, are two further trompe l'oeil drawings, added at a later date and introduced without any regard for the balanced arrangement of the original map. One of these shows a plan of Forte Urbano, the other a scroll-sized and extremely refined drawing in black of a blank shield surmounted by the papal arms (a fly drawn as though resting on the surface of the paper in the bottom left-hand corner does not make the meaning of this strange image any clearer).

The frescoes on the vault corresponding to the map of *Bononiensis Ditio* are: *Christ Reminding St. Peter of His Duty to Tend the Flock of the Faithful*; *St. Petronius Reviving a Workman Killed in a Building Accident*; *The Angels Bringing Bread to St. Dominic and His Brethren, Who Had None*; *View of the Monastery of San Michele in Bosco near Bologna*; and *View of the Sanctuary of the Virgin on Monte della Guardia near Bologna*.

129

Pl. 129. Panel showing *Bononiensis Ditio* (The Jurisdiction of Bologna), and two herms.

130

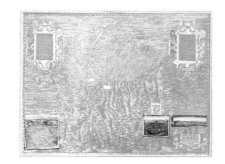

Bononiensis Ditio (The Jurisdiction of Bologna), details.
Pl. 130. Trompe l'oeil painting with plan of Bologna.
Pl. 131. Trompe l'oeil painting with Forte Urbano, built in 1628 on the border
with the Duchy of Modena.
Pl. 132. Trompe l'oeil painting with view of Bologna.

131

132

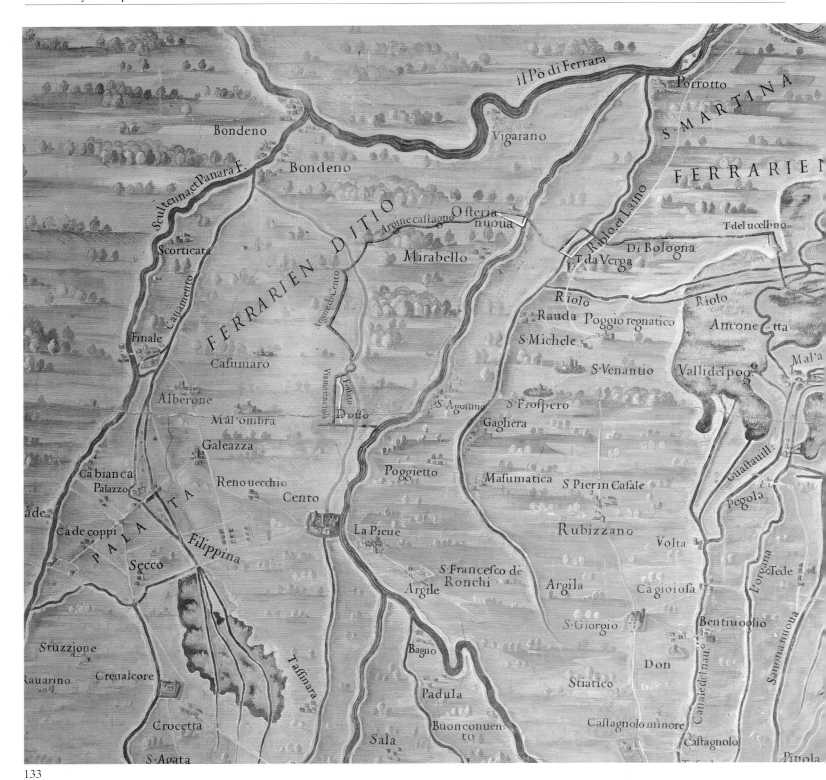

il Pò di Ferrara

Porrotto

S MARTINA

Bondeno

Vigarano

FERRARIEN

Bondeno

Sculteina,et Panara F.

Scorticata

Osteria

Argine castagno

nuoua

Riolo.et Laino

T del ucellino

FERRARIEN DITIO

Mirabello

T da Verga

Di Bologna

Riolo

Riolo

Finale

Cauamento

Rauda

Poggio regnatico

Anconetta

Casiumaro

Argine di Cento

S Michele

S Venantio

Valli del pog.º

Mal'a

Alberone

Via natraciola

Fossato

Dosso

S Agostino

S Prospero

Galeazza

Mal'ombra

Gagliera

Guastauilli.

Cà bianca

Palazzo

Renouecchio

Cento

Poggietto

Masumatica

S Pier in Casale

Rubizzano

Pegola

àde

Cà de coppi

PALATA

Filippina

La Pieue

Volta

Argila

L'organa

Tede

Secco

S Francesco de

Ronchi

Ca gioiosa

Stuzzione

Argile

S Giorgio

Canale del naui.

Taffinara

Bentiuoglio

Rauarino

Creualcore

Bagno

Don

Stiatico

Crocetta

Padula

Castagnolo minore

Castagnolo

Saturnanuoua

S Agata

Sala

Buonconuen
to

Pipola

Campo del però

FERRARIENSIS · DITIO

ella foffa

DITIO

Monifteriolo

Marara

S.Nicolò

Boccalione

Confandoli

Argenta

Ferrarien ditio
Sononien ditio

Traghetto

Valle del   Arcu di Rauena

ella Pegola

Valli di mare morto

Foffato Zaniolo

Baftia

M.ª di mezza
ualle

Muhnella

Volta

Valle di Diolo

Manzuola

T. de caualli

Durazzo

Portonouo

Barigella

Minerbio

Diolo

Selua

S·Mart ino

Mezolara

Curula

Argine

Buda

Cacciano   Riccardina

Budrio

Herculana   Fantuccia   ifterolo

Pl. 133. *Bononiensis Ditio* (The Jurisdiction of Bologna), detail.
The lower Bolognese plain between the rivers Santerno and Panaro.

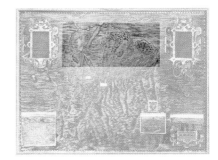

Flaminia
Romagna

This map, 10′6″ x 13′9″ (3.2 x 4.2 m), of the region Danti calls *Flaminia*, mostly corresponds to the region of Romagna. It is the earliest known chorographical representation of the region. The inscription in the bottom right-hand corner, which is original, states that the map illustrates only the part of the traditional *Flaminia* included in that province of the Papal State that for three centuries had been called Romagna (*Romandiola*).

The stele with pyramid in the lower left-hand corner is also part of the original design. This carries a fake epigraph composed around the middle of the 15th century and in 1476 placed on the so-called bridge of San Lazzaro, 2.2 miles (3.5 km) to the southeast of Cesena, by which Via Emilia crosses the Rubicon. On the steps at the base of the stele is the scale, which is equal to 9,000 paces and measures 19″ (48.5 cm), giving a ratio of 1:27,500.

As shown by the compass rose on the sea, the map is oriented with the north pointing upward but shifted to the left by 44°. The grid formed by the degree lines is therefore oblique. The latitudes range from 44° to 44°58′ along the left edge and from 42°58′ to 43°56′ along the right, while the longitudes range from 33°08′ to 34°51′ along the bottom edge and from 34°27′ to 36°12′ along the top.

The map is divided equally between lowland and mountain areas and both are quite accurately described. The part of the plain delineated most carefully and correctly is that along the coast, especially the partly marshy depressions that had begun to be reclaimed only a short time before. The coastline is well drawn and abuts the sea between the mouths of the Primaro and the Focara headland. On the sea, which is ruffled by an easterly wind, are three large coasters, possibly tartans. Along the coast are effective views of the three coastal cities, Ravenna, Cervia, and Rimini. The picture given of the coast to the north of the Savio is very different. The broken coastline here is partly the result of the sandbanks formed at the river mouths and partly of estuary juttings. Along the coast between the Savio, or more precisely between the salt pans at Cervia, and the Primaro, stretches a thick and almost unbroken band of pinewood, whose local divisions the map carefully marks.

The most minutely described portion of the plain is the low-lying area to the west of the coast between the rivers Sillaro and Savio, an area partly invaded by ponds and marshes that terminates in the north at the Po di Primaro. The topography of this area, changing year by year, is depicted with precision and care. In addition to the rivers, the map shows the drainage canals, mostly artificial, the numerous mill canals, the perimeters of the flooded *valli* (marshy area), and the side channels branching out into these from the riverbeds to carry off overflow and warp.

In the papal province of Romagna, east of the Senio, the map provides a clear record of the land reclamation begun by Clement VII (papacy 1523–1534) in 1531, and taken up again by Gregory XIII in 1578, in the *valli* between the Lamone and the broad band of sand dunes containing the San Vitale pinewood.

As regards the plain to the west of the coastal strip and low-lying areas, the map is considerably less informative about settlements. Those shown are for the most part linked to rivers or roadways. Thus, among them are the settlements lying along Via Emilia and along Via di Faenza, which leads from Ravenna to Via Emilia. Most of the minor settlements in the plain are named (sometimes slightly misspelled, e.g., *Russo* for Russi, *Cotognola* for Cotignola). However, their views are quite elementary and conventional, and only in a few instances is their rectangular medieval plan clearly recorded: see Medicina, Castel Guelfo (*C. Ghelfo*), Cotignola, and Castel Bolognese.

The major settlements along Via Emilia, whose names are written in Latin, are shown in small but striking perspective plans that give a good idea of their layout as well as their relation to the rivers at the mouths of the *valli*. Prominence is also given to the bridges where Via Emilia crosses these rivers and to the mill canals fed by them.

Along Via Emilia itself, an army composed of large battalions of foot soldiers, cavalry squadrons, and baggage wagons is marching from Faenza to Cesena and beyond, to the point where Via Emilia meets the river Rubicon, marked by a prominent inscription reading "*jacta est alea*" ("the die is cast"). It is thus the army of Julius Caesar setting out on its march to Rome in 49 B.C.

Another complex battle scene may be seen to the south of Ravenna, on either side of the river Ronco, accompanied by the inscription *Ravennae acerrima clades*. Numerous internal clues identify this as the battle that took place in 1512 between the French army and the combined Spanish and papal forces.

The mountain region is on the whole less thoroughly described, while with specific regard to its oro-hydrographic features some areas are more correct than others. The best delineated are the valleys of the Lamone and Santerno in the west, and those of the Savio, Marecchia, and of the two minor rivers, the Uso and Conca, in the east. The valleys in the Forlì area are less accurate; indeed, their proportions are quite wrong. The areas best described from the physical point of view are also those where most care is taken over the description of the settlements. These are generally placed high up, in the eastern valleys exclusively so. The perspective views representing these towns are often less stylized than those representing the smaller towns in the plain. They are sometimes even quite realistic. A certain number of the mountain settlements and one or two of those in the plain in the central and right-hand portions of the panel are marked with heraldic symbols, whose significance is clarified in the inscription on a scroll placed in the mountainous area and which bears the winged dragon from the Boncompagni coat of arms. The inscription states that the places marked with this symbol had been restored to the Church after having been expropriated from various less important nobles through a review of fiefs.

The frescoes on the vault corresponding to the map of *Flaminia* are: *The Holy Ghost Designating St. Severus Archbishop of Ravenna* and *The Fish Rising from the Water at St. Anthony's Sermon*.

Pl. 134. Panel showing *Flaminia* (Romagna), and two herms.

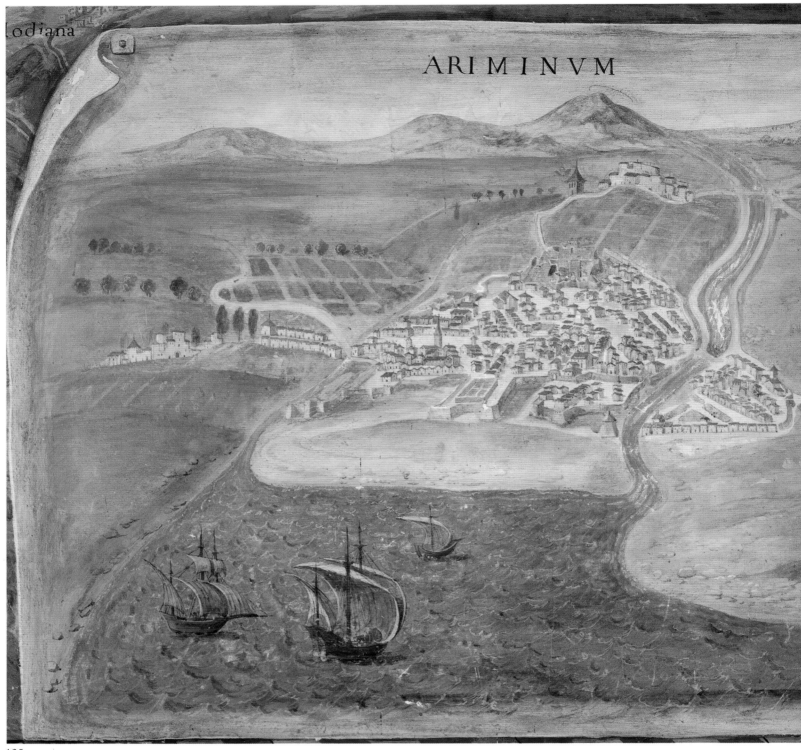

lodiana

ARIMINVM

135

Pl. 135. *Flaminia* (Romagna), detail. Trompe l'oeil painting with view of Rimini.

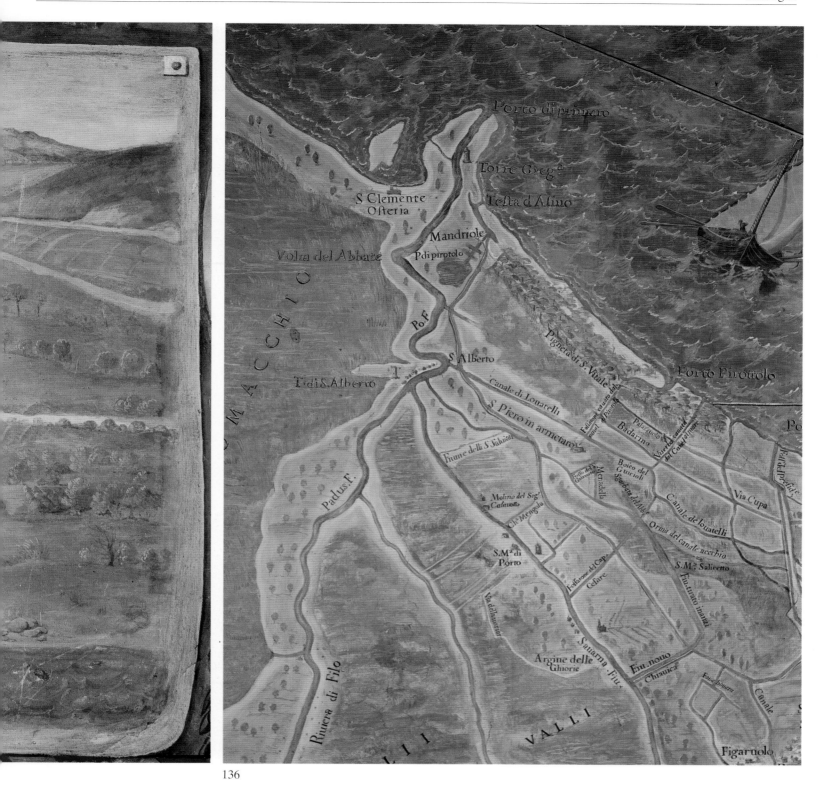

Porto di pimaro

Torre Greg.e

Testa d'Alino

S Clemente
Osteria

Mandriole

Volta del Abbate

P di pirotolo

C O M A C C H I O

Po.F

Pigneta di S. Vitale

Porto Pirotolo

S Alberto

T di S. Alberto

Canale di Louatelli

S Piero in armetaro

Padus. F.

Fiume delli S. Sakitat

Palazzuolo

Badarino

Boico del
Guicioli

Via Cupa

Menadella

Molino del Sig.r
Calan

Canale de Iouatelli

Ch. Mengola

Orma del canale uechio

S.Ma di
Porto

S.Ma Salicetto

Frattrato inanzi

Cesare

Via dellamaura

Argine delle
Ghiorie

Sattarna .Fiu.

En. nouo
Chiauica

Riuera di Filo

V A L L I

V A L L I

Figaruolo

136

Pl. 136. *Flaminia* (Romagna), detail. The southern part of the lagoons of Comacchio
and the plain between Ravenna and the Po di Primaro.

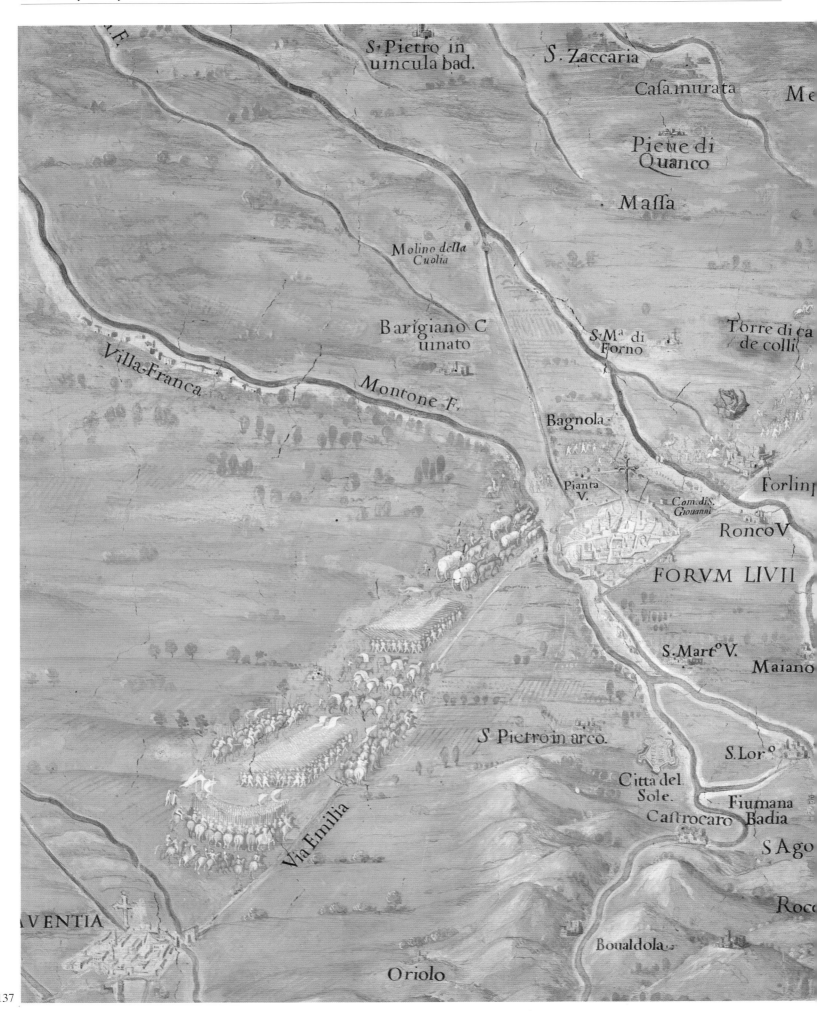

S. Pietro in
uincula bad.

S. Zaccaria

Cafa murata

Me

Pieue di
Quanco

Maffa

Molino della
Cuolia

Barigiano C
uinato

S. Ma di
Forno

Torre di ca
de colli

Villa-Franca

Montone F.

Bagnola

Pianta
V.

Com. di S.
Giouanni

Forlin

RoncoV

FORVM LIVII

S. Martº V.

Maiano

S. Pietro in arco.

S. Lorº

Citta del
Sole.

Fiumana

Caftrocaro Badia

S Ago

Via Emilia

Roco

AVENTIA

Bouaidola

Oriolo

137

144

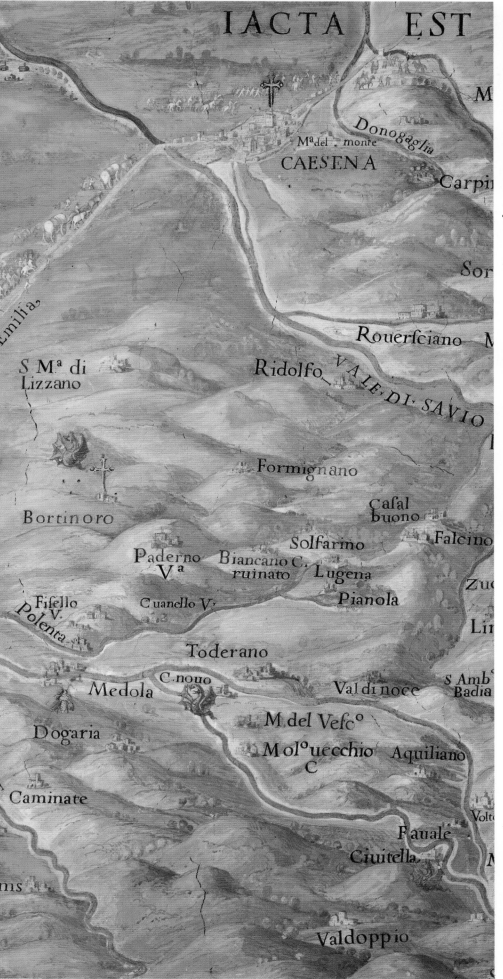

138

QVAE·LOCA·IN·DEPI T IS·TABVL
DRACONIS·AVREI·SIGNVM·
HVIC·SIMILE·OS T NDV
EA·GREGORIVS·XIII·P·O·M·
APOSTOLICAE·DITIONI·
RECVPERAVIT
ID·VOLVI·NESCIVS·NE·ESSES

139

Flaminia (Romagna), details.
Pl. 137. The march of Julius Caesar's army toward the Rubicon River along Via Emilia.
Pl. 138. The Republic of San Marino.
Pl. 139. Painted inscription stating that the places marked with a golden dragon were reclaimed for the Holy See by Pope Gregory XIII Boncompagni.

Urbini Ducatus
The Duchy of Urbino

This map, 10′9″ x 13′10″ (3.28 x 4.21 m), covers the entire Duchy of Urbino as it was until 1626, when, once the Della Rovere family had died out, it was expropriated by the Papal States. It overlooked the Adriatic Sea for more than 31.1 miles (50 km) between Cattolica and the Torre di Montignano (here *Torre Feltresca*) beyond Senigallia, and penetrated into the heart of the peninsula via valleys between the rivers Marecchia and Misa, extending to the west of the mountain range as far as the Gubbio plain. The spaces on the map not pertinent to this area are practically left void of names and chorographical markings.

The inscription found in the bottom right-hand corner, in white on a vermilion ground, is contained in a cartouche of extremely fine execution, although its festooned frame around which cherubs, sirens, and two figures of children hover grasping surveying instruments (cross-staffs and compasses) is a little overwhelming. The inscription refers to the two families who had governed the duchy "*beneficiario jure*" (i.e., according to feudal regulations) until 1626: first the Montefeltro until 1508, then the Della Rovere. It also mentions its final passing to the pope. This is therefore not the original inscription, of which the odd word written here and there in black is still visible below the vermilion ground, and which celebrated Urbino as a center of culture and its most illustrious representatives "*in Graphices, Architecturae et Picturae arte*."

In the bottom left-hand corner, a harmonious cartouche painted in several well matched colors and decorated with Barberini bees, contains the scale of 6,000 paces, measured on a bar 15″ (37.8 cm) in length, giving a ratio of 1:23,500. As may be seen from the compass rose in the top left-hand corner, the north is shifted by almost 30° to the left of the vertical axis of the map; the terrestrial coordinates are therefore not at right angles to the axes of the map. The edges of the map are graduated in minutes, numbered—with some gaps—at intervals of five. The surviving numbers show the latitudes to range from 43°17′ to 44°07′ along the left edge and from 42°39′ to 43°28′ along the right, while the longitudes range from 34°47′ to 36°07′ along the top edge and from 34°08′ to 35°36′ along the bottom.

The orography, with its massed, uniform cones, usually lit from the left, does not render the general effect of a change in the structure of the relief as one gradually leaves the coast (where particular emphasis is given to the Focara spur) and climbs the valleys to the bleak mountain backdrop forming the peninsular chain (note the inscription *Apenninus* at the left-hand edge of the panel by the Alpe della Luna). The few reliefs identified by name have no particular form to emphasize or distinguish them from their neighbors. The only geomorphological peculiarity of the region that is effectively stressed is that of the Furlo gorges, with the Pietralata mountain dropping sheer onto the river Candigliano, whose winding course it follows. The hydrography is both well and incisively drawn, dense, and for the most part correct. The river names are also numerous and correct. More precisely, in the parts of the duchy corresponding to Marche and Umbria, every watercourse of a certain length is identified by name; only the rivers of Montefeltro are not.

There are a large number of settlements numbering at least 350, which are generally named. Quite a few (the best known are given their Latin name) are shown in clearly drawn perspective plans: Pesaro (*Pisaurum*), Fano (*Fanum*), Senigallia (*Senogallia*), Urbino (*Urbinum*), Urbania (formerly Castel Durante, and here shown with the name of *Civitas Urbania* adopted by the city in 1636 in honor of Urban VIII), Sant'Angelo in Vado, Mercatello, Fossombrone (*Forum Sempronij*), Cagli (*Gallium*, properly *Callium*), Pergola, and Gubbio (*Eugubio*). The only area in which slightly less care has been taken over the description of the settlements is the Montefeltro area, which is better described in the map of *Flaminia*. Here the only settlement shown in reasonable detail is San Marino, distinguished by a quadrangle of walls and a reference to its three towers.

Not to be forgotten are the two "*barchi*," i.e., enclosed parks, marked on the flat floor of the Metauro Valley, one up-river from Urbania, the ducal park of the large villa built by Frederick II (1422–1482) to a design by Francesco di Giorgio Martini (1439–1502), then completed by Gerolamo Genga, and the other, again ducal, up-river from Fossombrone. One should also note the not inconsiderable number of bridges—fifteen or so—over the rivers, especially in the mountain area.

The map shows no boundaries, partly because some areas of the duchy are left out (e.g., the communes of Montefeltro to the west of the Marecchia) and (regarding other areas extending beyond its limits) partly for reasons of chorographical homogeneity. Thus, it incorporates the *contado* (rural district) of Fano, conquered by the papal forces in 1463 and here given its official name of *Vicariato*. The final section of the Metauro Valley, above which this *contado* lies, is, however, largely covered by a large scene depicting the Battle of Metauro in 207 B.C. between the Romans and the Carthaginians.

Above the scale in the bottom left-hand corner of the panel is an elegant horizontal panorama of Urbino, while in its center is a plan of Pesaro, both certainly added under Urban VIII.

The frescoes on the vault corresponding to the map of *Urbini Ducatus* are those showing *St. Peter Damian Writing the Rules of His Hermit Community* and *St. Ubald, Bishop of Gubbio, Freeing His City from a Siege*.

140

Pl. 140. Panel showing *Urbini Ducatus* (The Duchy of Urbino), and two herms.

VRBINVM

141

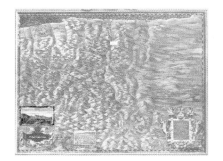

Pl. 141. *Urbini Ducatus* (The Duchy of Urbino), detail. Trompe l'oeil painting with view of Urbino.

142

143

144

Urbini Ducatus (The Duchy of Urbino), details.
Pl. 142. Plan of Urbania (*Civitas Urbania*).
Pl. 143. Plan of Cagli (*Gallium*).
Pl. 144. Plan of Pergola.

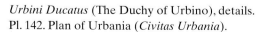

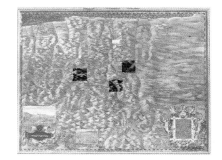

145

On the map, the following labels appear:

R I A T I

ntico

FANVM

Carignano

Cocoran V

Merauro. F

Arzilla.F

toceto

ano

alto

Saltara

S Lõgarino

ghello

Tauernella

S.Coftanzo

Mondolfo

S.raciola

R I A T O

Ceregia

C·CLAVDIVS·NERO
ASDRVBALE·OCCISO
QVINQVAGINTA·SEX·MIII
HOSTIVM·CARTAGINENSIVM
INTERFECIT
AN·ABV·COND·IƆXLV·II

Piaggie

A

Castel uecchio

M.Maggiore

Poggio

S.Giorgio

M·il·porco

Caualara

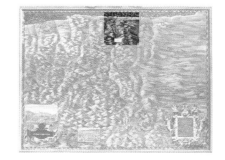

Pl. 145. *Urbini Ducatus* (The Duchy of Urbino), detail.
The battle at the river Metauro between the Romans and the Carthaginians (207 B.C.).

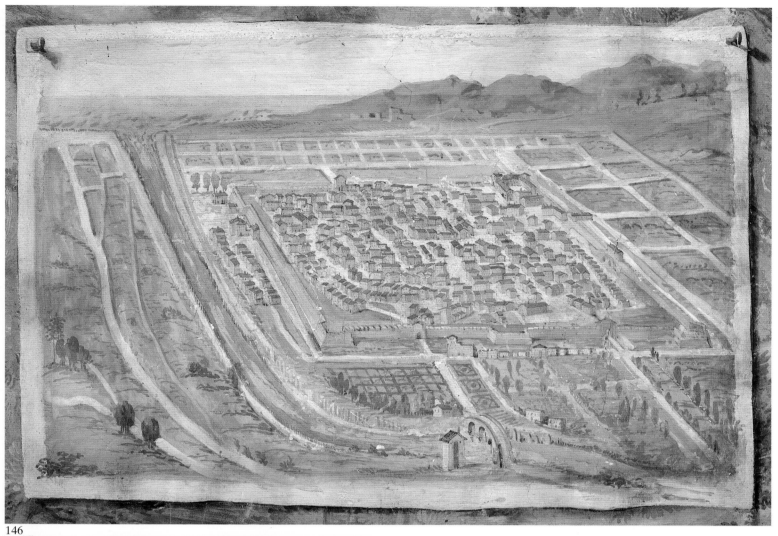

146

147

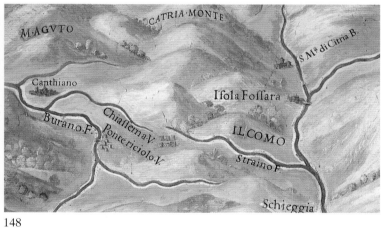

148

Urbini Ducatus (The Duchy of Urbino), details.

Pl. 146. Trompe l'oeil painting with view of Pesaro.

Pl. 147. Plan of Senigallia (*Senogallia*).

Pl. 148. Mount Catria and the valleys of the rivers Cesano and Burano.

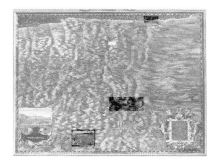

Picenum
Marche

In the Gallery, the present-day territory of the Marche is divided between three panels, two others for various reasons being specifically dedicated to the Duchy of Urbino and the area around Ancona. The rest of the region, depicted in a panel measuring 10'3" x 15'1" (3.13 x 4.6 m) is given its ancient name of *Picenum*. The term corresponds to the papal Marche in the second half of the 16th century, namely the territory ruled by the Church between Fano and Ascoli, thus excluding (as compared with today's boundaries) the Duchy of Urbino and Pesaro.

A fine cartouche in bottom left-hand corner, decorated with the winged dragon from Gregory XIII's coat of arms, shows the scale, along with an inscription in gold letters on a blue ground that also gives the reference parallel and meridian. In this map, 12,000 paces are equal to 16" (41.8 cm), giving a ratio of approximately 1:42,500. The marginal graduation goes from 22°24' to 43°53' latitude and from 35°15' and 38°8' longitude. The reference parallel—given as 43°20'—is therefore correct, whereas that of the meridian is mistaken, calculated at 36°45' instead of 36°35'.

In the top right-hand corner of the fresco, a 16-point compass rose in gold shows that the map is oriented with the north (or more precisely the northeast) pointing upward.

In the lower right-hand corner of the panel a fine cartouche, decorated with winged children and female figures, carries the original inscription referring to the fertility of the land and the dense population of the region and expressing the wish that Marche, now as in the past, can be of benefit to Rome and to the other Italian regions with its provisions and soldiers.

The fact that the frame of the cartouche with the celebrative inscription includes the Barberini bee is proof of work having been carried out during the papacy of Urban VIII. Whether this only concerned the decorative aspects of the panel or also affected the map as such is a difficult question. The fine wooded landscape along the bottom of the panel is reminiscent of Paul Bril, and so must be part of the original design.

The most recent restoration resulted in the rewriting of some place-names, some of which were evidently no longer understood, and these can still be seen half-canceled. Signs of a clumsy attempt at restoration can also be seen in the bottom right-hand corner of the fresco.

The cobalt-blue sea is limited to a strip at the top of the map, where three small galleys sail among the gold flourishes of the inscription *Hadriaticum Mare*. The surface of the fresco is, thus, almost entirely taken up with the greens of the regional territory, from which emerge the ocher and bluish-white cones used to depict the mountains in a conventional manner, while the patches of woods thicken and darken the tones in the band between Fano and Osimo. No boundaries are shown.

The orography merely indicates the mountainous nature of the region, without rendering its forms or identifying the principal structural elements, except in the case of Monte S. Vicino.

The hydrography is drawn in blue, with greater accuracy than the mountains and in considerable detail. The main watercourses of the region are all clearly recognizable, albeit with some imprecision of route, and nearly all are identified by name.

The coastline, low and without harbors, is shown realistically with the Ancona headland and Monte Conero standing out in the center. The latter is reasonably well depicted.

The settlements are shown in views, some of which are very accurate and of a decidedly cartographical character, not in the least conventional. Among the most attractive are the views of *Asculum*, *Auximum* (Osimo), *Fabriano*, *Recanetum* (Recanati), and *S. Severino*.

Three roads that cross at the ruins of *Helvia Ricina* are also shown. In the present state of the panel, the first of these apparently starts at Recanati, but time and possibly restoration in the last century have probably canceled the initial stretch starting from the coast, namely from Porto Recanati and the nearby ruins of Potentia as far as Loreto (*S. Maria Lauretana*). It then continues all along the Potenza Valley, toward Umbria, touching the remains of the Roman town of *Helvia Ricina*. From here the second road starts and, after having reached the Castello della Rancia, climbs the upper Chienti Valley toward Tolentino, going round S. Severino and Camerino, to meet up again with the first section. The third road runs perpendicular to the other two, crossing them at *Helvia Ricina* via Filottrano and Jesi, from which it now appears to begin. The first road connects the three archaeological sites marked on the map: besides *Helvia Ricina*, the site of the ancient *Pollonia* (Potenza Picena) and that of *Trea* (near the present Treia, marked on the map as *Montecchio*, the name it had from the 9th century until 1790), which is the site of the *Reliquie di Traiana*.

On the whole, the geographical content of the map is uneven, not only on account of the inadequately described road network, but also with regard to the distribution of the settlements. Although the lack of information in the Ancona area is made up for by the panel specifically dedicated to it, and in the case of Senigallia the same lack can be explained by the fact that the town and its territory were to remain an enclave of the Duchy of Urbino within the papal *Marca* until 1626, nothing justifies the thinning out of the settlements in other areas. The whole lower half of the map is practically deserted, but so are certain more circumscribed areas, such as the *Marca* of Fano. The settlements tend to be more concentrated especially inland from the coast between the *Nevola* (today the Misa) and the *Tenna* (repeated as *Terna*), an area for which the map provides an abundant supply of place-names.

The fresco on the vault corresponding to the map of *Picenum* is: *The Translation of the Holy House of Loreto.*

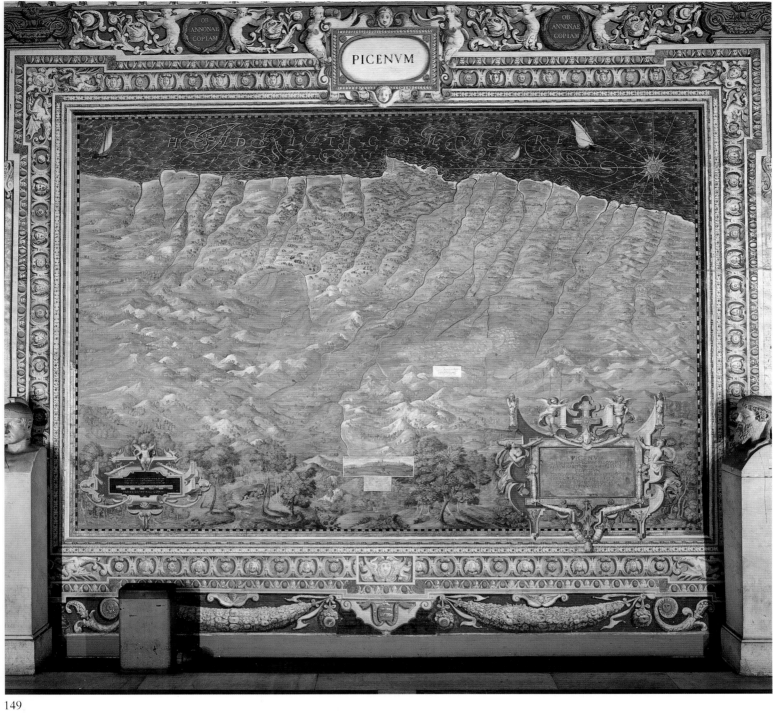

Pl. 149. Panel showing *Picenum* (Marche), and two herms.

150

Pl. 150. *Picenum* (Marche), detail.
Trompe l'oeil painting with a view of Macerata and a wooded landscape.

151

152

S. Mᵃ in Cafciano

Veftigi di Recina

S.chiodio
Abᵃ

Macerata

Reliquie di
Tracana

Serrauall

153

Picenum (Marche), details.
Pl. 151. Plan of Fermo (*Firmium*).
Pl. 152. Macerata and the ruins of the Roman township *Helvia Ricina*.
Pl. 153. Wooded landscape.

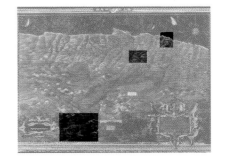

Anconitanus ager
The Territory of Ancona

Only a quarter of this panel, 10′4″ x 13′9″ (3.14 x 4.18 m), which is the only one in the Gallery to show a part of a larger provincial territory, has any chorographical significance, and this refers to a somewhat limited area, namely the *contado* (rural district) of Ancona lying between the rivers Esino and Potenza, a gently undulating terrain, extending inland between 9.3 and 12.4 miles (15 and 20 km). Almost half the panel is occupied by the sea (*Hadriaticus sinus*, regarded more as a gulf than as open sea). The left-hand side of the panel (inscribed *Piceni agri pars*, but this is not correct, since the region of *Picenum*, described in the adjacent panel, should be on the opposite side) is virtually blank, with some pleasant woodland scenes painted toward the bottom, but with no chorographical information of any kind.

As shown by the compass rose on the sea, the map is oriented with the north pointing upward. But the compass rose is somewhat inaccurate, as the north should be shifted by about 25 degrees to the left.

The graduation along the edges is not very clear (the minutes are mostly marked at intervals of five). The latitudes probably go from 43°24′ to 43°51′ and the longitudes from 36°10′ to 37°01′.

In the bottom right-hand corner is an altar with two putti playing with a monkey. The altar's top is strewn with instruments for topographical surveying (a metric rod, a pair of compasses, a mason's level, and a surveyor's cross), while on its face is the scale, measuring 18″ (45 cm) and equal to 4,000 paces, so giving a ratio of 1:13,000.

In the bottom left-hand corner is a cartouche with a richly decorated frame featuring festoons, masks, and figures and enclosing a celebrative inscription written in gold letters on a sky-blue ground, which praises the port of Ancona, described here as the principal city of Piceno. It also recalls the building work carried out by the Emperor Trajan around A.D. 105 to improve the port, and, quite recently, by Popes Gregory XIII and Urban VIII to fortify the city "*ingenti propugnacolo*"—namely by means of the Cittadella di Capodimonte, which was actually begun in the second quarter of the 16th century and was merely completed by the two popes. But this inscription, which therefore dates from the time in which Urban VIII was pope, was painted over another, some fifty years earlier (a transcription of which is in *Cod. Barb. Lat.* 1803, f. 6v). The original inscription dwelled on the Greek origins of Ancona and on the close relation between the city's name ("elbow" in Greek) and its position, on a headland that forms a sharp bend in the Adriatic coastline.

The map delineates the coastline very carefully, especially the mouths of the rivers (notice the breakwater to the left of the mouth of the Esino, still present a century ago, on which stands the Rocca Priora) and the windings and protrusions of the promontories (e.g., the rock of the Trave, the spur of Sirolo, and the tiny inlet of Portonovo). The orography of the promontory and the hill chain between the rivers Esino and Musone is very evocative (but the name of Monte Conero, the only mountain named, is given by mistake to a non-existent village). The hydrography is notably accurate, showing an unusual number of terminal branches on either side of the river Esino, where it crosses the plain of Chiaravalle. The map even shows drainage canals. Around forty settlements are marked with their names (mostly large country villages), and their positioning, mostly on high ground, is generally correct.

The layout of Ancona is shown in a fine perspective view, which particularly stresses the city walls and the harbor jetties. Farther inland, Jesi and Osimo are shown in smaller perspective views, which, nevertheless, resemble their actual forms. On the coast near the promontory—streaked under Mount Conero as if alluding to the unstable terrain—are Portonovo, Sirolo, and the two nuclei of Numana (which the map calls by its medieval name *Humana*), the upper town by the sea. Moreover, between the courses of the Musone and the Potenza—formerly close to the sea—there is a view of the Sanctuary of S. Maria at Loreto, a miniature version of the topography of the town painted on a scroll in the lower center of the panel, in such a way as to suggest its being nailed to the surface. Lastly, along the coast are several fortalices and watchtowers built as defence against the attacks of pirates: Rocca Priora, mentioned above, and two towers a little farther east in the direction of Ancona, another at the mouth of the Musone, and still another at the mouth of the Potenza. A little up-river from their mouths, two bridges cross the Esino and the Potenza.

In the top right-hand corner is a large expanse of sea, in which are sailing nine vessels, all of different kinds. In the center and to the left are coasters and possibly a fishing boat (note the deck covered with sacks on the coaster to the left). To the right there are at least three cargo ships and farther down another vessel of the cargo type being approached by a boat with oars but without a sail, loaded with sacks. The emphasis given to the sacks carried by these vessels may be meant as an allusion to the export of cereals that at that time was one of the main functions of the ports of the Marche.

The fresco on the vault corresponding to the map of *Anconitanus ager* is *St. Marcellinus, Bishop of Ancona, Saves the City from a Fire*.

154

Pl. 154. Panel showing *Anconitanus ager* (The Territory of Ancona), and two herms.

155

Pl. 155. *Anconitanus ager* (The Territory of Ancona), detail. Trompe l'oeil painting with view of Loreto.

156

Pl. 156. *Anconitanus ager* (The territory of Ancona), detail.
Two cargo ships and a sloop in the Adriatic Sea.

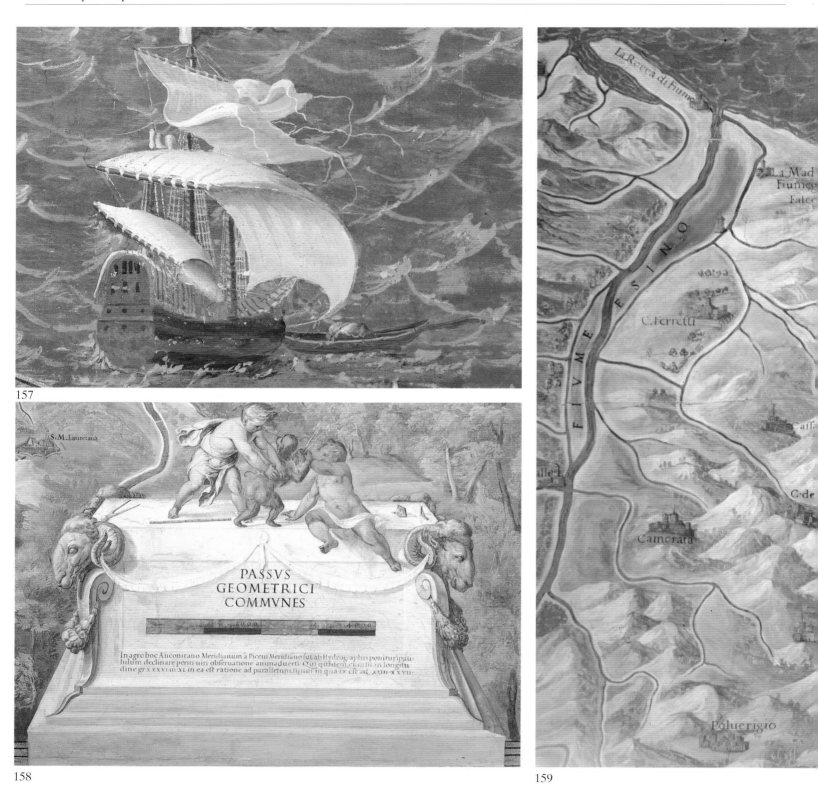

157

158

159

Anconitanus ager (The Territory of Ancona), details.
Pl. 157. A cargo ship and a sloop in the Adriatic Sea.
Pl. 158. Altar with cupids and metric scale.

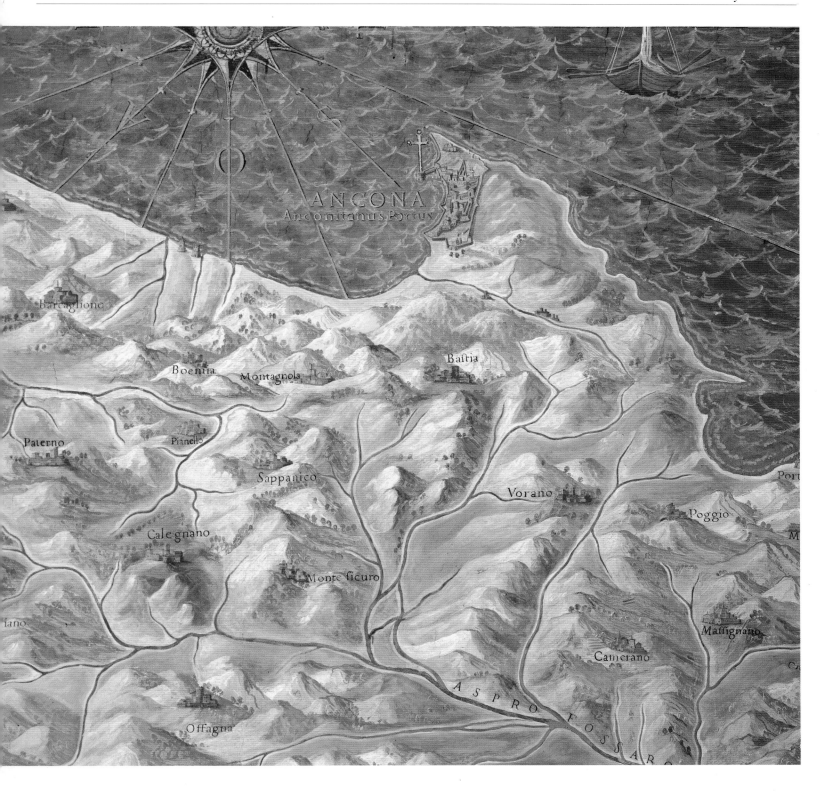

Pl. 159. *Anconitanus ager* (The Territory of Ancona), detail. The Adriatic coast between Falconara and Mount Conero with the hills between the rivers Esino and Aspio.

Aprutium
Abruzzo

The panel dedicated to Abruzzo measures 10′1″ x 13′4″ (3.08 x 4.06 m) and covers the territory between the Tronto and the Trigno, between the Adriatic Sea and the Sabini and Simbruini Mountains, and from Rieti to the basin of the Fucino. In the bottom left-hand corner a putto grasping a compass and seated on columnar altar holds a garlanded ribbon to which is tied a small inscription indicating the scale. This measures 13″ (32 cm) and is equal to 8,000 paces, giving a ratio of approximately 1:37,000.

A compass rose in blue and gold lies alongside a large elaborate cartouche with a celebrative inscription in gold letters on a purple ground in the cobalt-blue waters of the *Hadriaticum Mare*. It shows that the map is oriented with the north pointing upward. On the whole, the coast is fairly well drawn, although a less than happy graphical expedient is used to represent the differences between the coastline south of Francavilla al Mare with its occasional dunes and the higher coast farther north, resulting in exaggeratedly jagged and protruding forms. The Tremiti Islands are also shown close to the coast.

The orography is, as usual, conventional, although some reliefs are highlighted more by the fact that their names are marked than by pictorial means: e.g., Velino, Maiella, Mount Cavallo, Mount Corno. But there is no sign of the three chains that make up the specific configuration of the region. The Gran Sasso massif itself, which is probably what the name Mount Corno is to be taken to refer to, is given little emphasis.

The unsatisfactory representation of the relief in turn excludes the possibility of a successful characterization of the depressions between the mountains, except for that of the Fucino, its properly egg-shaped and sky-blue lake shown along with its tributary, and conspicuous on account of its size. Lake Scanno, on the other hand, is now scarcely legible on the fresco.

The hydrography is detailed and shows the main watercourses of the region, although these are not always named. Most are correctly depicted in their final stretches where they cross the coastal strip. The upper courses are sometimes less happily rendered, as in the case of the Amiterno, which forms an unlikely anastomosis to the south of Aquila, decoratively filled in with the slight suggestion of a wood. The rivers flowing into the Adriatic along the coast north of Pescara are on the whole better drawn. Here one finds not only the largest concentration of river names (*Tronto, Vibrata, Salinello, Tordino*) but also a tolerable level of accuracy (despite the lack of names) in the watercourses between the Vomano and the Pescara, with the confluence of the Fino and the Tavo, which forms the Salinello, clearly marked. Also shown are stretches of the Velino (which becomes swampy in the Rieti hollow), Aniene, and Liri (which runs through a not very clearly drawn Val Roveto under the name of Garigliano, thus contradicting the correct configuration of the Liri-Garigliano seen in the map of *Campania*).

Lastly, the short river without a name that rises near Leonessa and peters out after Cascia corresponds to the Corno,

whereas the *Buscio* is today's Tirino.

The settlements shown are fairly numerous and are for the most part both evenly and correctly distributed. The towns are, as usual, represented by means of often conventional perspective views painted in crimson, although these are carefully drawn and varied. As regards the main towns and cities there is an outstanding number of realistic plans and views, suggesting the use of special models: see Pescara, Sulmona, *Theate* (Chieti), Tagliacozzo, Rieti—with its crown of Franciscan foundations—and Aquila, whose plan is correctly positioned on the left bank of the Aterno, but oriented to the south, unlike both the map itself and the enlarged plan of the town in the bottom right-hand corner of the fresco.

Some views deserve special mention as they share an unusual form, an empty enclosure surrounded by buildings on one or more sides; these are Valva, Avezzano, and *Giardino*, the latter located near Cerchio and not identifiable from its place-name. There is reason to believe that the enclosure was used as a symbol to indicate archaeological sites that were still settlements in modern times.

Another settlement marked with an enclosure is *Amiterno*, the ancient Sabine *Amiternum* and Roman *municipium*. On the other hand, there is nothing in the view of Atri to suggest the town's descendence from *Hatria*, despite the fact that the town's *contado* (rural district) is marked *Hadrianus Ager*, an allusion to the fact that the Emperor Hadrian was born here.

Further references to the geography of the area in the classical period are the inscriptions regarding the Aniene, to the west of *Subiaco* and the Benedictine monasteries of *S. Scolastica, Sacro Speco, Fontes Aq(uae)*, and *Aquae Augustae Fons*. These inscriptions clearly refer to the *Anio Vetus* and to the *Anio Novus*, the former alluding to the Acqua Marcia Springs, the second to the channel leading to the monumental aqueduct restored in the time of Augustus.

The abundance of historical information regarding the classical period led Almagià to suppose that the panel had been added to by Holste, whose interest in the historical topography of the Abruzzo region is well known. However, considerations cast some doubt on the hypothesis. Firstly, the map does not show some important discoveries made by Holste. Secondly, Via Valeria is also missing, which, along with some of its *diverticula* (branches), was one of Holste's main objects of study in Abruzzo. Moreover, it is unusual for Danti to show an interest in historical geography. There are, however, some important similarities between the present panel and that of *Lucania*. Like the *Lucania* panel, that of *Aprutium* may therefore be based on an as yet unidentified source.

The frescoes on the vault corresponding to the map of *Aprutium* are: *The Hermit St. Peter of Morrone Receiving the News of His Election to the Papacy* and *St. Bernardine Orders the Bonfire of the Vanities*.

160

Pl. 160. Panel showing *Aprutium* (Abruzzo), and two herms.

161

162

163

164

Aprutium (Abruzzo), details.
Pl. 161. Altar with cupid and metric scale.
Pl. 162. Plan of Aquila.
Pl. 163. Plan of Rieti.
Pl. 164. Plan of Teramo.

licio

Dentella

AQVILA

165

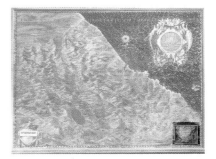

Pl. 165. *Aprutium* (Abruzzo), detail. Trompe l'oeil painting with view of Aquila.

Apulia
Northern Puglia

The panel, 10′4″ x 13′10″ (3.16 x 4.22 m), depicts northern Puglia, or to be more precise the ancient Capitanata, one of the three parts into which the Norman Duchy of Puglia and Calabria was divided, first under Angevin, then under Aragonese rule. The region shown includes the Gargano headland and the Tavoliere, from which it extends north over much of what is now Molise as far as the river Biferno and east over part of the Neapolitan Apennines, taking in the mountains of Sannio and Irpinia as far as Benevento.

As can be seen from the gold and blue 16-point compass rose in the upper right-hand corner, the map is oriented with the north pointing upward. The scale is in an ornate frame immediately below the richly decorated cartouche (which as usual carries an inscription, in gold letters on a blue ground).

The scale measures 14″ (34.5 cm) and is equal to a distance of 9,000 geometrical paces, thus giving a ratio of 1:38,600, as in the panel dedicated to the Salentine Peninsula, which completes the region of Puglia.

Below the scale are the reference parallel and meridian. These tally with the marginal graduation, which goes from 40°50′ to 42°9′ latitude and from 40°25′ to 42°38′ longitude.

The Barberini bees at the center of the compass rose suggest that some work was done on it—it is not possible to say of what kind or how extensive—during the papacy of Urban VIII.

Besides the usual cartouche, other conspicuous decorative features are the delicate wooded landscape painted along the bottom edge of the panel (a motif found in almost all the maps of the Kingdom of Naples) and, in the bottom right-hand corner, a polyhedron placed on an altar decorated with a bas-relief and resting on a console, which appears to protrude from the wall. Almagià suggested that the subject of the bas-relief might be an episode featuring St. Michael the Archangel, who is said to have appeared in a cave in Monte S. Angelo in Gargano, where he is venerated and which is marked on the map. In reality the relief shows the killing of Archimedes, so the altar is probably meant to represent his tomb.

The colors are the usual ones. The cobalt-blue sea, its broad brushwork suggesting the movement of the waves, which lighten toward their foaming crests, is sailed by a merchant xebec, a small cargo galley, a second cargo galley in the Adriatic, and a further small galley, its men at their stations, carrying merchandise and towing a sloop in the Gulf of Manfredonia.

Almagià—perhaps overharshly—considered the coastline and the lakes of Lesina and Varano "rather coarse." What is beyond question is that the source for this stretch of coastline seems to be different from that used for the coastline of the Salentine Peninsula, which is definitely drawn with greater precision. Above all, though the Gargano headland is well portrayed and immediately recognizable, its coastline is inaccurate.

The orography is represented in chiaroscuro, the light coming from the left. On the whole it is conventional but becomes more realistic in the Gargano massif (*Garganus Mons*). The coast is not sheer enough and in this area is particularly inaccurate. The

way the relief becomes more crowded in Sannio and the Matese Mountains is realistic, although its representation is mannered. None of the mountains are named.

The Tavoliere plain (*Capitinata*) is well differentiated from the mountainous Gargano and the Apennine areas. The border with the latter is largely rendered by means of the simple fading of the relief, while that with the former is clearly marked by the course of the Candelaro, which is reasonably well drawn.

The network of rivers is dense and fairly accurate, but like the orography, devoid of names, with the sole exception of the Ofanto (*Aufidius F[lumen] ho [sic] Lefanto*). The Biferno, which the inscription on the cartouche describes, along with Ofanto, as one of the region's borders, is also unnamed. Apart from the Candelaro, other recognizable features of the hydrography are the Carapelle, the Cervaro (which flows into a lagoon on the Siponto coast that may be identified as Lake Salso, later silted up by the Candelaro and the Cervaro), the Celone, the Triolo, the course of the Biferno (although this is perhaps confused with one of its affluents, the Cigno, with an independent watercourse, the Fortore), Val di Sangro, Valle del Trigno and the upper Valle del Volturno, the Tammaro, and perhaps the Calore (although the position of Benevento at the confluence of the Sabato with the Calore is not clear, on account of the obtrusive frame of the cartouche and the landscape surrounding it).

No roads or sheep tracks are shown. The settlements are marked with miniature perspective views, mostly conventional, but quite finished. Indeed, on the whole, the territory is depicted in a mannered way: a green or greenish yellow wash forms a ground for randomly placed patches of trees or hints of furrowed fields. The distribution of the settlements is generally accurate. However, one is struck by the fact that they are more concentrated in the mountain areas, especially in Molise, and scarce in the Tavoliere area, where the absence of Cerignola is also surprising. The view of Bovino (*Bouini*) is worth noting: it is not conventional like the others, but gives a close idea of the form of the town as it extends along the ridge between Valle del Cervaro and Valle del Biletra.

Completing the map in the bottom right-hand corner is a depiction of the Battle of Cannae, fought near the village of the same name (destroyed by the Normans in 1083) between the Romans and the Carthaginians in the year 216 B.C. The armies are drawn up on the right bank of the Ofanto according to the tactical pattern described in classical sources. On the left bank of the river are the two camps: the ordered Roman *castrum* with a square plan, surrounded by a trench and a palisade at the sides of which open the four gates, and inside which the legions are deployed in a rigid geometric scheme; more irregular and disordered is the Punic camp, inside the fencing of which everyday scenes are shown amid the multicolored tents, and animals, including three camels, roam behind the troops.

The fresco on the vault corresponding to the map of *Apulia* is *The Appearance of St. Michael the Archangel on Monte Gargano*.

Pl. 166. Panel showing *Apulia* (Northern Puglia), and two herms.

Maiora Romanorum Castra

Porta decumana

P.C.C.

Pedites extraordinarÿ

Pedites extraordinarÿ

Equites extraordinarÿ

Equites extraordinarÿ

VIA LATA

Milites turdes

Milites foreñfes

Equites
diuerfi

Pedites
Equites
diuerfi

Forum

Praetorium Quaestor.

Armamenta Fabefecerat:

Pedites
fociorū

Equites
fociorum

VIA LATA

VIA LATA

Pedites
fociorum

Equites
fociorum

Via

Pedites II le
gionis

Principes II
legionis

Via

Triarÿ II leg
Equites II
legionis

Via

Equites prima
legionis

Triarÿ II leg

Via

Principes pri
legionis

Pedites prima
legionis

Via

P.C.C.

Dexter Sector: I Legio

Latus

Porta quintana

Castra Punica

Fontana

Aufidius Flio Lefanto

Pugnæ Locus

L Ac

Equites Hifpani
et Galli

167

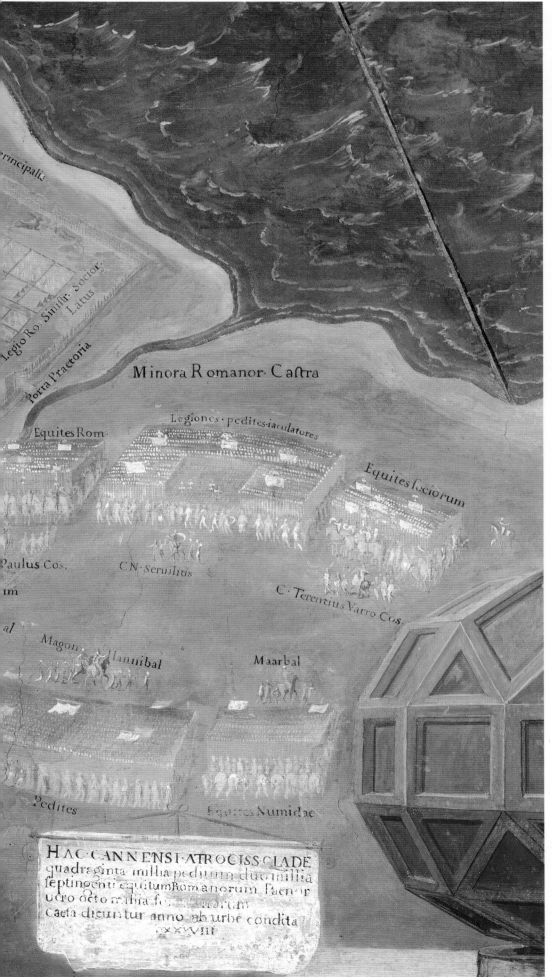

principalis

Legio Ro: Siniftr: Socior:
Latus

Porta Praetoria

Minora Romanor. Caftra

Equites Rom:

Legiones · pedites · iaculatores

Equites fociorum

Paulus Cos.

CN· Seruilius

um

C· Terentius Varro Cos.

al

Magon Hannibal

Maarbal

Pedites

Equites Numidae

HAC CANNENSI ATROCISS CLADE
quadraginta millia peditum duo millia
feptingenti equitum Romanorum Paenor
ucro octo millia fo . . norum
Caela dicuntur anno ab urbe condita
. . . . . .

168

169

Apulia (Northern Puglia), details.
Pl. 167. The Battle of Cannae
between the Romans and the Carthaginians
(216 B.C.).
Pl. 168. Lesina and Lake Lesina.
Pl. 169. View of Benevento.

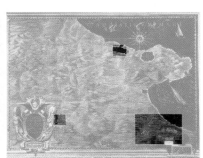

Sallentina Hydrunti Terra
Southern Puglia

The Salintine Peninsula is described in a special panel, 10′8″ x 13′10″ (3.25 x 4.22 m), distinct from that showing Puglia (*Apulia*). It covers the territory between the Murge Plateau and Capo di S. Maria di Leuca, a region made up of the Terra di Bari and the Terra d'Otranto.

A purple cartouche with a richly decorated gilt frame held by two winged putti and also featuring Barberini bees, carries an inscription giving the reference meridian and parallel and also contains a linear scale in black and gold measuring 18″ (46 cm) and equal to 12,000 geometrical paces, so giving a ratio of 1:38,600. Almagià (1952, p. 77) noted that a comparison with the actual distances gives a slightly smaller scale, on average between 1:46,000 and 1:50,000.

The 16-point gold compass rose in the upper center shows the map to be oriented with the north pointing upward. The Barberini bees decorating the cartouche showing the scale are evidence of restoration work carried out under Pope Urban VIII, but this was presumably limited to the retouching of the inscription giving the scale and reference parallel and meridian. There is no record of the map itself or of the large cartouche in the bottom left-hand corner having been modified.

A simple white scroll, painted to resemble a sheet of paper hung on the wall between the map and the border on the right-hand side of the fresco, carries a third inscription, in Latin. It refers to the attempt to find the most correct graduations during preparatory work on the cycle. The inner edge of the frame is graduated in minutes in gold and purple: from 39°45′ to 41°5′ latitude and from 41°50′ to 44°9′ longitude, which tallies with the reference meridian and parallel given.

The peninsula is shown between the Adriatic and Ionian Seas. On the two seas, painted in cobalt-blue, sail numerous vessels: in the Adriatic, a large cargo boat with two lateen sails, a galley towing a sloop, and a small galley, and in the Gulf of Taranto, a merchant galley, and a galleon with its sails swelling in the direction opposite that of the sails and standards of a nearby vessel.

The coastline, picked out in light ocher, is reasonaby well drawn and certainly more plausible and accurate than in other maps of the provinces of the Kingdom of Naples. Nonetheless, it is not as accurate as Almagià considered it, who, however, was right to think it was modeled on nautical charts. This was probably the origin of the excessively jagged coastline, especially in the stretch between Molfetta and Brindisi and at particular points, such as Capo d'Otranto or Capo Spulico. The mainland is shown as basically flat or with little relief and painted in delicate tones of green, here and there shading into ocher. The only area with more rise and fall is that on the edge of the territory between Conversano and Altamura (the map does not convey the latter's position atop an eminence), while four cone-shaped mountains are given greater prominence (though not very faithfully drawn), in northern Murgia, near Minervino. No mountain names are given.

The hydrography is limited to the *Tara et Japigio Flumen*, corresponding to the Bradano, which marks the boundary with

Basilicata, and the *Galese rio*, which after a short course flows into the Mare Piccolo di Taranto. The final stretch of the *Lofanto* (Ofanto) appears in the top left-hand corner of the map and marks the limit of the area mapped but also that of karst Puglia, which ends at the Tavoliere plain.

The settlements are represented with views that are well differentiated from one another, but are mostly mannered. The perspective plans of the larger settlements, on the other hand, are often faithful, if somewhat simplified, and reproduce the form of the urban perimeter.

With regard to the distribution of the settlements, the geographical content of the map is somewhat uneven. At least three zones can be distinguished.

The Terra di Bari appears correct, but in actual fact there are numerous errors of position and frequent lacunae. Serious mistaken positions are given to a considerable number of inland settlements: *Castellana* is found to the northwest of Putignano, instead of to the northeast, and on the same latitude as *Gioia* (Gioia del Colle); *Noia* (Noicattaro), Rutigliano, and Conversano are not in right relation to one another; Bitetto, Grumo, and Toritto (*Turito*), which lie on the terraces sloping down toward the Bari coast, are mistakenly aligned with *Cassiano* (Cassano) and a place called *S. Ermo* (it is not clear which town is meant, but it is to be hoped that it is not Santeramo, which would be in entirely the wrong position here); and lastly, *Martina* (Martina Franca) and Putignano are too far inland. The Maltese crosses placed above Putignano and Fasano mark the fiefs of the Order of the Hospital of St. John of Jerusalem.

The Terra d'Otranto can be divided into two areas, which are differently described. Toward Taranto, the Murge Plateau has very few place-names, and on the whole the map betrays a patchy and somewhat confused knowledge of the area.

The third zone—the extreme tip of Salento—is more thoroughly, and also more precisely, described, although there are some inaccuracies (e.g., the positions of *Capertino*, or Copertino, and Leverano are reversed and slightly too far west). The description becomes especially detailed in the Salentine Murge, between Gallipoli, S. Maria di Leuca, and Capo d'Otranto and little more incomplete between Lecce, Corigliano (*Congliano*), and Muro Leccese.

The map also shows the routes of some roads. Chief among these is a final extension to Via Appia, which terminated at Brindisi, joining it to Taranto and branching into two roads between Mesagne (*Misiagrio*) and Grottaglie so as to take in Latiano (*Luciano*) and Francavilla on the one hand and Oria on the other. A second road runs almost perpendicular to this one between Taranto and Gravina and near Castellaneta crosses a further roadway, which has partially been canceled, probably in the course of restoration in the 19th century.

The fresco on the vault corresponding to the map of *Sallentina Hydrunti Terra* is *St. Anselm Refuting the Errors of the Heretics during the Council of Bari*.

170

Pl. 170. Panel showing *Sallentina Hydrunti Terra* (Southern Puglia), and two herms.

171

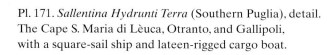

Pl. 171. *Sallentina Hydrunti Terra* (Southern Puglia), detail.
The Cape S. Maria di Lèuca, Otranto, and Gallipoli,
with a square-sail ship and lateen-rigged cargo boat.

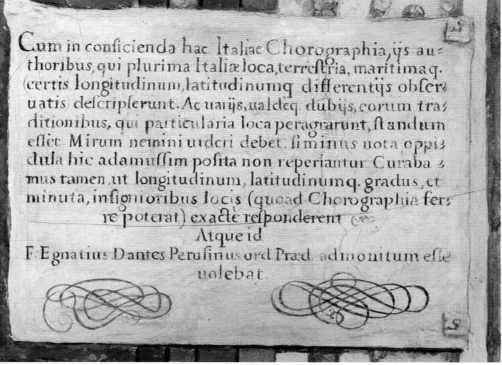

172

173

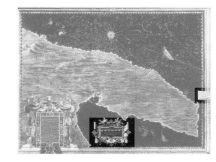

Sallentina Hydrunti Terra (Southern Puglia), details.
Pl. 172. Trompe l'oeil document in which Danti claims authorship of the original decorative scheme of the Gallery and stresses the accuracy of the coordinates used in the maps.
Pl. 173. Metric scale.

Civitas Vetus
Civitavecchia

This view, 9'4" x 3'7" (2.85 x 1.1 m) of the city and port of Civitavecchia in Lazio is surmounted by an angel bearing a standard upon which is written *Portus Traianus ad Centum Cellas* ("Trajan's port at *Centum Cellae*," the ancient name for the city).

The scale is not shown, and the border is not graduated. Though the points of the compass rose are not marked, the map is in fact oriented with the east pointing upward. In the center of the compass rose is a medallion bearing a portrait of Pope Urban VIII in profile and an inscription commemorating his part in the reordering of the city and port. There is no record of the panel's having been restored, but the fact that the compass rose is unmarked is probably due to its having been repainted. The present panel dates from 1634, as shown by the inscription in the gilt frame.

The port and the city of Civitavecchia are shown in conventional perspective, with the surrounding hills and the Monti della Tolfa in the background. They are represented in the manner of topographical painting, without cartographical features or conventional symbols. The image probably derives from drawings made during the rebuilding of the port under Urban VIII between 1627 and 1634. The benefits that this brought the city are listed both in the framed inscription and in another placed within the city.

In the sea in front of the port, a large raft with a standard bearing the letters S.P.Q.R. is seen carrying an obelisk from Egypt to Rome.

The raft has two masts with banners and square sails, 26 pairs of oars (without oarsmen), and an anachronistic bar rudder, like the ones on the two smaller vessels accompanying it: one, a much smaller craft with neither crew or sail, transporting a stone parallelepipe, and a little, modern cargo ship, with two masts, square sails, and two ribbons on the mast to prow. The modern ship is not flying identifiable colors, but the two smaller crafts fly the banner of ancient Rome.

The view of the city (which at this time had less than 3,000 inhabitants) places as much emphasis as possible on the port in the foreground and thus celebrates the pope responsible for its renovation. The enclosed body of water to the left is the Darsena Romana or Roman dock, built by Trajan around A.D. 106 and restored to full working order in 1513 during the papacy of Leo X (papacy 1513–1521). Facing it is the fortress, now called the Forte Michelangelo, which was built by Antonio da Sangallo the Younger (1483–1546) and whose main tower was completed by Michelangelo Buonarroti (1475–1564) in 1535. At the end of the eastern pier (the Molo del Bicchiere) is the Lanterna or lighthouse built in 1608 by Paul V (papacy 1605–1621) and restored under Urban VIII, while at the end of the western is the lighthouse built under Urban VIII. The Antemurale Traiano, the breakwater that closed the Roman port, was also restored by the pope, who in addition built the wall closing the mouth of the port and the external fortifications on its east side. The rest of the bastioned walls and external fortifications date back to the preceding century.

The drawing is both meticulous and faithful—indeed, this may be the reason why the renovated port seems disproportionately large in comparison with the small number of sailing ships actually making use of it, despite the fact that Civitavecchia was the port of Rome and also served the alum mines of Tolfa. The few vessels shown are in dry dock on the beaches, and the dock is empty. And Urban VIII's vast new external fortifications—the imposing "*opera a corno*" dating from between 1627 and 1630—has been furnished with a washhouse and is given over to the thoroughly domestic function of drying laundry. This was where the new town would develop in the 18th century, around the church of S. Francesco, built at the beginning of the 17th century and later to become the cathedral of the city. The garrison is performing a drill on one of the bastions, and modest emplacements of cannon are arranged on the walls facing the sea.

Another of the repairs carried out by Urban VIII is not itself visible in the view but is commemorated in an inscription written on a small scroll—the restoration of the underground aqueduct built in 1588 by the architect Giovanni Fontana (1540–1614) for Sixtus V, whose water flowed from a fountain found at the exact spot where the scroll is placed in the view.

The meticulous drawing allows us to reconstruct the layout of a part of the city that has now completely vanished. The gates and towers of the medieval city walls are drawn in a particularly detailed way.

PORTVS
TRAIANVS
AD
CENTVM CELLAS

Preceding page:
Pl. 174. Panel showing *Civitas Vetus*
(Civitavecchia), and two herms.

Pl. 175. *Civitas Vetus* (Civitavecchia),
detail. Roman cargo ship,
reconstructed in the form of a raft,
transporting the Montecitorio
obelisk to Rome.
175

Genua
Genoa

The view of the city of Genoa is placed in the area to the left of the door leading to the Sistine Chapel. The door's marble molding, together with the carved frame of the cartouche above it, thus acts as an irregularly shaped border to the right side of the fresco. The other three sides are framed by the usual decorated border, creating a rectangle of approximately 10′2″ x 4′9″ (3.1 x 1.44 m).

The view covers the area between the Bisagno, the gully of Val Polcevera, the stretch of sea beyond the gulf, and the mountain behind the city, beyond which a delicate and morphologically varied landscape fades at the horizon into a blue sky in which whitish or pinkish cirrus clouds gather here and there. Amid the clouds two mythical winged griffins support a standard bearing the inscription: "*Genua / maritimae Liguriae caput / navalis militiae studio / et civium virtute / atque opulentia / inclyta / munitissimis nuper / exaedificatis moenibus / tutam / clarissimae Reipublicae / sede(m) praebet*" ("Genoa, capital of maritime Liguria, renowned for the pride she takes in her fleet and for the excellence and wealth of its citizens, offers with its strongly fortified walls, not long built, a safe base for the Illustrious Republic").

The panel does not show the scale, nor is it graduated. Its orientation is not marked, but is with the north pointing upward.

The whole panel was certainly repainted during the papacy of Urban VIII, for the city is shown enclosed within the long perimeter of the new walls, begun in 1626 and completed in 1632, and the inscription on the standard held by the two griffins refers to their recent construction.

The city is placed about a third of the way up from the bottom of the panel and acts as a link between the mountain behind it, dotted here and there with settlements, and the sea in front of it. Brush-strokes of varying size and direction—and light, foaming crests—convey the difference between the movement of the waves within the gulf, where the port lies, and out at sea, where two ships are sailing, a three-masted war galley, armed with cannons and with six men at their stations, and a galleon also armed with cannons. In the roadstead of the port other ships ride at anchor at the jetties and in the dock. And it is from the sea that the city and port are seen, from a viewpoint high up on the horizon. The buildings and the layout of the streets are painted with elegant precision: pale gray-toned hues (almost a kind of *grisaille* with a sprinkling of ocher here and

there) cleverly mark the transition from the deep green of the sea to the lighter greens of the countryside surrounding the town, darkened at times to convey the shade of the deeper valleys and woods, and elsewhere rubbed with terre verte to represent the harsh, mountainous Genovese land.

The city center is enclosed within the old walls, beyond which there are signs of expansion, especially along certain roadways. The high viewpoint allows the whole of the countryside outside the walls to be seen, while a skillful use of color, proportion, and perspective underlines the territorial continuity between the town and its hinterland, which is not even interrupted by the new city walls as they wind up the mountain to the top of Monte Peraldo, the structure of their ramparts accurately portrayed. On the contrary, the rough triangle formed by these long walls as they climb away from the city seems to incorporate it into the mountains, whose forms, divided up by many small valleys, they highlight in a topographically plausible manner. At the same time, the dwellings scattered outside both old and new walls, most of which are concentrated in the Bisagno Valley, give the impression of a gradual thinning out of the urban structure. Again (and less obviously) the roadways leaving the town for the mountain hardly ever form a network—in other words they exclusively connect the city and its hinterland.

This panel is clearly more pictorial than cartographical in approach. The layout of the city is clearly seen, as too are certain specific buildings (e.g., at the western extremity of the city within the old walls, the square-shaped Monastero dello Spirito Santo, still without its western wing, the Magazzini del Grano opposite this, its four blocks already complete, the Loggia dei Banchi, between the port and the cathedral of S. Lorenzo, S. Maria Assunta di Carignano, the new Pescheria on the jetty, and the Arsenale). This enables one to see the main changes in the structure of the city between 1581 and 1636. Foremost among these were the opening, in the northwestern part of the city, of the new road from Porta di S. Tommaso to the Guastato, the repair of the wall, and opening of a road, between the Ponte degli Spinola and the Ponte dei Calvi and between the latter and the Darsena, the renovation of the Banchi and the remodeling of the jetty, and the building of the walls and the new Pescheria. These details confirm that the fresco was entirely repainted in the 1630s, probably after 1636 (the date of the latest of the changes illustrated).

GENVA
MARITIMAE · LIGVRIAE · CAPVT
NAVALIS · MILITIAE · STVDIO
ET · CIVIVM · VIRTVTE
ATQVE · OPVLENTIA
IN · CLYTA
MVNITISSIMIS · NVPER
EXAEDIFICATIS · MOENIBVS
TVTAM
CLARISSIMAE · REIPVBLICAE
SEDĒ · PRAEBET

PARIET
PIC

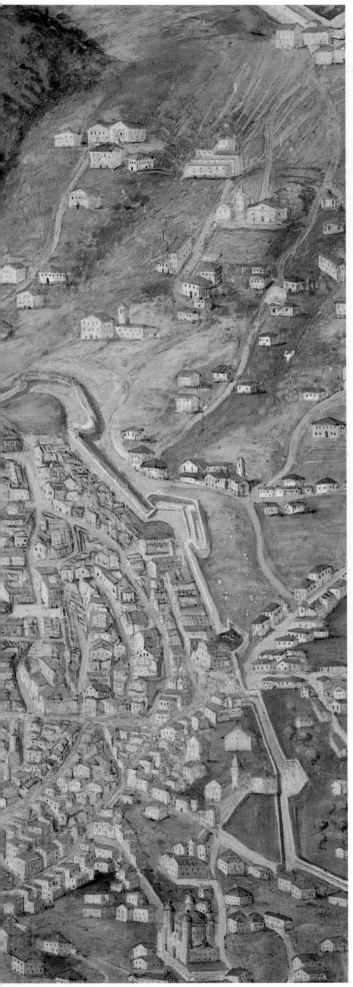

177

178

Page 179:
Pl. 176. Panel showing *Genua* (Genoa)
with a herm.

Genua (Genoa), details.
Pl. 177. The city and its port.
Pl. 178. Galleon in the Gulf of Genoa.

Venetia
Venice

This panel, 10′3″ x 4′10″ (3.1 x 1.48 m), can be divided horizontally into two areas of almost equal size. The upper shows an expanse of bright sky with solar reflections at the edges of the horizon, and the lower the lagoon dotted with islands and closed at the bottom by the mainland.

The Lion of St. Mark dives from the heavens with a scroll clutched between its paws carrying the legend: "*Venetiae Civitas admirabilis post eversam ab Attila Hunnor(um) rege Aquileiam, condita anno a salute hominibus restituta CCCCLIIII*" ("Venice splendid city, founded in the year 454 after the birth of Christ, after Aquileia was destroyed by Attila, King of the Huns").

In the lagoon is a bird's-eye view plan drawn in perspective of Venice, oriented with the north pointing upward but slightly shifted to the right. Around the large curved form of the main body of Venice, their names usually written in gold, are the islands of the lagoon, both toward the mainland (San Michele, Murano, San Nicola, Mazzorbo, San Francesco, Burano, Torcello) and toward the Lido (Giudecca, San Giorgio, Grazia—which is not named—Sant'Elena, San Servolo, San Lazzaro, the old leper island [*Lazzaretto vecchio*], San Clemente, Santo Spirito, Poveglia). Two almost deserted sections of the Lido are shown, with scattered huts, and a small portion of Chioggia (a Chioggia unusually surrounded by walls and lacking internal canals) projects into the panel in the bottom left-hand corner. The island of *Malamocho* is rather strangely shown as totally separate from the Lido (certainly not the case in the 16th century), and next to it is an unrecognizable bastioned island called *Podestario* (unless it is to be taken as the beginnings of the Bastione Campana).

The lagoon between the Lido and the main islands is shown as a geometrical pattern formed by waves of unvarying shape and size. Across it sail several large boats (a xebec, a galley, and a galleon) and smaller vessels (two resembling tartans). Other very small boats (perhaps also tartans) sail among the islands farther north.

At the northwestern end of the lagoon there is a panorama of the Padua-Treviso plain and behind it a very faint whitish outline of mountains. It is an imaginary panorama, for it omits the scalloped edges of the sandbanks between the plain and the lagoon, while it shows a non-existent eroded escarpment where the plain (which appears flecked with bodies of standing water) descends to the sea. The sandbar that extends into the lagoon from the mainland toward the island of San Secondo is also imaginary.

The strength of this painting lies in its being almost a miniature portrayal of the city. A great many of the best known religious and civil buildings are recognizable, as too is the minute network of canals and streets, many bridges, the buildings of the Arsenale, and the convent gardens—especially at Canaregio, along the Giudecca, and in the outlying islands.

One's first impression is that the source for the map is the splendid plan by Jacopo de' Barbari (1440–1516) published in the year 1500. However, the picture of the city it gives is up-to-date. It must therefore derive from a source that, while modeling itself on de' Barbari's plan, shows the city at a more recent date. Closest to it, Almagià thought, was Paolo Forlani's map, engraved by Bolognino Zalterio in 1566. But from a stylistic point of view it is clear that several decorative features—such as the lion, the sky in which it flies, the anonymous depiction of the mainland and possibly even the orderly waves of the lagoon—date from the 17th century.

VENETIAE CONDITA
CIVITAS ANNO
ADMIRABILIS A·SALVTE
POST·EVERSAM HOMINIBVS
AB·ATTILA RESTITVTA
HVNNOR·REGE CCCCLIIII
AQVILEIAM

DICAVIT
AVIT

180

Pl. 179. Panel showing *Venetia* (Venice).

Pl. 180. *Venetia* (Venice), detail. Venice and its surrounding islands.

Ancona
Ancona

The upper half of the map, 9'4" x 3'7" (2.85 x 1.08 m), is filled by the sky, its noonday brightness emerging between clouds of all kinds. A flying cherub bears a standard with the words: "*Ancon civitas dorica cum portu Traiani*" ("Ancona, a city founded by the Dorians, with the port of Trajan"). The inscription evokes the city's Hellenic origins and marine functions in every era.

Below this large sky, and compressed between it and an equally large space given over to the sea, is a perspective view of the city, which forms an arc as it stands on the undulating relief of its headland, displaying its port and extensive fortifications.

At the two opposite ends of the view, are two scrolls with inscriptions. That on the left, given the form of a cloth held up by a cherub, says: "*Urbanus VIII pont. max. domum ad expurgandum merces et advenas morbi suspicione construxit*" ("Pope Urban VIII constructed a building where the soundness of the goods can be checked and people from foreign ships can be examined so as to ensure no epidemics are introduced"). That to the right, nailed to the shore of the headland, reads: "*Urbanus VIII pont. max. propugnaculum ad tutelam arcis et portus Traiani*" ("Pope Urban VIII [raised] the citadel to defend the old town and the port of Trajan"). However, the references in the two inscriptions to the construction of the lazaretto and the system of fortifications culminating in the citadel as projects (mainly) promoted by Urban VIII smacks of flattery. For Urban VIII is not among the popes who played a significant role in remodeling Ancona. There were already two lazarettos a century before his papacy—one near the Arsenale (now the naval shipyard) and one originally placed near the rocks of S. Agostino and later transferred (after being damaged by a landslide) to the S. Lucia bastions. They were both modernized by Orazio Paciotto in the last quarter of the 16th century. The wall alongside the jetty that protected the port area and the ramparts along the seafront protecting the city were already in use, as they appear in the painting, after the middle of the 16th century. The citadel was based on a design by Antonio da Sangallo the Younger in 1532 and completed—as shown in the fresco—in the last years of the 16th century. Regarding these important features of the city's military and sanitary defence system, Urban VIII was merely engaged in restoration work.

The panel clearly shows the church of S. Ciriaco, almost isolated on top of the 109-yard-high (100-meter-high) eminence—the Guasco—that terminates the headland. At the foot of the latter can also be seen the Arsenale, while farther left, at the beginning of the jetty, is Trajan's arch. In the central part are the major religious buildings (among those most clearly visible are S. Francesco delle Scale, S. Maria della Piazza, the church of the Sacramento, and the group of buildings around S. Agostino) and civic ones (the Palazzo degli Anziani and the Loggia dei Mercanti stand out). Farther to the right on the Astagno relief—the innermost one on the headland—care has been taken over the drawing of the citadel, along with its trenches. To the west of Astagno are the hazardous escarpments that over a fairly wide area descend sharply to the sea.

The picture must therefore have been painted during the papacy of Urban VIII and is faithfully derived from a fine panorama engraved in wood in 1632 by Domenico Castelli from a drawing by Vincenzo Ricci, illustrating an event of the previous year, when the queen of Hungary set out from the port of Ancona in a Venetian ship. In Ricci's detailed drawing, the waters of the port are crowded with boats shooting salvos (more than twenty large vessels can be counted, surrounded by numerous smaller boats). In the present map, on the other hand, there are no more than ten vessels, few of which are cargo boats and most being slender war galleys sailing outside the port or nearby (the silhouettes of other boats are seen on the horizon).

Indeed, one has the impression that the port itself is almost deserted. Leaving the port free of boats, with their succession of masts, sails, and rigs, the anonymous painter merely wished to further focus attention on the city front overlooking the port. However, this area of empty water between the bastions and the medieval jetty closing it to the north curiously echoes the complaint made by Giacomo Fontana in a report addressed to Sixtus V in the years 1588–90 (and also found in documents of the first quarter of the 17th century) regarding the serious reduction in mercantile traffic and (in sharp contrast with the celebrative intent of the map) the irreversible decline of this center of papal commerce.

ANCON
CIVITAS
DORICA
CVM PORTV
TRAIANI

182

183

Preceding page:
Pl. 181. Panel showing *Ancona* (Ancona), and two herms.

Ancona (Ancona), details.
Pl. 182. The north end of the port with the Arsenale and the Trajan's Arch.
Pl. 183. The south end of the port with the city walls and the fortress.

188

184

Pl. 184. *Ancona* (Ancona), detail. Sailing and rowing boats in the port.

Tremitae
Tremiti Islands

This is a view, 3'12" x 4'8" (1.21 x 1.41 m), of the Tremiti Archipelago off the coast of Puglia. Toward the bottom of the panel, as though on a rectangular sheet nailed to the surface, is a view of the ruins of the ancient port of Ostia. The scale is not shown. The view is oriented with the north pointing upward, as can be seen from the compass rose, whose rays are marked with the initial letters of the half- and quarter-point winds.

There is no record of the panel having been modified or restored. The part of the panel representing the Tremiti is graduated along its edges, and each minute numbered. The degrees are no longer legible. The coordinates probably range from 42°37' to 42°43' latitude and from 41°28' to 41°32' longitude.

The three islands (San Domino, San Nicola, and Caprara) and a part of the *Credazzo* rock (Cretaccio) are shown in perspective. The land is painted in green and brown, the sea and sky in blue and white, the names and the compass rose are in gold.

The view is modeled on an engraving by Natale Bonifazio da Sebenico, printed in Venice in 1574, which shows the monks of San Nicola resisting attack by a Turkish fleet in August 1567. The naval battle is shown in the foreground: galleys flying the crescent moon sink a sailing ship flying the Neapolitan flag, while galleys flying the St. Andrew's cross of the local fleet hasten to the scene.

The panel gives a vivid picture of the island landscape, with its imposing cliffs dominated by the abbey of San Nicola, entrusted by Gregory XIII to the Lateran Canons Regular of San Frediano in Lucca. San Domino is uninhabited except for a few peasants whose houses are scattered along the road that still runs along the ridge of the island. Caprara, on the other hand, is inhabited by wild rabbits. Despite the graduations along its edges, the panel is not cartographical at all. In addition to representing the islands, it emphasizes the importance of one of Gregory XIII's many attempts to renew the Church (the recovery of the abbey of San Nicola, which had long been abandoned) with a view to the defence of Christendom against the Turkish threat.

The trompe l'oeil drawing, 23" x 44" (59 x 112 cm), included in the panel also forms part of the original iconographic scheme of the Gallery and commemorates Gregory XIII's restoration of the splendors of ancient Italy for the good of his subjects. It shows the ruins of the Roman port of Ostia as they were at the time the panel was painted: "*Romani Portus reliquiae (sic) An(no) X Pontificatus Gregori XIII P(ontifici) M(aximi) descriptae*" ("The remains of the port of Rome, described in the tenth year of the papacy of Gregory XIII Pontifex Maximus"). It is a companion to the view of the port in its original state included in the panel showing Elba. The present view is oriented with the south pointing upward. It dates from either 1581 or the start of 1582 and is by Danti himself, who made the preparatory drawings on the spot.

ROMANI · PORTVS · RELIQVIAE
AN · X · PONTIFICATVS · GREGORII · XIII · P · M · DESCRIPTAE

Tevere F.

Fiumicino

Casello

ROMA
AN·X̄·PONTIFICA

186

Preceding page:
Pl. 185. Panel showing *Tremitae* (Tremiti Islands), and two herms.

Pl. 186. *Tremitae* (Tremiti Islands), detail.
Trompe l'oeil painting with the ruins of the Roman port of Ostia.

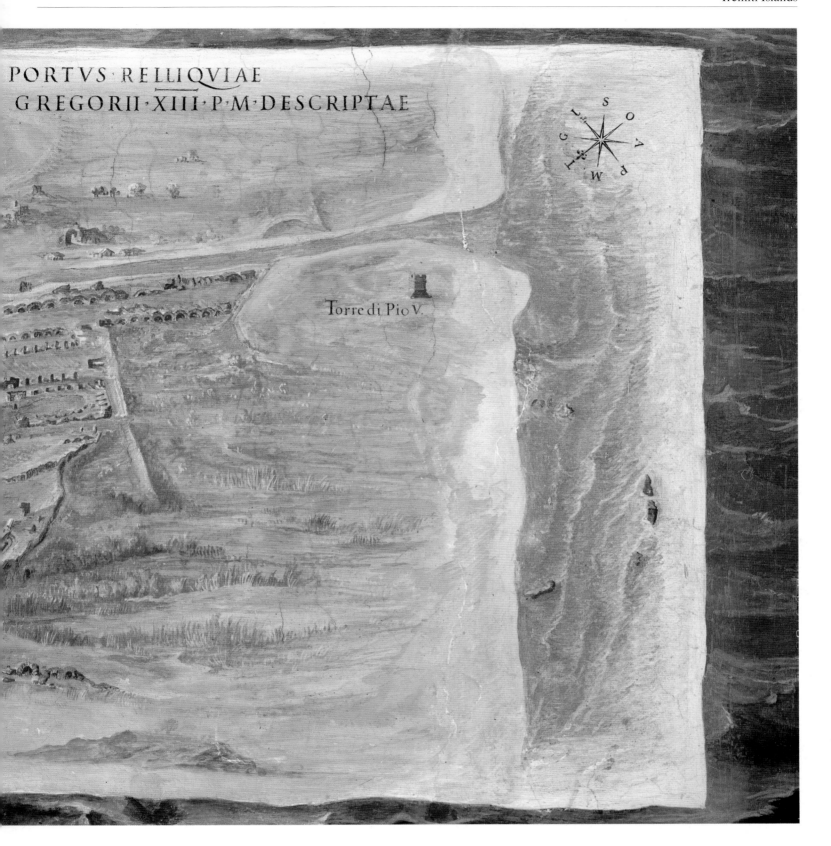

PORTVS·RELLIQVIAE
GREGORII·XIII·P·M·DESCRIPTAE

Torre di Pio V.

Corfu
The Isle of Corfù
and Trompe l'oeil Drawing with the Battle of Lepanto (1571)

The upper part of the panel shows the Ionian island of Corfù, with a part of the Albanian coast (*Epiri Pars*, Epirus), but without any chorographic details. The trompe l'oeil drawing below depicts the Battle of Lepanto (7 October 1571). Above the map of the island, 9'9" x 4'9" (2.98 x 1.44 m), is an angel bearing a scroll inscribed with the title of the picture: "*Classis Turcarum ad Crocyleium profligata*" ("The Turkish Fleet defeated near Crocyleium").

The scale is not shown. As can be seen from the compass rose, marked with the initial letters of the winds, the map is oriented with the north (*T[ramontana]*) pointing upward.

There is no record of the panel having been modified or restored. However, the absence of symbols on the flags suggests that it has been somewhat hastily repainted. The graduation along the edges is in minutes, numbered at intervals of five. The degrees are not shown.

The form of the coastline certainly derives from a nautical chart. The orography is conventional and uses various shades of green and brown. The littorals are outlined in ocher, while the hydrography and sea are in blue, the latter highlighted in white. The settlements are represented by buildings, either isolated or in groups. Churches and castles are in painted in crimson. There is a vast area of ruins around the inlet of *Necro Talassa*. The city and the fortress of Corfù are taken from drawings made on the spot and are shown in perspective. Place-names are in Italian, except for *Mare Ionium* (Ionian Sea), and are written in black and gold.

This image of Corfù is derived from a popular print of the period that was published in various editions, both in Rome and in Venice. It is almost identical to the one published in Ortelius's *Theatrum Orbis Terrarum* (1570), even though the orientation is somewhat different.

Apart from the view of the Fortezza Vecchia, built by the Venetians in 1550, the depiction of Corfù is conventional.

Indeed, the ruins are simply a visual translation of the inscription *borghi diffatti* (*sic*, for *disfatti*, ruined) in the original map. For the cartographer, the most important feature of the island was clearly the fortress, which consolidated the island's role as a bulwark of Christendom (Corfù had resisted a Turkish attack in 1537).

The Battle of Lepanto (now called Naupaktos, at the mouth of the Gulf of Corinth), is one of the glories of the Church particularly celebrated at this end of the Gallery. The angel above the image matches the one over the depiction of the siege of Valletta. He holds the palm of martyrdom in his right hand and in his left a crown of laurels symbolizing the victory of Christendom over Islam. This victory was the result of diplomatic action on the part of Pope Pius V and was officially celebrated as decisive, even though it did not even bring about the recovery of the Venetian possession of Cyprus, which had fallen to the Turks the previous year (1570) after a long period of resistance.

The great battle between the fleet of the Holy Alliance (Spain, the Holy See, Venice, Savoy, Parma, Malta, Tuscany, Genoa, and Urbino), commanded by Don John of Austria (1547–1578), and the Ottoman fleet took place at the mouth of the Gulf of Patras, thus not far from Homer's *Crocyle*, which Strabo placed on the island of Levkás (Santa Maura), but which is not otherwise identifiable. The title of the panel therefore features a learned reference. In the drawing, the battle takes place in a conventional landscape and is represented according to an equally conventional, though well established and well known, iconographic model. It is in fact modeled on an engraving by Antonio Lafrery (1512–1577), published in Rome toward the end of the year 1571. The battle is shown back to front, with Ucchiali on the right wing of his fleet and Andrea Doria on the left of his, when their positions should be actually reversed.

CLASSIS·TVRCARVM
AD·CROCYLEIVM·PROFLIGATA

IONIVM MARE

EPIRI PARS

Corfu

LEVCHIMME

Chiarenza

Lepanto

Dardanelli

Patras

QVAM

Chiarenza

Sragno

Occhiali

Isole de Curzolari

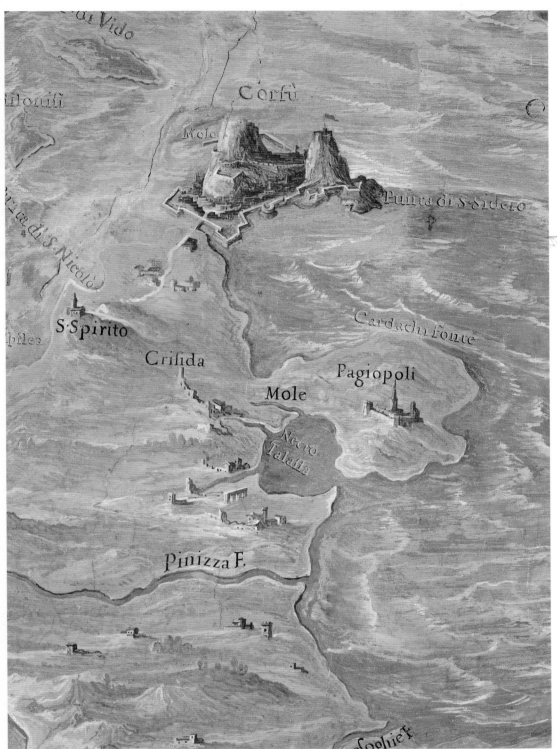

189

Page 195:
Pl. 187. Panel showing *Corfu* (The Isle of Corfù) and a trompe l'oeil painting of the Battle of Lepanto.

Corfu (The Isle of Corfù), details.
Pl. 188. Trompe l'oeil painting of the Battle of Lepanto (1571).
Pl. 189. The city and the Venetian fortress of Corfù.

Malta
The Isle of Malta
and Trompe l'oeil Drawing with the Siege of Valletta by the Ottoman Fleet (1565)

The upper part of the panel, 6'10" x 4'7" (2.08 x 1.39 m), shows the island of Malta with Comino, Cominotto, a part of Gozo, and the *Aphricum Mare* (Strait of Sicily). The lower shows the siege of Valletta by the Ottoman fleet (1565). Set into the lower left-hand corner is a plan of the city of Valletta (*Melita*).

The scale is not shown. The panel is variously oriented: the map of Malta has the southwest (*A[ustro]*) pointing upward, while the siege of Valletta has the northeast pointing upward (*G[reco]*), as may be seen from the separate compass rose, which is marked with the initial letters of the winds. The orientation of the plan of Valletta is not marked, but it has the southeast pointing upward.

There is no record of the panel having been modified or restored. However, the plan of Valletta might be a later addition, and the Turkish and Christian symbols on the tents and the flags have relatively recently been crudely repainted. The graduations along the edges are in minutes, numbered at intervals of five. The degrees are not shown.

The cartographic representation of the island has the usual conventional features: terrain and relief are in green and brown, coastlines in ocher, hydrography in blue, and the sea in blue highlighted in white. The settlements are represented by groups of buildings in crimson. The following are shown in plan: *La Città* (Città Vecchia, the old capital of the island); *Valletta Città Nova* (La Valletta, built between 1564 and 1571), of which only the massive walls are shown, culminating in the star-shaped fortress of Sant'Elmo; the fortified *Borgo S. Mich(ele)e* (Senglia) and *C(astel) S. Angelo* (La Vittoriosa); and the *Giardino del Gran Mastro*. The coastline is taken from nautical charts and so emphasizes inlets and projections but in general tends to round off the form of the larger island. None of the islands is given a name. Place-names are in black and gold and written in Italian with the exception of *Aphricum Mare* (Strait of Sicily). The angel with the sword and book has the white cross and the red surcoat of the Knights of Malta. The book is inscribed *Melita obsidione liberata* ("Malta freed from siege").

The map of Malta seems to have been derived from the one published in Rome in 1551 by Lafrery and reprinted by Lafrery himself on the occasion of the Turkish siege of 1565. The map in Ortelius's *Theatrum* (1570) is identical, but the orientation has been overturned and the place-names have been garbled in the process of being transcribed. The same image of the island may be seen in the Sala delle Guardie in the Palazzo Farnese at Caprarola (Viterbo). The depiction of the siege of Valletta is based on another engraving by Lafrery, *Ritratto dello istesso disegno mandato da Malta dove sono annotate le cose più nobili*, published in Rome in 1565.

The best images of the territory offered by the panel are not found in the map, but in the representation of the siege.

Valletta is represented by its fortifications only, as in fact it must have appeared in those days; it is still without an urban infrastructure, its place taken here by the encampment and emplacements of the Turkish heavy artillery, marked out by means of the banner with the crescent moon. The encampments and batteries of cannon on land are also Turkish; the Knights of Malta are left merely with the fort of Sant'Elmo and the two fortified suburbs. The Turkish fleet, made up mainly of double- and single-mast galleys, has disembarked its cannon and is crowding the Marsa Muscetto and the bay, blockading the Knights' fleet. The siege, which lasted from 25 May to 7 September 1565, was one of the great events in the naval history of the Mediterranean in the 16th century. It was lifted by the "*grand soccour*" of Christendom—that is the arrival of a fleet put together by various Christian rulers—and the flight of the Turkish ships.

The map of Malta has the characteristics common to all contemporary maps of the island (of which, however, it is the best), e.g., stylized relief and settlements, an exclusive concern with the fortifications, the absence of other humanmade constructions, boundary lines, or information regarding the use to which the territory was put. Place-names alone are supplied in abundance. A bulwark of the Christian faith, Malta has an important role within the Gallery cycle (and in 16th-century cartography in general) on account of its fortifications and their function, clearly illustrated in the depiction of the siege.

Here, the alternation of fortified areas with unprotected zones, like the inlets and projections of the extremely broken bay are shown up well, thanks to the disposition of the armies using them. Similarly, the irrelevance of the islands in purely territorial terms (the power of the Knights of Malta was exclusively naval, and their real territory the sea) is highlighted by the great press of shipping that extends to the horizon. Owing to the functions of war (the disembarking of cannon, the disposition of the military encampments), we are also given an idea of the various modes of access to the island and the roadways around the capital, features not represented at all in the map of the island.

According to Almagià, the plan of Valletta (*Melita*) may have been added at a later date, since the design of the fortifications does not completely correspond to that in Lafrery's and Ortelius's images and probably illustrates a subsequent phase in their development. Also, the layout of the streets and houses, elsewhere omitted, is shown here. But it should also be pointed out that the plan of the city is an important part of the panel taken as a whole; in Lafrery's and Ortelius's pictures of Malta, it is precisely the housing that is missing, and housing is an aspect that Danti normally considered of the greatest importance (see, for example, the *Sicilia* panel, the best and most up-to-date aspect of which are the plans of the cities). It is therefore possible that (as in other maps in the Gallery cycle) Danti did not have enough time to supplement the various cartographical sources available to him and that he simply superimposed them on one another, in the hope that the combined image would be acceptable and informative.

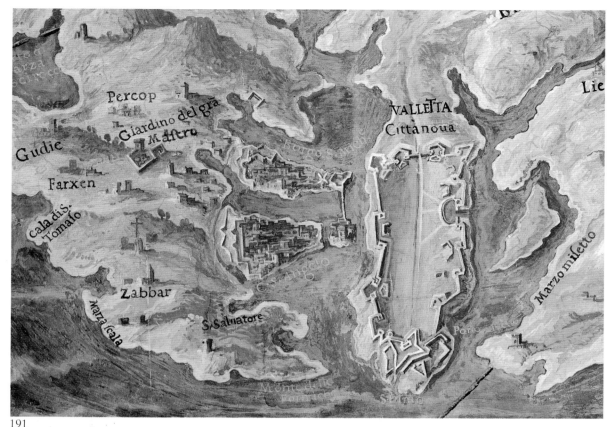

191

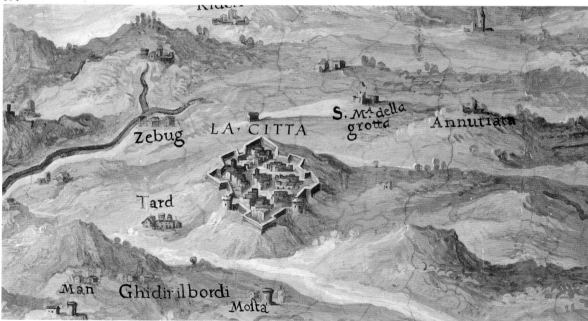

192

193

Preceding page:
Pl. 190. Panel showing *Malta* (The Isle of Malta) and a trompe l'oeil painting
of the siege of Valletta by the Ottoman fleet (1565).

Malta (The Isle of Malta), details.
Pl. 191. The walls of Valletta and the fortified township on the bay.
Pl. 192. Città Vecchia, a former capital of Malta.
Pl. 193. Trompe l'oeil painting showing the siege of Valletta
by the Ottoman fleet (1565) and the plan of the city.

Ilva
The Isle of Elba
and Trompe l'oeil Drawing with Reconstruction of the Ancient Port of Ostia

This panel, 10'5" x 4'7" (approx. 3.17 x 1.4 m), shows the Isle of Elba in the Tyrrhenian Sea (*Tyrrhenum Mare*). Set into the lower part is a trompe l'oeil drawing of a reconstruction of the port of Claudius at Ostia in Roman times.

The scale is not shown. The map is oriented with the south (*O[stro]*) pointing upward, as can be seen from the 16-point compass rose, marked with the initials of the eight principal winds. There is no record of the panel's having been modified or restored, but the inscription *Tyrrhenum Mare* must date from during the papacy of Urban VIII.

The panel is graduated along its edges in minutes, numbered at intervals of five. The coordinates range from 41°55' to 42°28' latitude and, probably, from 43°48' to 44°7' longitude.

High ground is represented in a pictorially pleasing but unfaithful manner, and no names are given. Relief and plains are shown in varying shades of green, the coasts are outlined in light ocher, and the promontories and inlets along the coast are greatly accentuated. Settlements are represented by more or less numerous groups of houses in crimson with stylized churches and towers. *Cosmopolis*, the fortress at Portoferraio built by Cosimo I, Duke of Tuscany (1519–1574), is shown in perspective, with the great Forte Stella in the foreground. Geographical names are given in Italian (except, as usual, for the name of the sea) and are painted in black and gold. The compass rose is in gold.

The map is probably modeled on a nautical chart with some chorographic features. It has nothing in common with the map of Elba in Ortelius's *Theatrum Orbis Terrarum* (1570). Danti probably procured the necessary material himself during his long stay in Tuscany. The Elba in Magini's *Italia* of 1620 is derived from this *Ilva* by Danti.

No historical events are shown. The territory is depicted in a conventional manner; the only important element is the great fortress of *Cosmopolis* at Portoferraio, center of the Medici occupation of a part of the island, which was built by Giovanni Battista Bellucci (known as "il San Marino") and by Giovanni Camerini for Cosimo I in 1546. No other humanmade constructions are shown, and this particular orientation was probably chosen as the one that would best show off the fortress. *Cosmopolis* was another bulwark of Christendom and had resisted a Turkish attack in 1553.

The trompe l'oeil drawing showing a reconstruction of the ancient port of Ostia (A.D. 41–54) is hung, like a sail, from the mast of a large cargo raft at sea and shows the hypothetical reconstruction of the Roman port of Ostia during the reign of Claudius (*Romanus portus a Claudio Imp[eratore] constructus*), with the south pointing upward. It is a companion to the representation of the same port in 1581–82, facing it from the other side of the Gallery in the lower part of the panel showing the Tremiti Islands. The image, about 23" x 38" (approx. 57.5 x 95.5 cm), is derived from Stefano Du Perac's engraving *Claudii et Traiani Imp(eratorum) admirabilium portuum Ostiensium ortographia per Stephanum Du Perac*, printed in Rome by Lafrery in 1575.

ROMANVS PORTVS
CON

195

Preceding page:
Pl. 194. Panel showing
Ilva (The Isle of Elba).

Pl. 195. *Ilva* (The Isle of
Elba), detail. Trompe
l'oeil painting with a
reconstruction of the
port of Ostia as it was in
the time of the Emperor
Claudius (A.D. 41–54).

Bibliography

MANUSCRIPTS

DANTI E. *Anemographia* (before 1576). Florence, Biblioteca Riccardiana, Ms. Riccardiano 2834.

DANTI E. *Anemographia F. Egnatii Dantis OSD. In Anemoscopium Vaticanum horizontale, ac verticale instrumentum ostensorem ventorum* (6 February 1581). Vatican City, Biblioteca Apostolica Vaticana, Cod. Vat. Lat. 5647.

DANTI E. *Scritti sui venti* (before 1576). Florence, Biblioteca Nazionale Centrale, Ms. Mgl. XI 121 ff., fols. 332r–344v.

HOLSTENIO L. *Iscrizioni originali della Galleria con annotazioni di L. Holstenio* (ca. 1636). Vatican City, Biblioteca Apostolica Vaticana, Cod. Barb. Lat. 1803.

—. *Iscrizioni della Galleria delle Carte geografiche* (1662). Vatican City, Biblioteca Apostolica Vaticana, Cod. Barb. Lat. 2008.

PUBLISHED SOURCES

ACKERMAN J. *The Cortile del Belvedere.* Vatican City: Libreria Editrice Vaticana, 1954.

ALBERTI L. *Descrittione di tutta Italia.* Bologna: Anselmo Giaccarelli, 1550.

ALBERTI L. *Descrittione di tutta l'Italia et isole pertinenti ad essa . . .* (with an introduction by Borgaruccio Borgarucci). Venice: G. B. Porta, 1581.

ALMAGIÀ R. "La pittura geografica dell'Italia nel palazzo Farnese di Caprarola." *Rivista Geografica Italiana* (1919): pp. 133–137.

ALMAGIÀ R. *L'Italia di Giovanni Antonio Magini e la cartografia dell'Italia nei secoli XVI e XVII.* Naples and Città di Castello: Comitato Geografico Nazionale Italiano, 1922.

ALMAGIÀ R. *Monumenta Italiae Cartographica.* Florence: Istituto Geografico Militare, 1929.

ALMAGIÀ R. *L'opera geografica di Luca Holstenio.* Studi e testi series, vol. 102. Vatican City: Libreria Editrice Vaticana, 1942 (reprinted 1984, in Modena).

ALMAGIÀ R. *Carte geografiche a stampa di particolare pregio o rarità dei secoli XVI e XVII esistenti nella Biblioteca Apostolica Vaticana.* Monumenta Cartographica Vaticana series, vol. 2. Vatican City: Libreria Editrice Vaticana, 1948.

ALMAGIÀ R. *Le pitture murali della Galleria delle carte geografiche* Monumenta Cartographica Vaticana series, vol. 3. Vatican City: Libreria Editrice Vaticana, 1952.

BAGROW L. *A. Ortelii Catalogus Cartographorum* (consists of several volumes). Gotha, 1928–1930.

BAGROW L., L. A. SKELTON. *Meister der Kartographie.* Frankfurt am Main and Berlin, 1985.

BAROZZI J. *Le due regole della prospettiva pratica con i comentarii del R. P. M. Egnatio Danti.* Rome, 1583.

BERTOLINI G. L. "Su l'edizione italiana dell'Ortelio." In *Scritti . . . in onore di G. Della Vedova*, pp. 295–305. Florence, 1908.

BIONDO F. *Italia illustrata.* Venice: Bernardinus Venetus de Vitalibus, 1503.

BRAUN G., F. HOGENBERG. *Civitates Orbis Terrarum in aes incisae et excussae.* 6 vols. Colonia 1572–1618, (facsimile edition of *Theatrum Orbis Terrarum*, vol. 1 Amsterdam, 1965).

BROC N. *La geografia del Rinascimento* (edited by C. GREPPI). Modena, 1989. Translation of *La géographie de la Renaissance 1420–1620.* Paris, 1986.

CHENEY I. "The Galleria delle Carte Geografiche at the Vatican and the Roman Church's View of the History of Christianity." *Renaissance Papers*, 1989 (1990): pp. 21–37.

CODAZZI A. *Le edizioni quattrocentesche e cinquecewntesche della "Geografia" di Tolomeo.* Milan, 1950.

CORNINI G., A. M. DE STROBEL, M. CRESCENZI SERLUPI. "Il Palazzo di Gregorio XIII." In *Il Palazzo Apostolico Vaticano*, edited by C. PIETRANGELI, pp. 150-167. Florence, 1992.

DANTI E. *La prospettiva di Euclide. Nella quale si tratta di quelle cose, che per raggi diritti si veggono: et di quelle, che con raggi reflessi nelli specchi appariscono. Tradotta dal R. P. M. Egnazio Danti Cosmografo del Seren. Gran Duca di Toscana. Con alcune sue annotazioni di luoghi più importanti. Insieme con la Prospettiva d'Eliodoro Larisseo cavata dalla Libreria Vaticana, e tradotta dal medesimo nuovamente data in luce.* Florence: Giunti, 1573.

DANTI E. *Le due regole della prospettiva pratica di M. Iacopo Barozzi da Vignola, Con i comentari del RPM Egnatio Danti. . . .* Rome: Francesco Zannetti, 1583.

DANTI E. *Le Scienze Matematiche ridotte in tavole dal Rev. P. Maestro Egnatio Danti publico professore di esse nello Studio di Bologna.* Bologna: Appresso la Compagnia della Stampa, 1577.

DANTI E. *Trattato del radio Latino. Istrumento giustissimo et facile più d'ogni altro per prendere qual si voglia misura, et positione di luogo; tanto in Cielo come in Terra: il quale, oltre alle operationi proprie sue, fa anco tutte quelle della Gran Regola di C. Tolomeo, et del antico Radio Astronomico, inventato dall'illustrissimo et eccellentissimo signor latino Orsini, con li Commentari del reverendo padre maestro Egnatio Danti da Perugia, Hoggi Vescovo di Altari, et da esso di nuovo ricorretto, et ampliato con molte nuove operationi.* Rome: Marc'Antonio Moretti and Iacopo Brianzi, 1585.

DANTI E. *Trattato dell'uso et della fabbrica dell'Astrolabio di F. Egnatio Danti dell'Or. di S. Domenico con l'aggiunta del Planisferio del Roias*. Florence: Giunti, 1569.

DANTI E. *Usus radii Latini, seu Isogonii, instrumenti mathematici certissimi simul et facillimi . . . cum commentariis . . . Ignatii Dantis. . . .* Wurzburg: Typis Georgii Fleishmanni, 1602.

DANTI V. *Il primo libro del trattato delle perfette proporzioni di tutte le cose che imitare e ritrarre si possano con l'arte del disegno, dedicato a Cosimo Duca*. Florence, 1567. Modern edition: P. BAROCCHI. *Trattati d'arte del Cinquecento fra Manierismo e Controriforma*. Scrittori d'Italia series, vol. 1. (Other authors included in this volume: Varchi, Pino, Dolce, Danti, Sorte.) Bari: Laterza, 1960.

DELUMEAU J. *Vie économique et sociale de Rome dans la seconde moitié du XVIe siècle* (consists of several volumes). Paris, 1957–1959.

HARLEY J. B. "Maps Knowledge and Power." In *The Iconography of Landscape. Essays on the Symbolic Representation, Design and Use of Past Environments*, edited by D. COSGROVE and S. DANIELS, pp. 277–312. Cambridge, 1988.

HARLEY J. B. "Silences and Secrecy: the Hidden Agenda of Cartography in Early Modern Europe." *Imago Mundi* 40 (1988): pp. 57–76.

HARLEY J. B., D. WOODWARD, eds. *Medieval Europe and the Mediterranean* (pp. 286–370). Chicago, 1987.

HOLSTENIUS L. *Epistulae ad diversos* (edited by I. F. BOISSONADE). Paris, 1817.

KARROW R. W. *Mapmakers of the Sixteenth Century and their Maps. Bio-Bibliographies of the Cartographers of Abraham Ortelius*. Chicago, 1993.

KOEMAN C. *The History of Abraham Ortelius and his "Theatrum Orbis Terrarum."* Lausanne, 1964.

KRETSCHMER K. *Die italienische Portolane des Mittelalters*. Berlin, 1909.

MAGINI G. A. *Italia*. Bologna, 1620 (facsimile edition with an introduction by R. ALMAGIÀ, *Theatrum Orbis Terrarum*, Amsterdam, 1974).

MERCATOR G. *Atlas, sive cosmographicae meditationes de fabrica mundi et de fabricati figura*. Duisburg, 1595.

MEURER P. H. *Fontes Cartographici Orteliani. Das "Theatrum Orbis Terrarum" von Abraham Ortelius und seine Kartenquellen*. Weinheim, 1991.

MORELLO G. "La Galleria delle Carte Geografiche e la Torre dei Venti." In *Il Palazzo Apostolico Vaticano*, edited by C. H. PIETRANGELI, pp. 186–195. Florence: Nardini, 1992.

ORTELIUS A. *Theatrum Orbis Terrarum*. Antwerp: Plantjin, 1570.

ORTELIUS A. *Epistulae* (edited by J. HESSEL). Cambridge, 1887.

PARTRIDGE L., R. STARN. *Art of Power: Three Halls of State in Italy, 1300–1600*. Berkeley and Los Angeles: University of California Press, 1992.

PARTSCH J. *Philipp Clüver der Beründer der historischen Länderkunde*. Wien und Omütz, 1891.

PASTOR VON L. *Storia dei papi*. 15 vols. Rome, 1910–1934. In particular, see vol. 9 (1925).

PIETRANGELI C., ed. *Il Palazzo Apostolico Vaticano*. Florence: Nardini, 1992.

PRINZ W. *Galleria. Storia e tipologia di uno spazio architettonico* (edited by C. VIA CIERI). Modena: Franco Cosimo Panini Editore, 1988. (Translation of *Die Entstehung der Galerie in Frankreich und Italien*. Berlin, 1977).

REDIG DE CAMPOS D. *I Palazzi Vaticani*. Bologna, 1967.

RIPA C. *Iconologia*. Rome, 1603.

ROSE P. L. *The Italian Renaissance of Mathematics. Studies on Humanists and Mathematicians from Petrarch to Galileo*. Geneva, 1975.

SCHULTZ J. *La cartografia tra scienza e arte. Carte e cartografi nel Rinascimento italiano*. Modena: Franco Cosimo Panini Editore, 1990.

SCHULTZ J. "Maps as Metaphors. Mural Map Cycles of the Italian Renaissance." In *Art and Cartography. Six Historical Essays*, edited by D. WOODARD, pp. 97-113. Chicago and London, 1987. Italian edition: "Mappe come metafore: cicli murali cartografici nell'Italia del Rinascimento." In *La cartografia tra scienza e arte. Carte e cartografi nel Rinascimento Italiano*. Modena: Franco Cosimo Panini Editore, 1990.

SCHÜTTE M. *Die Galleria delle Carte Geografiche im Vatikan. Eine ikonologische Betrachtung des Gewölbeprogramms*. Hildesheim, 1993.

TAJA A. *Descrizione del Palazzo Apostolico Vaticano*. Rome, 1750.

THOMASSY R. "Les papes geographes et la cartographie du Vatican." In *Nouvelles Annales des voyages et des sciences geographiques* series. Paris. See especially vol. 1, pp. 151–172 (part II); vol. 2, pp. 7–47 (part III); vol. 3, pp. 266–269 (appendix); and vol. 4, pp. 57–129 (part I).

VAES M. "Matthieu Bril 1550-1583." *Bulletin de l'Institut historique belge de Rome* 8 (1928): pp. 228–331.

WAUWERMANS H. E. *L'école cartographique belge et anversoise du XVI siécle*. Amsterdam, 1895.

ZIPPEL G. "Cosmografi al servizio dei Papi nel Quattrocento" *Bollettino della Società Geografica Italiana* 47 (1910): pp. 843–53.